ComeHomeAmerica.us

Historic and Current Opposition to U.S. Wars and How a Coalition of Citizens from the Political Right and Left Can End American Empire

Edited by
George D. O'Neill, Jr.
Paul Buhle
Bill Kauffman
Kevin Zeese

Publishers Notes

Copyright October 2010
Titan Publishing Company LLC
P. O. Box 112
Lake Wales FL 33859-0112

First Edition, First Printing
ISBN 978-0-9830316-0-4
Library of Congress Control Number: 2010940153

Cover art by Gary Dumm and Cover color by Laura Dumm.

R1

For further information please visit our web site:
ComeHomeAmerica.us

The Cover

Come Home America, the title of this book and the ComeHomeAmerica.US website, was the 1972 presidential campaign slogan of Senator George McGovern. It originated with the famed anti-Vietnam War speech of Dr. Martin Luther King, Jr., who is featured on the cover. Most recently it was the title of a book by William Greider, who participated in the right-left meeting described in this book.

On the cover are other notable anti-war and peace advocates from the last century. Many others could have been chosen; this is meant to be a representative sample of the types of people who have opposed war and empire, not the top anti-war advocates of all time. Also on the cover are:

Robert La Follette represented Wisconsin as a member of the U.S. Congress from 1884 to 1890. He served as the state's Governor from 1901 to 1906 and as a U.S. Senator from 1906 to 1925. He was a vocal opponent of U.S. entry into World War I, viewing it as a pretext for the enrichment of corporations on the backs of the poor. He was a leading Midwestern progressive opponent to Woodrow Wilson throughout the war. "Fighting Bob" was the Progressive Party presidential candidate in 1924; reduction of military spending and opposition to war were key planks of his platform.

Jeannette Rankin was the first woman elected to Congress and the first woman elected to a national legislature in any western democracy. She served two widely separated terms (1917-1919 and 1941-1943). A Republican, she was an outspoken opponent of war, voting against the declarations of both World War I and World War II. (In the latter case hers was the only vote in opposition.) Both votes cost her re-election but she remained an active citizen and spokeswoman for peace. In 1968, she led more than five thousand women in a protest in Washington, DC against the Vietnam War.

Smedley Butler was the most decorated Marine in history. He participated in military actions in the Philippines, China, Nicaragua, Cuba, Haiti, Mexico, the Caribbean and France, where he served during World War I. By the end of his career he had received 16 medals, five of which were for heroism. He was twice recipient of the Congressional Medal of Honor for acts in China and Haiti. After retiring in 1931, he became an anti-war advocate who described war as a racket and his military career as a "racketeer for big business, who could have taught Al Capone a thing or two." He spoke out against war profiteering and was a supporter of the Ludlow Amendment, which would have required a nationwide referendum before sending Americans off to war.

Robert Taft, known as "Mr. Republican," was a U.S. Senator from Ohio for 14 years beginning in 1939 and a prominent conservative statesman who was a major proponent of non-interventionism. He believed America should avoid any involvement in European or Asian wars and concentrate instead on solving problems in the United States. He believed that a strong U.S. military, combined with the natural geographic protection of the Atlantic and Pacific Oceans, was sufficient to protect America. Taft was an early critic of the Cold War; his last speech before his death in 1953 warned against committing U.S. troops to the Asian mainland. He failed in his quest to win the presidential nomination of the Republican Party in 1940, 1948 and 1952.

Eugene V. Debs was a union leader from Indiana. He was founder of the American Railway Union and a founding member of the Industrial Workers of the World (the "Wobblies"). Debs ran five times for president representing the Socialist Party. He was a strong opponent of war who was sentenced to ten years in prison for a speech he gave on June 16, 1918, in Canton, Ohio, opposing World War I and urging resistance to the military draft. Debs ran for president from prison in 1920, receiving nearly one million votes. In 1921 President Harding commuted his sentence after President Wilson had refused to do so.

Jane Addams was the first American woman to be awarded the Nobel Peace Prize, which she received in 1931 for her work trying to realize her aspiration to rid the world of war. She was a noted author, and a leader in the causes of woman suffrage and world peace. She opposed World War I; the year after it began, she was elected national chairman of the Woman's Peace Party and president of the Women's International League for Peace and Freedom. She was chosen by an International Woman's Conference in The Hague to head the commission to find an end to World War I.

Ron Paul is a Republican congressman from Texas (1977, 1978-1984, 1988 to present). He ran for president in 1988 as a Libertarian and 2008 as a Republican. Paul, a strict constitutionalist, is an outspoken opponent of war as well as the Patriot Act, the draft and torture, describing himself as a non-interventionist, not an isolationist. Paul believes the Republican Party has lost its way: "There's a strong tradition of being anti-war in the Republican Party. It is the constitutional position. It is the advice of the Founders to follow a non-interventionist foreign policy, and stay out of entangling alliances, be friends with countries, negotiate and talk with them and trade with them."

Joan Baez is a singer, songwriter and activist whose music has often dealt with social issues. Baez was a vocal opponent of the Vietnam War. In 1964, she endorsed tax resistance by withholding 60% of her 1963 income taxes. In 1964, she co-founded the Institute for the Study of Nonviolence. In 1967 Baez was arrested twice for blocking the entrance of the Armed Forces Induction Center in Oakland, California, resulting in her serving more than a month in jail. She joined Cindy Sheehan at Camp Casey in Texas protesting the Iraq War in 2005.

Mark Twain, the pen name for Samuel Clemens, is one of America's greatest humorists, lecturers and authors. After supporting American imperialism in Hawaii and the Philippines, Twain reversed course and in 1899 became a leading voice against U.S. militarism, imperialism and empire. He was a vice president of the American Anti-Imperialist League. He wrote and spoke against war, most notably in "The War Prayer," which was rejected for publication until 1916, six years after his death.

Opening Statement

This book was prepared for a meeting of people from across the political spectrum who oppose war and militarism. The book presents views from the right, left and radical center, views that reflect those of many Americans which are not represented in the political dialogue in Congress or the White House, or the mainstream media. Throughout American history there have been times when movements developed that were outside the limited political dialogue of the two major parties, such as the abolitionists, the Anti-Imperialist League, the Non-Partisan League, and aspects of the Old Right and the New Left. Sometimes those movements have broken through and created paradigm shifting moments. Some of the materials in this book describe the Populist Movement of the late 1800s to provide an example of the type of movement that can influence politics, even though it starts outside of the "acceptable" political spectrum. Our hope is that this meeting will be the first step toward building effective advocacy against war and militarism which pulls in the majority of Americans who recognize that war should truly be a last resort limited to the real defense of our Nation.

> *Of all the enemies of true liberty, war is, perhaps, the most to be dreaded, because it comprises and develops the germ of every other. War is the parent of armies; from these proceed debts and taxes; and armies, and debts, and taxes are the known instrument for bringing the many under the domination of the few.—James Madison*

Foreword

This book is a compilation of essays resulting from an unprecedented gathering of unlike-minded people who are alarmed about the destructive consequences of our country's runaway militarism. The Across the Political Spectrum Conference Against War and Militarism, was held in Washington, D.C. on February 20th, 2010. The participants were from the right and the left; most had not previously collaborated. It is our hope that this book of essays begins to close the divide between people of different political and philosophical persuasions who are working to make our foreign policy more peaceful, less expensive, and better for Americans and the world.

I was a Cold War hawk. I remember conversing in the 1980s about the wickedness of the Soviet regime. We were appalled that the commissars required the citizens to show identification in order to travel from city to city. We sneered that the Soviets listened in on telephone conversations, and were shocked when we heard about the Gulag. We laughed with self-righteousness when the Soviets justified the above with the claim that they were just protecting the homeland. Due to our wars, our government now does that too. We are an efficient free-market economy, which enables our government to access and record far more telephone conversations and financial transactions than the inefficient Soviet system was able to record. Just protecting the homeland.

When I was in my twenties, I took a trip to Guatemala, where there were military police in the airport toting Thompson machine guns. I smugly thought to myself how nice it was to be an American who doesn't experience these base displays of government power in public places. Because of our wars, now we do too.

There are soldiers in full combat regalia toting automatic weapons in train stations, airports, and important government installations. Even in rural Florida, where I live, our sheriff's department's SWAT team has its very own armored vehicle, which they proudly display at school fairs. We look and act like the third-rate military dictatorships that we have denigrated over the years and have felt compelled to invade or destabilize because of their militaristic behavior. Again, just protecting the homeland.

For years we have witnessed our leaders admonishing other countries for committing human rights abuses. Yet our government on a daily basis deploys troops in countries around the world. These troops are regularly sent to invade private homes and roughly drag the occupants into the street. Sometimes they drag them to prison camps to be held for years without any due process of law. Too many times these actions are based on a rumor or just a tip. When they don't invade houses that are rumored to contain "suspected terrorists," they just blow them up with smart bombs and kill all the occupants. All this is excused by our political leaders as necessary collateral damage and essential to protect the homeland. For some reason it is much more excusable to slaughter innocents when smart bombs are used. What is our example—the Soviet Union?

As a tragic aside: The government apologists, justify the slaughter of innocent bystanders using the fantastic logic that states: all civilians know the U.S. military is searching for and destroying terrorist leaders. Therefore, civilians should know better than be in a house containing suspected terrorist leaders because there is a risk the house will be destroyed at any time. It is the civilians' responsibility to avoid being killed by smart bombs.

Due to the Cold War, our government has become accustomed to interfering with the governments of weaker nations around the world. Our government agents have regularly engaged in activities designed to destabilize countries and insert political leaders who are "friendly to U.S. interests." Interestingly, those "friendlies" usually turn out to be corrupt and detrimental to our interests. Both Shahs of Iran were our guys. Manuel Noriega and Saddam Hussein were at one time our guys. So many times our corrupt "friendlies" have set the stage for people like Fidel Castro, Ayatollah Khomeini, and the Ortega brothers. We supported and trained the Taliban fighters to kill Soviets. Now they kill Americans. When will we stop?

Our latest "friendly leader," President Karzai, has a brother who is reputed to be a big player in the Afghani opium trade. How must we look to the Afghanis, Iraqis, Iranians, Somalis, and the rest of the world? Our leaders preach about freedom and democracy yet we act with arrogance and use deadly force in and against weaker nations. Our leaders act very much like the Soviet regime we spent many lives, many dollars, and many years "defeating." In our case it is acceptable behavior because we are just protecting the homeland.

The political elite think they fool us with talk about exit strategies from their many "police actions," even though we are still quartering troops in lands invaded during the 19th century Spanish American War. We have many tens of thousands of soldiers still deployed across Europe, sixty-five years after the end of the Second World War and twenty years after the demise of the Soviet Union. Our troops still occupy Korea, sixty years after that UN police action. We have more than 700 foreign military bases in all, with hundreds of thousands of personnel stationed abroad. When the Soviet Union collapsed, NATO was redefined and NATO forces have been sent out to occupy and bomb rather than be disbanded. There is always an excuse for more militarism, not less.

The Washington elites arrogantly talk about American exceptionalism and America's responsibility to police the world and make it "safe for democracy." Yet what example are we setting? We are engaged in the same old killing and destruction, while hiding behind moralistic excuses.

I hope this book helps raise awareness of the extent of the destruction war brings upon our own country, and to people in foreign lands. Let us work to gain a consensus to stop this profligate waste of lives, financial resources, and the steady erosion of our civil rights. America is better than this.

George D. O'Neill, Jr.
Lake Wales, Florida
September 2010

Acknowledgements

Thank you to Bill Kauffman, Kevin Zeese, and Paul Buhle for their patience and great advice in editing this project.

Kevin Zeese and Bill Kauffman for all their efforts helping to organize the February, 20th, 2010 conference.

Katrina vanden Heuvel from *The Nation* and Kara Hopkins and Daniel McCarthy from *The American Conservative.*

All the wonderful participants of the conference, who were willing to cross ideological lines and work with those who hold some very different views. Also thank you to the writers who were unable to attend the conference and contributed essays to this book.

Also my babies, Catharine, Georgie, Roger, and Phoebe, who were not only helpful, but understanding of the hours spent working on the project.

George D. O'Neill, Jr.

I join George O'Neill, Jr. in all the acknowledgments above but need to add one. Thank you to George O'Neill, Jr. for reaching out across political lines to bring all of us together. We share the hope that these first steps lead to an end to wars of aggression, the closure of U.S. military bases around the world and a significantly smaller military budget sufficient for the real *defense* of the nation.

Kevin Zeese

Table of Contents

* indicates post-conference contribution

Building an Across the Political Spectrum Movement Opposed to War and Empire

LESSONS FROM HISTORY

Ain't My America: The Long, Noble History of Antiwar Conservatism and Middle-American Anti-Imperialism

Bill Kauffman

Introduction: I'll Just Stay Here, Thanks

Left stands for peace, right for war; liberals are pacific, conservatives are bellicose. Or so one might conclude after surveying the dismal landscape of the American Right in the Age of Bush II.

Yet there is a long and honorable (if largely hidden) tradition of antiwar thought and action among the American Right. It stretches from ruffle-shirted Federalists who opposed the War of 1812 and civic-minded mugwump critics of the Spanish-American War on up through the midwestern isolationists who formed the backbone of the pre-World War II America First Committee and the conservative Republicans who voted against U.S. involvement in NATO, the Korean conflict and Vietnam. And although they are barely audible amid the belligerent clamor of today's shock-and-awe Right, libertarians and old-fashioned traditionalist conservatives are among the sharpest critics of the Iraq War and the imperial project of the Bush Republicans.

Derided as isolationists—which, as that patriot of the Old Republic Gore Vidal has noted, means simply people who "want no part of foreign wars" and who "want to be allowed to live their own lives without interference from government"—the antiwar Right has put forth a critique of foreign intervention that is at once gimlet-eyed, idealistic, historically grounded, and dyed deeply in the American grain. Just because Bush, Rush, and Fox are ignorant of history doesn't mean authentic conservatives have to swallow the profoundly un-American American Empire.

Rooted in the Farewell Address of George Washington, informing such conservative-tinged antiwar movements as the Anti-Imperialist League, which said no to U.S. colonialism in the Philippines, finding poignant and prescient expression in the extraordinary valediction in which President Dwight Eisenhower warned his countrymen against the "military-industrial complex," the conservative case against American Empire and militarism remains forceful and relevant. It is no museum piece, no artifact as inutile as it is quaint. It is plangent, wise, and deserving of revival. But before it can be revived, it must be disinterred.

A note, first, on taxonomy. To label is to libel, or at least to divest the subject of individuating contradictions and qualifications. I have found that the most interesting American political figures cannot be squeezed into the constricted and lifeless pens of liberal or conservative. Nor do I accept the simpleminded division of our lovely and variegated country into red and blue, for to paint Colorado, Kansas, and Alabama requires every color in the spectrum. Right and Left have outlived their usefulness as taxonomic distinctions. They're closer to prisons from which no thought can escape.

Yet the terms are as ubiquitous as good and evil, and in fact many on the Right do think, Latinately, of their side as dexterous and the Left as sinister. I say it's time for a little ambidexterity. So my "Right" is capacious enough to include Jeffersonian libertarians and Jefferson-hating Federalists, Senators Robert Taft and George McGovern (yes, yes; give me a chance), dirt-farm southern populists and Beacon Streeters who take hauteur with their tea and jam, cranky Nebraska tax cutters and eccentric Michigan tellers of ghostly tales, little old ladies in tennis shoes marching against the United Nations and free-market economists protesting the draft. My subjects are, in the main, suspicious of state power, crusades, bureaucracy, and a modernity that is armed and dangerous. They are anti-expansion, pro-particularism, and so genuinely "conservative"—that is, cherishing of the verities, of home and hearth and family—as to make them mortal (immortal?) enemies of today's neoconservatives.

Above all, they have feared empire, whose properties were enumerated well by the doubly pen-named Garet Garrett: novelist, exponent of free enterprise and individualism, and a once-reliable if unspectacular stable horse for the *Saturday Evening Post.* Writing in 1953, he set down a quintet of imperial requisites.

> 1. *The executive power of the government shall be dominant.*
> 2. *Domestic policy becomes subordinate to foreign policy.*

> 3. *Ascendancy of the military mind, to such point at last that the civilian mind is intimidated.*
> 4. *A system of satellite nations.*
> 5. *A complex of vaunting and fear.*

Between "Constitutional, representative, limited government, on the one hand, and Empire on the other hand, there is mortal enmity," wrote Garrett, who did not burst with confidence that the former would vanquish the latter. He wrote in the final days of the Truman administration. The executive bestrode the U.S. polity. Militarism and the cult of bigness held sway. The blood rivers of Europe had yet to run dry. More than fifty thousand American boys had died—for what?—on the Korean peninsula. Truman had refused to obtain from Congress a formal declaration of war; future presidents would follow suit. The dark night of Cold War was upon us. This was what our forebears had warned against.

Why did these men (and later women) of the "Right" oppose expansion, war, and empire? And, in contemporary America, where have all the followers gone?

From the Republic's beginning, Americans of conservative temperament have been skeptical of manifest destiny and crusades for democracy. They have agreed with Daniel Webster that "there must be some limit to the extent of our territory, if we are to make our institutions permanent. The Government is very likely to be endangered...by a further enlargement of its already vast territorial surface." Is it really worth trading in the Republic for southwestern scrubland? Webster's point was remade, just as futilely, by the Anti-Imperialist League. It was repeated by those conservatives who supplied virtually the only opposition to the admission of Hawaii and Alaska to the Union. As the Texas Democrat Kenneth M. Regan told the House when he vainly argued against stitching a forty-ninth star on the flag, "I fear for the future of the country if we start taking in areas far from our own shores that we will have to protect with our money, our guns, and our men, instead of staying here and looking after the heritage we were left by George Washington, who told us to beware of any foreign entanglements."

Expansion was madness. John Greenleaf Whittier compared its advocates to hashish smokers.

The man of peace, about whose dreams
The sweet millennial angels cluster,
Tastes the mad weed, and plots and schemes,
A raving Cuban filibuster!

George W. Bush, it is rumored, preferred coke to hash, but his utopian vision of an American behemoth splayed across the globe would be, to conservatives of eras past, a hideous nightmare.

Robert Nisbet, the social critic who was among the wisest and most laureled of American conservatives, wrote in his coruscant *Conservatism: Dream and Reality* (1986): "Of all the misascriptions of the word 'conservative' during the last four years, the most amusing, in an historical light, is surely the application of 'conservative' to the [budget-busting enthusiasts for great increases in military expenditures]. For in America throughout the twentieth century, and including four substantial wars abroad, conservatives had been steadfastly the voices of non-inflationary military budgets, and of an emphasis on trade in the world instead of American nationalism. In the two World Wars, in Korea, and in Viet Nam, the leaders of American entry into war were such renowned liberal-progressives as Woodrow Wilson, Franklin Roosevelt, Harry Truman and John F. Kennedy. In all four episodes conservatives, both in the national government and in the rank and file, were largely hostile to intervention."

In the two decades since Nisbet's observation the historical amnesia has descended into a kind of belligerent nescience. Today's self-identified conservatives loathe, detest, and slander any temerarious soul who speaks for peace. FDR and Truman join Ronald Reagan in the trinity of favorite presidents of the contemporary Right; those atavistic Old Rightists who harbored doubts about U.S. entry into the world wars or our Asian imbroglios (scripted, launched, and propagandized for by liberal Democrats) are dismissed as cranks or worse. Vice President Dick Cheney, lamenting the August 2006 primary defeat of the Scoop Jackson Democratic senator Joseph Lieberman, charged that the Democrats wanted to "retreat behind our oceans"—which an earlier generation of peace-minded Republicans had considered a virtuous policy consistent with George Washington's adjuration to avoid entanglements and alliances with foreign nations.

Felix Morley, the *Washington Post* editorialist who would have been a top foreign-policy official in the Robert Taft administration, wrote in 1959: "Every war in which the United States has engaged since 1815 was waged in the name of democracy. Each has contributed to that centralization of power which tends to destroy that local self-government which is what most Americans have in mind when they acclaim democracy."Alas, Dick Cheney, the draft-dodging hawk, the anti-gay-marriage grandfather of a tribade-baby, is not an irony man.

I will consider the anti-expansionists of the early Republic in the first chapter. My focus in this book, however, is on "conservative" anti-imperialists of the twentieth century—the American Century, as that rootless son of missionaries Henry Luce dubbed it. The men and women whom I shall profile regarded Lucian expansion, conquest, and war—whether in the Philippines in 1900 or Vietnam in 1968—as profoundly un-American, even anti-American. The American Century, alas, did not belong to the likes of Moorfield Storey, Murray Rothbard, or Russell Kirk. But the American soul does.

These brave men and women also insisted, in the face of obloquy and smears, that dissent is a patriotic imperative. For questioning the drive to war in 1941, Charles Lindbergh would be called a Nazi by the FDR hatchet man Harold Ickes, and for challenging the constitutionality of Harry Truman's Korean conflict, Senator Robert Taft would be slandered as a commie symp by *The New Republic*. Patrick J. Buchanan would be libeled as an anti-Semite for noting the role that Israel's supporters played in driving the United States into the two (the first two?) invasions of Iraq, and the full range of anti-Iraq War right-wingers would be condemned as "unpatriotic conservatives" by *National Review* in April 2003. Same as it ever was. As Senator Taft lamented in January 1951 during the brief but illuminating "Great Debate" over Korea and NATO strategy between hawkish liberal Democrats and peace-minded conservative Republicans, "Criticisms are met by the calling of names rather than by intelligent debate."

In pre-imperial America, conservatives objected to war and empire out of jealous regard for personal liberties, a balanced budget, the free enterprise system, and federalism. These concerns came together under the umbrella of the badly misunderstood America First Committee, the largest popular antiwar organization in U.S. history. The AFC was formed in 1940 to keep the United States out of a second European war that many Americans feared would be a repeat of the first. Numbering eight hundred thousand members who ranged from populist to patrician, from Main Street Republican to prairie socialist, America First embodied and acted upon George Washington's Farewell Address counsel to pursue a foreign policy of neutrality.

As the America Firsters discovered, protesting war is a lousy career move. Dissenters are at best calumniated, at worst thrown in jail: for standing against foreign wars and the drive thereto Eugene V. Debs was imprisoned (World War I), Martin Luther King Jr. was painted red and spied upon (Vietnam War), and those who have spoken and acted against the Bush-Cheney Iraq War have been subject to a drearily predictable array of insults and indignities.

It has long been so. Edgar Lee Masters, the *Spoon River Anthology* poet and states'-rights Democrat who threw away his career by writing a splenetic biography of Abraham Lincoln decrying Honest Abe as a guileful empire builder, recalled of the Spanish-American War: "There was great opposition to the war over the country, but at that time an American was permitted to speak out against a war if he chose to do so." Masters had lived through the frenzied persecutions of antiwar dissidents under the liberal Democrat Woodrow Wilson. He had little patience with gilded platitudes about wars for human rights and the betterment of the species. He knew that war meant death and taxes, those proverbial inevitabilities that become shining virtues in the fog of martial propaganda. Masters, in the argot of today's war party and its publicists, was a traitor, a cringing treasonous abettor of America's (and freedom's!) enemies.

Yet Masters and his ilk were American to the core, and the antiwar Middle Americanism they represented has never really gone away. It surfaced even during Vietnam, that showpiece war of the best and brightest establishment liberal Democrats. Although most conservative Republicans were gung-ho on Vietnam, discarding their erstwhile preference for limited constitutional government, the right-wing antiwar banner was carried by such libertarians as Murray Rothbard (who sought, creatively, to fuse Old Right with New Left in an antiwar popular front) and the penny-pinching Iowa Republican congressman H. R. Gross, who said nay to the war on the simple if not wholly adequate grounds that it cost too much.

The Iraq wars of the Presidents Bush have rekindled the old antiwar spirit of the Right, though it is easy to miss in the glare of the bombs bursting in the Mesopotamian air. Indeed, Bush Republicans and pro-war Democrats have fretted mightily over recent surveys from the Council on Foreign Relations showing that the American people are reverting to—horrors!—isolationism, which the CFR defines invidiously as a hostility toward foreigners but which I see as a wholesome, pacific, and very American reluctance to intervene in the political and military quarrels of other nations.

The old American isolationism endures, despite the slurs, despite its utter absence within the corridors of power. President George W. Bush, as messianically interventionist a chief executive as we have ever endured, took out after the bogeyman in his 2006 State of the Union address: "Our enemies and our friends can be certain: The United States will not retreat from the world, and we will never surrender to evil. America rejects the false comfort of isolationism." And America, or rather its masters, chooses the bloody road of expansion and war.

The men who write the words that thud from Bush's mouth felt compelled to rebuke nameless isolationists because, as a Pew Research Center survey of October 2005 found, 42 percent of Americans agreed that the U.S. "should mind its own business internationally and let other countries get along the best they can on their own." As a Pew press release noted, over the last forty years "only in 1976 and 1995 did public opinion tilt this far toward isolationism."

Democrats were "twice as likely as Republicans to say the U.S. should mind its own business internationally," a sign of just how successful Bush and the neoconservatives have been in reshaping the GOP mind, as it were. (A decade earlier, Pew found no substantial difference in isolationist attitudes among Republican and Democratic partisans.)

Despite the Wilsonian tattoo issuing from the White House and repeated assertions that the U.S. military is constructing a democratic Middle East, Pew found that "promoting democracy in other nations" comes in dead last in the foreign-policy priorities of Americans. Only 24 percent of respondents affirmed that goal, as compared to 84 percent who favored "protecting jobs of American workers" and 51 percent who placed "reducing illegal immigration" atop their list. These latter two are classic themes of the isolationist Right, as embedded, for instance, in the presidential campaigns of Patrick J. Buchanan.

There is nothing freakish, cowardly, or even anomalous about these Middle Americans who are turning against foreign war. They are acting in the best traditions of their forebears. But those forebears have been disgracefully forgotten. The history of right-wing (or decentralist, or small-government, or even Republican) hostility to militarism and empire is piteously underknown. The traditions are unremembered. Which is where this book comes in.

The Bush-whacked Right is incorrigibly ignorant of previous "Rights." For all they know, Robert Taft may as well be Che Guevara. Yet there is a good deal of subsurface grumbling by the Right, among Republican operatives (who understand the potential of an anti-interventionist electoral wave); D.C.-based movement-conservatives, who recall that in the dim mists of time they once spoke of limited government as a desideratum; and at the grassroots level, where once more folks are asking the never-answered question of the isolationists: why in hell are we over there?

Bill Clinton lamented after his 1997 State of the Union address, "It's hard when you're not threatened by a foreign enemy to whip people up to a fever pitch of common, intense, sustained, disciplined endeavor." Old-style conservatives would deny that this is *ever* a legitimate function of the central state. "Sustained, disciplined endeavor" driven by a populace at "fever pitch" and organized by a central state is fascistic. It ill befits the country of Ken Kesey and Bob Dylan and Johnny Appleseed. It sure as hell ain't my America.

I should own up to my own biases. I belong to no political camp: my politics are localist, decentralist, Jeffersonian. I am an American rebel, a Main Street bohemian, a rural Christian pacifist. I have strong libertarian and traditionalist conservative streaks. I am in many ways an anarchist, though a front-porch anarchist, a chestnut-tree anarchist, a girls-softball-coach anarchist. My politics are a kind of mixture of Dorothy Day and Henry David Thoreau, though with an upstate New York twist. I voted for Nader in 2004 and Buchanan in 2000: the peace candidates. I often vote Libertarian and Green. I am a freeborn American with the blood of Crazy Horse, Zora Neale Hurston, and Jack Kerouac flowing in my veins. My heart is with the provincial and with small places, and it is from this intense localism that my own isolationist, antiwar sympathies derive. I misfit the straitjackets designed by Fox News and the *New York Times*. So does any American worth the name.

You can have your hometown or you can have the empire. You can't have both. And the tragedy of modern conservatism is that the ideologues, the screamers over the airwaves, the apparatchiks in their Beltway viper's den, have convinced the Barcalounger-reclining *National Review* reader that one must always and forever subordinate one's place, one's neighborhood, whether natal ground or beloved adopted block, to the empire.

It isn't true! It never has been true. There is nothing conservative about the American Empire. It seeks to destroy—which is why good American conservatives, those loyal to family and home and neighborhood and our best traditions, should wish, and work toward, its peaceful destruction. We have nothing to lose but the chains and taxes of empire. And we have a country to regain.

Review of *Ain't My America*
Fewer Bases, More Baseball

Ain't My America: The Long, Noble History of Anti-War Conservatism and Middle-American Anti-Imperialism,
Bill Kauffman, Metropolitan, 274 pages

Daniel McCarthy

Bill Kauffman writes prose—history, novels, journalism—but he is a poet and a prophet. His task in *Ain't My America* is to remind us of who we are: a Republic, not an empire, a nation of families and towns, not barracks and bases. Kauffman writes to restore conservatives to their senses. No more war, please. Remember your ancestors. Remember Jefferson and John Quincy Adams, Russell Kirk and Robert Nisbet. What has passed for the Right since the Cold War isn't right in any sense, and Kauffman sets out to prove it.

Antiwar, "Little America" conservatism was present at the creation of the Republic. Revolutionaries like Patrick Henry, having thrown off the yoke of British empire, were not about to set up a centralized fiscal-military state in the former colonies. "I abominate and detest the idea of government, where there is a standing army," George Mason told Virginia's ratifying convention.

Unfortunately, Anti-Federalists like Mason and Henry set the practical as well as philosophical precedent for future conservatives—they failed. A stronger central government with heightened war-making powers, sufficient to put down Whiskey rebels—tax rebels, actually—and Daniel Shays, took root. Even so, the victorious Federalists were no imperialists. On the contrary, they opposed Thomas Jefferson's designs to build an inland "Empire of Liberty" with the Louisiana Purchase. "As you extend your limits you increase the difficulties arising from a want of that similarity of customs, habits, and manners so essential for its support," warned Connecticut Federalist Roger Griswold. Neighbors might be friends; strangers had to be unified by laws.

Neither Federalists nor Jeffersonian Republicans were consistently antiwar. The former raised a navy, and taxes, under John Adams to fight a Quasi-War with France. Republicans invaded Canada and kicked off the War of 1812. The most implacable opponent of that conflict—a foe of almost all militarism and expansion, in fact—was John Randolph of Roanoke, a Republican himself, as well as "a habitual opium user, a bachelor who seems to have nurtured a crush on Andrew Jackson," Kauffman tells us, and an exemplary American conservative. The history of Randolph and his fellow dissident Republicans, the Tertium Quids, is samizdat in George Bush's America. "Today, most of those old battles are forgotten," neocon Robert Kagan assures us, "No one recalls that John Randolph of Roanoke and John Taylor of Caroline—more Jeffersonian than Jefferson himself—railed against the War of 1812." Not so, Bob. Bill Kauffman remembers, and he won't let America forget.

Partisans of peace in the Old Republic included poets as well as statesmen. Kauffman not only writes with literary flair of his own, he quotes generously from antiwar poets and songwriters. "Once upon a time in America," he says, "poets engaged in public discourse and sought consulates instead of endowed chairs." William Cullen Bryant abominated the War of 1812; Emerson and John Greenleaf Whittier took their stands against the Mexican War.

The Little America tradition remained strong, if at all turns unsuccessful, through the Spanish-American War, the opposition to which, most notably the Anti-Imperialist League, was filled with classical liberals like Yale sociologist William Graham Sumner and was funded by (mostly) small businessmen—a conservative coalition. "They spoke for… a land of creeks, not oceans; shops, not factories; modesty and sly humor, not bluster and brass," Kauffman writes. And this was no mere protest movement: prominent politicians like Democratic ex-president Grover Cleveland and such stalwart Republicans as Senators Justin Morrill of Vermont—a founder of the Grand Old Party, no less—and George Frisbie Hoar of Massachusetts supported the cause.

Resistance to U.S. entry into World War I arose from many of the same segments of society that had stood against the Spanish-American War. "The opposition to the war came mostly from farmers, old-school classical liberals, pacifists, Main Street Republican isolationists, and socialists," Kauffman relates. But this time, "The balance tilted leftward":

"The Left distinguished itself in 1917, while the Right, as it would in future conflicts, threw in with a liberal war president. That it took Socialists to circulate a pamphlet with the libertarian title *No Conscription, No Involuntary Servitude, No Slavery* is an indictment of the individualistic Right."

The ranks of old-guard Republicans like Morrill and Hoar had thinned by 1917, leaving right-wing antiwar sentiment to be expressed by such unsavory figures as Mississippi arch-segregationist Sen. James Vardaman. He damned Wilson's interventionism and denounced "the un-American principle of compulsory military training." That cost him his Senate seat—an equally segregationist hawk replaced him.

After Woodrow Wilson's misadventure, opposition to further bleeding America for Europe multiplied. The anti-interventionists of the interwar years had a sense of humor: satirical Veterans of Future Wars chapters sprang up on 584 college campuses, along with local variations such as the Future Profiteers and Future Golddiggers. These young doves were also budget hawks; according to Kauffman, they believed "a policy of preemptive fiscal conservatism would stop war before it started."

As World War II approached, the America First Committee assembled. It was the largest antiwar organization in U.S. history—and is perhaps the most maligned. Drawing on the work of historians Wayne Cole and Justus Doenecke, Kauffman sets the record straight: America First was not anti-Semitic or pro-German. A single unvetted speech by Charles Lindbergh asserted that "the three most important groups who have been pressing this country toward war are the British, the Jewish and the Roosevelt administration." Lindbergh had his defenders, a young Kurt Vonnegut among them, but leaders of America First like John T. Flynn, the anti-New Deal journalist who was head of the New York chapter, were aghast. Kauffman argues that this anomalous speech should not besmirch the organization: Lindbergh "was one man in the last broad peace movement in American history, almost a million strong."

Even during the Cold War, when an interventionist anti-Communism largely defined the Right, antiwar conservatives persevered. Felix Morley, co-founder of *Human Events,* was one of them. Others included traditionalist conservatives Russell Kirk and Robert Nisbet, who made little attempt to conceal their thoughts about what militarism meant for the nation's social order. "Nothing has proved more destructive of kinship, religion, and local patriotism," wrote Nisbet, "than has war and the accompanying military mind."

In Congress, there was Sen. Robert A. Taft—known as "Mr. Republican," though he narrowly lost the party's presidential nomination in 1952—and Taft's even more anti-interventionist '52 campaign manager, Nebraska Congressman Howard Buffett, father of Warren and an uncompromising foe of war and government growth (or do I repeat myself?). There was also Congressman H.R. Gross (R-Iowa), noted in his *New York Times* obituary for his "tight-fisted approach to fiscal matters and his strong isolationist views on foreign policy." Gross "railed against the space program, foreign aid, congressional junkets abroad, and every post office and bridge he could find," says Kauffman. And Kentucky Republican Eugene Siler, a devout Baptist, cast the sole "no" vote in the House against the Gulf of Tonkin Resolution. (Gross voted "present.")

Taft died in 1953, Buffet in 1964. Siler retired in '65, and Gross stepped down a decade later. A new crop of antiwar Republicans succeeded them—Oregon Sen. Mark Hatfield, Illinois Sen. Charles Percy, Kentucky Sens. John Sherman Cooper and Thruston B. Morton. But the real spiritual successors to the Old Right, Kauffman argues, were on the other side of the political spectrum: "The words of Buffett, of Morley, of Taft, could be discerned in the tunes of the New Left." Not coincidentally, the only antiwar candidate to win the nomination of either major party during the Cold War was a man of the Left, South Dakota Sen. George McGovern.

Then again, Kauffman suggests, this "soft-spoken man of the prairies" may have been "the most conservative of the serious presidential aspirants" of the era, "after Bob Taft and Eugene McCarthy." Kauffman is a persuasive McGovern revisionist, and old George's recent Wall Street Journal op-ed "Freedom Means Responsibility" certainly struck a libertarian chord: "under the guise of protecting us from ourselves," he wrote, "the right and the left are becoming ever more aggressive in regulating behavior." Acid, amnesty, and abortion? Or antiwar, anti-centralist, and authentically American?

The end of the Cold War should have been the end of the imperial Right. But it wasn't. Instead things got worse instead of better under two Bushes and two terms of Clinton. Today, writes Kauffman,

"The Republicans in the age of George W. Bush have become a war party, nothing less and certainly nothing more. Dissident GOP voices are rare and unwelcome echoes. Among the Democrats, it is the most culturally conservative national figures (Senators Robert Byrd of West Virginia and James Webb of Virginia) who have the guts and convictions to take on the Bush policy of hyperinterventionism."

Eleven House Republicans voted against Gulf War 2: The Phantom Menace. Only two of them are still in office—though, thankfully, they are the two most conservative: Ron Paul of Texas and Jimmy Duncan of Tennessee. They have since been joined in dissent by North Carolina's Walter Jones, who has owned up to making a mistake in voting for the war. These three almost seem the last of their breed. "Together, the Christian Right and the neoconservatives dedicated the GOP—exiled from Main Street—to war and empire" Kauffman laments. "Iraq II was only the beginning—or so they prayed."

The antiwar Right is used to losing: we have about 200 years' experience in that line. The marvel is that we have survived at all against the most efficient killing machine ever invented—the modern state. Failure has had a steep price, but the cost of not resisting would have been even greater. Kauffman's last chapter shows what war has done to our families, our towns, our culture—even our night skies, as war-perverts dream of planting missiles on the moon. "The social costs, in forms ranging from the nationalization of child care to booming divorce rates are monuments to the hypocrisy of conservatives," Kauffman writes. That some of the most trenchant conservative critics of militarism have been sociologists—William Graham Sumner, Robert Nisbet, Allan Carlson—is no accident. Taxes, divorce, juvenile delinquency, anomie, and rootlessness are just a few of the wages of war. "No agency of the government has done as much to destroy the traditional American family as has the Department of Defense," Kauffman concludes.

Like our once-federated Republic, we've been folded, spindled, and mutilated, but the antiwar Right is not giving up. The cause of Little America—of Batavia, New York and Sedalia, Missouri, and everywhere dear to a native son's heart—is too great to surrender. Ain't My America is a book every conservative, and certainly every TAC reader, should own—and give to friends. For Bill Kauffman reminds us that we have a long and joyous tradition to live up to.

THE EMPIRE VS LITTLE AMERICA

Conference Remarks

Bill Kauffman

Senator William Fulbright, the only good national Democrat named Bill ever to come out of Arkansas, said in 1967, "The price of empire is America's soul, and that price is too high."

War, expansion, the maintenance of a large standing army: these corrupt a country, as poets from James Russell Lowell to Wendell Berry have tried to tell us. The Vietnam or Iraq War may level villages across the sea but back home, in our villages, they unleash an insidious poison, too. They make our places less liveable. From the pit of the Cold War Edmund Wilson, the Sage of Boonville, New York, lamented that "our country has become today a huge blundering power unit controlled more and more by bureaucracies whose rule is making it more and more difficult to carry on the tradition of American individualism."

In Boonville as in Emporia as in Sauk Centre, the little places that give America soul were ravaged and denuded by the machine of perpetual war.

War effaces and perverts the very bases of healthy community life. It elevates impermanence and rootlessness to virtues. It forcibly uproots people; it distorts natural economic patterns, causing artificial regional booms and busts—witness the histories of Detroit and Kentucky; it spreads venereal disease, if not democracy; it separates husbands from wives and parents from children; it leads to a spike in the divorce rate among service personnel and it nationalizes their children in what the Pentagon, with its usual tonedeafness to Orwellian rings, calls "the Total Army Family." Welcome to the Brave New World.

A militaristic state is a centripetal machine that sucks all power to the center. Smaller bodies, grass-roots democratic institutions, are devitalized, wiped out. All political decisions of consequence are made at a level impossibly remote from real life. People we don't know—people who have no desire or even means to know us—make life or death decisions about us.

America is the sum of a thousand and one little, individuated places, each with its own history and accent and stories. A politician who understands this will act in ways that protect and preserve these real places. She will ask the question that never gets injected into national debates over the wisdom of America's constant wars—namely, What are the domestic costs? Loving her block, she will not wish to bomb Iraq. Loyal to a neighborhood, she will not send its young men and women across the sea to kill and die for causes wholly unrelated to local life. It's been a long time since a Republican or Democratic presidential nominee acknowledged the primacy of home over the empire. You'd have to go back to Mitchell, South Dakota's George McGovern and "Come Home, America," and before him to the man who, in a just world, would have been the Republican nominee in 1948 or '52, Senator Robert A. Taft of Ohio, Mr. Republican.

Today we have these rootless politicos babbling on about "the homeland"—a creepy totalitarian phrase that, pre-Bush, was never applied to our country and which we should ridicule at every opportunity before it is permanently implanted in our national vocabulary. As the manufacture of political opinions and the directing of the political parties has become centralized in imperial Washington, the old skepticism of a powerful central state and respect for out of the way places, the provinces, has seemingly vanished.

But it is in these places—and they are urban as well as rural—that a healthy antiwar movement can grow. I say "healthy" because it is more than just "anti" something: it is based in love. This sentiment has suffused anti-expansion and antiwar movements throughout our history. It was captured in G. K. Chesterton's wonderful novel *The Napoleon of Notting Hill,* when he said that "the supreme psychological fact about patriotism... [is] that the patriot never under any circumstances boasts of the largeness of his country, but always, and of necessity, boasts of the smallness of it."

This was the kind of patriotism that animated the Anti-Imperialist League, which in opposing U.S. conquest of the Philippines spoke for a Little America, a land of creeks, not oceans; shops, not factories; modesty and sly humor, not bluster and brass. The Anti-Imperialists thought that, say, Indianans had enough to occupy them in Indiana—they had rich enough lives in the Hoosier state—that they did not need to send their young men across the sea to kill foreigners and plant the American flag atop a mound of Filipino corpses.

Bush, McCain, Hillary Clinton, Obama—the rootless class that runs this government—what do they love, other than the wielding of power? They stand on nothing. They have no ground under their feet. They have tanks and bombs but they have no soul.

They view Little America as a source of cannon fodder and tax dollars, though they are occasionally frustrated by our "isolationism"—that is, our reluctance to kill or be killed by foreigners. This is benighted. So we are hectored to take our eyes off those things nighest and focus them on Baghdad, Hanoi, Teheran, who knows what's next. A warfare state centralizes and vulgarizes culture: it despises the local, exalts the national, focuses on the remote. So cherishing, protecting, little and local things becomes a subversive act. Love, finally, is the most potent enemy of the empire.

And the love which sustains this Little America is reasserting itself. At farm markets. In community-supported agriculture. Homeschooling. The reflorescence of regional literature. Something is happening and Mr. Jones—or Mr. Obama, or Mr. Romney—doesn't know what it is. Wendell Berry calls this new decentralism a "redemptive" movement, though he acknowledges that "in terms of standing and influence [it] is hardly a side at all. It doesn't have a significant political presence. It is virtually unrepresented in our state and federal governments. Most of its concerns are not on the agenda of either major party."

But it's out there. And a mind our own business, stay out of foreign wars, love what is nighest unto you ethos is part of this emerging decentralist spirit. The Little America is waking up. And it is fertile territory in which to plant the flag of peace.

Classical Liberalism and the Anti-Imperialist League: The First Left-Right Coalition

By David T. Beito

The year 1898 witnessed the birth of the first significant left-right antiwar coalition in U.S. history, the American Anti-Imperialist League. Few political organizations ever had a more ideologically diverse, or distinguished, membership. The League welcomed participation from across the ideological divide. Unlike many modern antiwar organizations, it bent over backwards to avoid any official organizational statements on domestic or economic issue that might alienate either the antiwar right or left. Hence, the League quickly attracted such accomplished Americans as Samuel Gompers, the head of the American Federation of Labor, author Mark Twain, socialist writer William Dean Howells, philosopher William James, and settlement house leader Jane Addams. Andrew Carnegie, the second richest man in the United States, was the group's financial angel.

Although the League spanned the political spectrum, classical liberals were unusually well represented. Only two years before its founding, many of them had defected from the Democratic Party and voted for the presidential candidate of the National Democratic (or Gold Democrats) Party rather than support the champion of free silver, William Jennings Bryan. The most notable example was former president Grover Cleveland, a champion of the gold standard, freer trade, and author of endless vetoes, who was one of the League's forty-one vice presidents. A fellow vice president of the League was William Graham Sumner, a Yale anthropologist, sociologist, and economist as well as the best known American exponents of laissez faire. Few have more effectively described the pitfalls of empire. In his seminal speech in 1899, "The Conquest of the United States by Spain," Sumner declared that "My patriotism is of the kind which is outraged by the notion that the United States never was a great nation until in a petty three months' campaign it knocked to pieces a poor, decrepit, bankrupt old state like Spain. To hold such an opinion as that is to abandon all American standards, to put shame and scorn on all that our ancestors tried to build up here, and to go over to the standards of which Spain is a representative."

Moorfield Storey, the League's president for three decades, also had a long record as a classical liberal activist. His career began just after the Civil War as secretary to the legendary Senator Charles Sumner of Massachusetts and was capped off by his election as president of the American Bar Association in 1896. Although he was white, Storey later served as the first president of the National Association for the Advancement of Colored People. According to his biographer, his views "included pacifism, anti-imperialism, and racial egalitarianism fully as much as it did laissez-faire and moral tone in government." American imperialists, Storey charged, had recklessly thrown aside "that wise policy of non-intervention" and turned the United States into a European style "military power, burdened with a standing army and enormous navy, threatened with complications thousands of miles away, and exposed to constant apprehension." Under imperialism, he predicted, "taxation must increase, our currency must become disordered, and worse than all, the corruption which threatens us cannot fail to spread." Of course, not all members shared Storey's anti-racism. Some, such as Benjamin "Pitchfork" Tillman, rejected empire because it would incorporate "inferior races" in the U.S. The League was better than most on issues of race, however, during perhaps the most racist period in American history.

By its second year, the League boasted thirty-one thousand members and a half million contributors. Although it had more defeats than victories, imperialists underestimated it at their own peril. The League and other anti-imperialists came within only two votes of defeating the Treaty of Paris and fell just one vote short of securing a Senate amendment to give the Philippines independence. U.S. Vice President Garett Hobart had to cast the deciding vote.

Later in 1899, a showdown between Edward Atkinson, a classical liberal, and the might of the federal government rocketed the League back into the headlines. Atkinson was no stranger to political controversy. In his youth, he had helped raise funds to equip John Brown's insurgent army in Kansas. After the Civil War, he was perhaps the leading publicist for free-market causes, such as free trade. Atkinson rejected the traditional gold standard in favor of the radical free market goal of a divorce between government and banking. He went on to become a founder of the league and a prominent officer. At age seventy-one, this wealthy fire insurance executive and textile manufacturer, showed no signs of trimming his sails. He boldly wrote the Secretary of War informing him that he planned to mail anti-imperialist pamphlets to American soldiers in the Philippines. The Postmaster General immediately banned the pamphlets from the Manila mails. For a time, the McKinley administration considered hauling the old man up on sedition charges but backed off for fear of turning him into a martyr. Atkinson revelled in the controversy which only served to stimulate more requests for more pamphlets from the general public.

The presidential election of 1900 tested the strength of the League's commitment to a cross-ideological coalition. Although William Jennings Bryan, the Democratic candidate, ran on a strongly anti-imperialistic platform, members found it hard to forgive his last-minute support for the hated Treaty of Paris in 1899. Many anti-imperialist gold bugs recoiled at Bryan's free silver views. Although some members toyed with a third-party strategy, the League (including most of its Gold Democratic contingent) ultimately endorsed Bryan. Putting aside the merits of this decision, the modern antiwar movement could learn from this willingness to put aside egos and intense disagreements on domestic issues and unite behind a greater goal.

After McKinley's easy victory over Bryan in November, the League struggled on against ever greater odds. It had a brief second wind during the bloody Philippine-American War just after the turn of the century. Over four thousand Americans died, more than in the entire Spanish American War. The Filipino civilian death toll may have been as high as a million. Armed with extensive evidence of American atrocities, anti-imperialists pressed for a Senate investigation but this effort faltered after a determined counterattack by President Theodore Roosevelt and his allies who branded them as "sickly sentimentalists." Roosevelt's solid victory in the 1904 election dealt another major blow to the League. The Philippine insurgency had already waned by that time and it seemed that most Americans either supported foreign-policy interventionism or were indifferent to it.

The League shared some of the blame for its decline. Early on, it made the strategic mistake of centering its agenda on ending colonies in a formal sense (especially in the Philippines), rather than opposing the use of all American military force overseas. Despite some rhetorical flourishes, for example, the League did little of substance to fight the repeated deployment of U.S. troops in Mexico, Haiti, Nicaragua, the Dominican Republic, and other non-colonies in the first two decades of the Progressive Era. Another strategic mistake was the League's close alignment with the Democratic Party. This proved to be especially fatal during the Woodrow Wilson administration. Casting aside the previous critique of overseas entanglements, most (but not all) of the League's officers supported what they depicted as Wilson's "anti-imperialist" crusade to make the world "safe for democracy." By the end of the war, the League was little more than a letterhead. It met for the last time in 1920 and disappeared with Storey's death in 1929.

Any of the League's shortcomings, however, must be put into a broader historical context. From the beginning, it had to struggle against a seemingly insurmountable tide of imperialism during the first two decades of the twentieth century. It is amazing that it did so well under the circumstances. It came within a whisker of getting Philippine independence in 1899 and gave the public a much-needed source of information about American atrocities in the Philippines. At the very least, the League served to soften the worst excesses of American empire during the period. Without the League, it is probable that the U.S. would have annexed even more territories including possibly Cuba. The greatest lesson that the League can offer the peace movement today, however, was its admirable and sustained effort to reach out to anti-imperialist Americans across the ideological spectrum.

Bibliography

Beisner, Robert L. 1968. *Twelve against Empire: The Anti-Imperialists, 1898–1900.* New York: McGraw-Hill.

Beito, David T. and Beito, Linda Royster. 2000. Gold Democrats and the Decline of Classical Liberalism. *Independent Review.* (Spring): 555-575.

Foner, Philip S. 1984. *The Anti-Imperialist Reader: A Documentary History of Anti-Imperialism in the United States.* New York: Holmes and Meier Publishers.

Harrington, Fred H. 1935. The Anti-Imperialist Movement in the United States, 1898-1900. *Mississippi Valley Historical Review 22* (September): 211-230.

Lanzar, Maria C. 1930. The Anti-Imperialist League. *Philippine Social Science Review 3* (August):7–41.

Schirmer, Daniel B. 1972. *Republic or Empire: American Resistance to the Philippine War.* Cambridge, Mass.: Schenkman.

Sumner, William Graham. 1919. *War and Other Essays.* Albert Galloway Keller, ed. New Haven: Yale University Press.

Thompson, J.A. 1971. An Anti-Imperialist and the First World War: The Case of Albert J. Beveridge. *Journal of American Studies* (August): 133-150.

Welch, Richard E., Jr. 1974. American Atrocities in the Philippines: The Indictment and the Response. *Pacific Historical Review* (May): 233-253.

Woods, Thomas E. Jr. 2006 *The Anti-Imperialist League and the Battle Against Empire.* The Mises Institute. The Anti-Imperialist League and the Battle Against Empire—Thomas E. Woods, Jr.—Mises Institute http://mises.org/daily/2408#ixzz0msyGZQWY

David T. Beito is professor of history at the University of Alabama and the author of *Black Maverick: T.R.M. Howard's Fight of Civil Rights and Economic Power* (Urbana: University of Illinois Press, 2009); *From Mutual Aid to the Welfare State: Fraternal Societies and Social Services, 1890-1967* (Chapel Hill: University of North Carolina Press, 2000); and *Taxpayers in Revolt: Tax Resistance during the Great Depression* (Chapel Hill: University of North Carolina Press, 1989). He is also the chair of the Alabama State Advisory Committee of the U.S. Commission on Civil Rights.

The Anti-Imperialist League and the Battle Against Empire

By Thomas E. Woods, Jr.
December 15 2006

In April 1898 the United States went to war with Spain for the stated purpose of liberating Cuba from Spanish control. Several months later, when the war had ended, Cuba had been transformed into an American protectorate, and Puerto Rico, Guam, and the Philippines had become American possessions.

When the US government decided not to grant independence to the Philippines, Filipino rebels led by Emilio Aguinaldo determined to resist American occupying forces. The result was a brutal guerrilla war that stretched on for years. Some 200,000 Filipinos lost their lives, either directly from the fighting or as a result of a cholera epidemic traceable to the war.

That American forces were engaged in a colonial war to suppress another people's independence led to a great deal of soul-searching among important American thinkers, writers, and journalists. What eventually became the American Anti-Imperialist League began at a June 1898 meeting at Boston's Faneuil Hall, where people concerned about the colonial policy that the US government may choose to adopt in the wake of the war gathered to speak out against the transformation of the United States into an imperial power. The League was formally established that November, dedicating its energies to propagating the anti-imperialist message by means of lectures, public meetings, and the printed word.

Those who later became anti-imperialists could be found both among supporters and opponents of the Spanish-American War of 1898. William Jennings Bryan was a good example of the former, and Moorfield Storey of the latter. It is on this latter group of anti-imperialists that I wish to dwell for a moment, since what they had to say about war is liable to sound eerily familiar.

Storey was quite an interesting figure: an accomplished lawyer and graduate of Harvard Law School as well as president of the

American Bar Association, he was a supporter of laissez faire and a well-known advocate of the gold standard and free trade. Storey, who was white, was also the first president of the National Association for the Advancement of Colored People (NAACP) from 1909 until 1915. He spoke at the Boston meeting presided over by Bradford, and went on to become both a vice president of the New England Anti-Imperialist League and, later, president of the national organization.

Now consider Storey's words in April 1898, on the eve of the Spanish-American War, for it was these sentiments that animated his and so many others' anti-imperialist work:

> *This Club [the Massachusetts Reform Club] never met under circumstances more calculated to create the gravest anxiety in every patriotic man than tonight, and by patriotic man I do not mean him who measures his country's greatness by the extent of her territory, the size of her armies, the strength of her fleets, or even by the insolence with which she tramples upon her weaker neighbors, but him who knows that the true greatness of a nation, as of a man, depends upon its character, its sense of justice, its self-restraint, its magnanimity, in a word upon its possession of those qualities which distinguish George Washington from the prize-fighter—the highest type of man from the highest type of beast.*

Carl Schurz, who among other things was the first German-born American to serve in the US Senate, was likewise deeply involved in the league as an officer as well as firmly opposed to the Spanish-American War. He wrote in April 1898,

> *The man who in times of popular excitement boldly and unflinchingly resists hot-tempered clamor for an unnecessary war, and thus exposes himself to the opprobrious imputation of a lack of patriotism or of courage, to the end of saving his country from a great calamity, is, as to "loving and faithfully serving his country," at least as good a patriot as the hero of the most daring feat of arms, and a*

far better one than those who, with an ostentatious pretense of superior patriotism, cry for war before it is needed, especially if then they let others do the fighting.

Schurz recalled a verse from James Russell Lowell, writing about the Mexican War of 1846–48:

The side of our country must ollers be took.
An' President Polk, you know, he is our country.

"Again in our own time," Schurz reported, "we hear with the old persistency the same old plea to the voters of the nation to be loyal to the country, right or wrong. And when we probe the matter—nor is much probing necessary—we find that we are being urged to be loyal not to the country right or wrong, but to President McKinley right or wrong." To fit the present situation, Schurz suggested amending Lowell's lines to read,

The side of our country must ollers be took,
An' Mister McKinley, you know, he is our country.

We can fill in Lowell's verse today easily enough.

Among the best-known members of the Anti-Imperialist League was Mark Twain, who served as vice president from 1901 until his death in 1910. One of Twain's most compelling antiwar writings, a short story called "The War Prayer," was considered too radical to be published in Twain's lifetime. "I don't think the prayer will be published in my time," Twain said. "None but the dead are permitted to tell the truth."

"The War Prayer" was a vivid commentary on the misappropriation of religion on behalf of nationalistic causes. It begins with a church service in which the pastor calls down the blessings of God upon American military forces and concludes with, "Grant us the victory, O Lord our God!"

A frail old man makes his way into the church and, waving the pastor aside, explains that he has spoken with God Himself, who wishes to hear the other half of that prayer—the half that was only in their hearts and uttered but implicitly.

> *O Lord our Father, our young patriots, idols of our hearts, go forth to battle—be Thou near them! With them—in spirit—we also go forth from the sweet peace of our beloved firesides to smite the foe. O Lord our God, help us to tear their soldiers to bloody shreds with our shells; help us to cover their smiling fields with the pale forms of their patriot dead; help us to drown the thunder of the guns with the shrieks of their wounded, writhing in pain; help us to lay waste their humble homes with a hurricane of fire; help us to wring the hearts of their unoffending widows with unavailing grief; help us to turn them out roofless with little children to wander unfriended the wastes of their desolated land in rags and hunger and thirst, sports of the sun flames of summer and the icy winds of winter, broken in spirit, worn with travail, imploring Thee for the refuge of the grave and denied it—for our sakes who adore Thee, Lord, blast their hopes, blight their lives, protract their bitter pilgrimage, make heavy their steps, water their way with their tears, stain the white snow with the blood of their wounded feet! We ask it, in the spirit of love, of Him Who is the Source of Love, and Who is the ever-faithful refuge and friend of all that are sore beset and seek His aid with humble and contrite hearts. Amen.*

The story ends abruptly, with the people considering the man a lunatic—and, presumably, carrying on as before.

It is sometimes said of the anti-imperialists that they cared more about the effects that colonialism would have on the character of America and Americans than they did about its effects on the peoples who were held as colonies. This is not entirely fair to the anti-imperialists, who were genuinely horrified at the treatment the Filipinos received at the hands of American forces and who sought to investigate conditions there.

The Nation's E. L. Godkin, for instance, declared that the US government had substituted "keen effective slaughter for Spanish old-fashioned, clumsy slaughter." William James was astonished that his country could "puke up its ancient soul…in five minutes." Andrew

Carnegie wrote to a friend who favored expansion: "It is a matter of congratulation…that you have about finished your work of civilizing the Fillipinos [sic]. It is thought that about 8000 of them have been completely civilized and sent to Heaven. I hope you like it."

In 1901, the League passed a resolution instructing its executive committee "to use its best efforts in promoting a petition to the President of the United States that General Aguinaldo should be permitted to come to this country under safe conduct, to state the case of his people before the American Congress and nation." Needless to say, Theodore Roosevelt ignored this appeal.

Over the next several years the League focused on discovering and disseminating the truth about the fate of the Filipinos under American occupation. They publicized firsthand testimonies of tortures like the "water cure" that US forces employed. Thus according to Private A.F. Miller of the Thirty-second United States Volunteers,

> *this is the way we give them the water cure; lay them on their backs, a man standing on each hand and each foot, then put a round stick in the mouth and pour a pail of water in the mouth and nose, and if they don't give up pour in another pail. They swell up like toads. I'll tell you it is a terrible torture.*

George Kennan, the special investigator of the *Outlook,* wrote in 1901:

> *The Spaniard used the torture of water, throughout the islands, as a means of obtaining information; but they used it sparingly, and only when it appeared evident that the victim was culpable. Americans seldom do things by halves. We come from here and announce our intention of freeing the people from three or four hundred years of oppression, and say "We are strong and powerful and grand." Then to resort to inquisitorial methods, and use them without discrimination, is unworthy of us and will recoil on us as a nation. It is painful and humiliating to have to confess that in some of our dealings with the Filipinos*

> *we seem to be following more or less closely the example of Spain. We have established a penal colony; we have burned native villages near which there has been an ambush or an attack by insurgent guerillas; we kill the wounded; we resort to torture as a means of obtaining information.*

These were the kinds of things the anti-imperialists wanted to bring into the public eye.

By and large, however, the American public was unmoved. One anti-imperialist writer pondered the meaning of this indifference:

> *What is the significance of such silence? Do we realize that amidst all the sunshine of our rich, prosperous life we are being weighed in the balance of a true civilization, of eternal justice—and are being found wanting? It is the product of arbitrary government authority without justice, force from which the lifeblood of righteousness and truth has run out.*

Some were in fact quite hostile to the league and its mission. According to the commander of the New York chapter of the Grand Army of the Republic, all league members should have their citizenship stripped from them and be "denied the protection of the flag they dishonor." Teddy Roosevelt described the anti-imperialists as "simply unhung traitors, and…liars, slanderers and scandalmongers to boot."

The league carried on all the same. Edward Atkinson, who had been involved in the league since the Faneuil Hall meeting, actually inquired with the War Department to get a list of soldiers serving in the Philippines in order to send them some of his antiwar writings. He wrote:

> *In this morning's paper a correspondent of the* Boston Herald *states that the Departments are going to "expose" the Anti-Imperialist League and others who have as alleged stirred up discontent among the troops in Manila. I do not think the Executive Committee of the Anti-Imperialist League has yet taken any*

> *active measures to inform the troops of the facts and conditions there. The suggestion is, however, a valuable one and I have sent to Washington today to get specific addresses of officers and soldiers to the number of five or six hundred so that I may send them my pamphlets, giving them my assurance of sympathy. I shall place the same lists in charge of the Executive Committee of the League to keep up the supply.*

He never heard back.

So he went ahead and sent some at least to a limited group of officers and American officials and others in the Philippines, as a start. The Postmaster General ordered that all Atkinson pamphlets heading for Manila be seized from the mails. Atkinson then thanked the government for all the attention, pointing out that interest in his pamphlets had risen dramatically throughout the country. He wrote,

> *I think the members of the Cabinet have graduated from an asylum for the imbecile and feeble-minded. They have evidently found out their blunder because the Administration papers suddenly ceased their attacks on me all on the same day, and I miss the free advertisement. I am now trying to stir them up again to provoke another attack.*

Some sectors of the league were reluctant to support Atkinson's activities, though some individual anti-imperialists did, as did the league's Chicago branch. But he continued his work, observing in 1899 that his latest pamphlet was his "strongest bid yet for a limited residence in Fort Warren."

As early as 1896, Atkinson had written to the *New York Evening Post* with a suggestion for a petition to be drawn up to the US Congress along the following lines:

> *It is requested that an act may be passed to the effect that any citizen of the United States who proposes to force this country into a war with Great Britain or with any other country on a dispute about boundaries or any other similar issue, shall be immediately*

> *conscripted or entered upon the army roll for service from the beginning to the end of any such war when it shall occur. It is suggested that Senators of the United States shall be assigned to the position of general officers in this addition to the army upon the ground that their military capacity must certainly be equal to their political intelligence...It is next suggested that Representatives in Congress shall be assigned to the command of brigades....Of course, men who in high public position have...expressed such an earnest desire to assert and defend the honor of the country at any cost, would most enthusiastically vote for this enactment and would immediately enroll themselves for active service in the field.*
>
> *This proposal for the immediate enrollment of the Jingo army will at once develop the sincerity of purpose of the advocates of aggression and violence by their enlistment. An indirect but great benefit would then ensue by the removal of these persons from the high positions in which they have proved their incapacity to deal with questions of peace, order and industry and to given them the opportunity to exert and prove their military prowess.*

Atkinson, like Storey, was for laissez faire—an important strain in anti-imperialist thought. Here was the old liberal tradition in all its wonderful consistency: in favor of private property and peace, and against looting and empire. George E. McNeill put it more simply: "Wealth is not so rapidly gained by killing Filipinos as by making shoes." Andrew Carnegie even offered to purchase the independence of the Philippines with a check for $20 million—the amount the US government had paid Spain for the islands. The *New York Times* denounced the offer as "wicked." (Is the *New York Times* ever right about anything?)

At the same time, labor leaders like Samuel Gompers belonged to the league, as did other people who by some standards belong to the Left, like Jane Addams and William James. It was a cross-ideological organization against empire.

And yet, for all their tireless work, the anti-imperialists by and large failed to spark the national discussion about the role of the US government in the world that we have needed to engage in ever since. Today, that debate takes place only between neoconservatives and realists, both of whom agree on the need for some kind of major US military presence over much of the globe. Not only is nonintervention not even considered, but it is also enough to get you written out of polite society—what are you, some kind of extremist?

(It may be worth considering someday exactly what opinions do get you branded an extremist, and what don't. It's evidently all right to favor incinerating innocent people in all kinds of scenarios, from Hiroshima to Vietnam—no one who favored those things has since been considered beyond the pale in mainstream political and media circles—but if you resolutely refuse to incinerate anyone, you're selfish and irresponsible, and so of course will not appear on television alongside such luminaries as Newt Gingrich and Joe Biden, in whose selflessness and statesmanship you are unworthy to bask.)

In *Freedom and Federalism* (1959), Old Right journalist Felix Morley suggested that the process of empire-building was

> *essentially mystical. It must somehow foster the impression that a man is great in the degree that his nation is great; that a German as such is superior to a Belgian as such; an Englishman, to an Irishman; an American, to a Mexican: merely because the first-named countries are in each case more powerful than their comparatives. And people who have no individual stature whatsoever are willing to accept this poisonous nonsense because it gives them a sense of importance without the trouble of any personal effort.*

Morley, a co-founder of *Human Events* newspaper, added that empire-building amounted to

> *an application of mob psychology to the sphere of world politics, and how well it works is seen by considering the emotional satisfaction many English long derived from referring to "the Empire on which the sun never*

> *sets." Some Americans now get the same sort of lift from the fact that the Stars and Stripes now floats over detachments of "our boys" in forty foreign countries.*

(Ah, the old days, when it was only forty.)

States have successfully managed to persuade their subject populations that they themselves are the state, and therefore that any insult to the honor of the state is an insult to them as well, any questioning of its behavior or intentions a slap in their very own faces. It becomes second nature for many people to root for their state in a way that does violence to reason and fact. They will defend the most contorted, ludicrous claims—claims they themselves would have dismissed with scorn had they come from Saddam Hussein or the 1980s Soviet Union—if necessary to vindicate the honor of the men who rule them.

The few noble exceptions aside, just flip through a few modern right-wing magazines to see what I mean. It is impossible to speak sensibly about foreign policy when a third of the population (at least) is absolutely committed to digging up anything it can find to vindicate arguments even its own leaders no longer bother to defend. How is conversation possible with someone who contends that hundreds of thousands of casualties, a Shi'ite-dominated regime, and regional chaos were worth it because we found a negligible amount of chemical agent in Saddam's Iraq?

President Polk, he is our country—that was bad enough. President McKinley, he is our country—that was much worse. But what genuine American patriot, in the sense to which Moorfield Storey referred, could bring himself to say, "George W. Bush, he is our country"? That alone reminds us of how important it is to oppose empire with every ideological tool at our disposal.

Reprinted from Mises.org.

Platform of the Anti-Imperialist League; October, 1899

We hold that the policy known as imperialism is hostile to liberty and tends toward militarism, an evil from which it has been our glory to be free. We regret that it has become necessary in the land of Washington and Lincoln to reaffirm that all men, of whatever race or color, are entitled to life, liberty, and the pursuit of happiness. We maintain that governments derive their just powers from the consent of the governed. We insist that the subjugation of any people is "criminal aggression" and open disloyalty to the distinctive principles of our Government.

We earnestly condemn the policy of the present National Administration in the Philippines. It seeks to extinguish the spirit of 1776 in those islands. We deplore the sacrifice of our soldiers and sailors, whose bravery deserves admiration even in an unjust war. We denounce the slaughter of the Filipinos as a needless horror. We protest against the extension of American sovereignty by Spanish methods.

We demand the immediate cessation of the war against liberty, begun by Spain and continued by us. We urge that Congress be promptly convened to announce to the Filipinos our purpose to concede to them the independence for which they have so long fought and which of right is theirs.

The United States have always protested against the doctrine of international law which permits the subjugation of the weak by the strong. A self governing state cannot accept sovereignty over an unwilling people. The United States cannot act upon the ancient heresy that might makes right.

Imperialists assume that with the destruction of self-government in the Philippines by American hands, all opposition here will cease. This is a grievous error. Much as we abhor the war of "criminal aggression" in the Philippines, greatly as we regret that the blood of the Filipinos is on American hands, we more deeply resent the betrayal of American institutions at home. The real firing line is not in the suburbs of Manila. The foe is of our own household. The attempt of 1861 was to divide the country. That of 1899 is to destroy its fundamental principles and noblest ideals.

Whether the ruthless slaughter of the Filipinos shall end next month or next year is but an incident in a contest that must go on until the Declaration of Independence and the Constitution of the United States are rescued from the hands of their betrayers. Those who dispute about standards of value while the Republic is undermined will be listened to as little as those who would wrangle about the small economies of the household while the house is on fire. The training of a great people for a century, the aspiration for liberty of a vast immigration are forces that will hurl aside those who in the delirium of conquest seek to destroy the character of our institutions.

We deny that the obligation of all citizens to support their Government in times of grave National peril applies to the present situation. If an Administration may with impunity ignore the issues upon which it was chosen, deliberately create a condition of war anywhere on the face of the globe, debauch the civil service for spoils to promote the adventure, organize a truth suppressing censorship and demand of all citizens a suspension of judgement and their unanimous support while it chooses to continue the fighting, representative government itself is imperiled.

• • •

We propose to contribute to the defeat of any person or party that stands for the forcible subjugation of any people. We shall oppose for reelection all who in the White House or in Congress betray American liberty in pursuit of un-American gains. We still hope that both of our great political parties will support and defend the Declaration of Independence in the closing campaign of the century.

We hold, with Abraham Lincoln, that "no man is good enough to govern another man without that mans consent. When the white man governs himself, that is self-government, but when he governs himself and also governs another man, that is more than self-government that is despotism." "Our reliance is in the love of liberty which God has planted in us. Our defense is in the spirit which prizes liberty as the heritage of all men in all lands. Those who deny freedom to others deserve it not for themselves, and under a just God cannot long retain it."

Populist Party Platform (1892)

The People's party, more commonly known as the Populist party, was organized in St. Louis in 1892 to represent the common folk—especially farmers—against the entrenched interests of railroads, bankers, processers, corporations, and the politicians in league with such interests. At its first national convention in Omaha in July 1892, the party nominated James K. Weaver for president and ratified the so-called Omaha Platform, drafted by Ignatius Donnelly of Minnesota.

Assembled upon the 116th anniversary of the Declaration of Independence, the People's Party of America, in their first national convention, invoking upon their action the blessing of Almighty God, put forth in the name and on behalf of the people of this country, the following preamble and declaration of principles:

Preamble

The conditions which surround us best justify our cooperation; we meet in the midst of a nation brought to the verge of moral, political, and material ruin. Corruption dominates the ballot-box, the Legislatures, the Congress, and touches even the ermine of the bench.[1]

The people are demoralized; most of the States have been compelled to isolate the voters at the polling places to prevent universal intimidation and bribery. The newspapers are largely subsidized or muzzled, public opinion silenced, business prostrated, homes covered with mortgages, labor impoverished, and the land concentrating in the hands of capitalists. The urban workmen are denied the right to organize for self-protection, imported pauperized labor beats down their wages, a hireling standing army, unrecognized by our laws, is established to shoot them down, and they are rapidly degenerating into European conditions. The fruits of the toil of millions are badly stolen to build up colossal fortunes for a few, unprecedented in the history of mankind; and the possessors of these, in turn, despise the Republic and endanger liberty. From the same prolific womb of governmental injustice we breed the two great classes—tramps and millionaires. The national power to create money is appropriated to enrich bond-holders; a vast public debt payable in legal-tender currency has been funded into gold-bearing bonds, thereby adding millions to the burdens of the people.

Silver, which has been accepted as coin since the dawn of history, has been demonetized to add to the purchasing power of gold by decreasing the value of all forms of property as well as human labor, and the supply of currency is purposely abridged to fatten usurers, bankrupt enterprise, and enslave industry. A vast conspiracy against mankind has been organized on two continents, and it is rapidly taking possession of the world. If not met and overthrown at once it forebodes terrible social convulsions, the destruction of civilization, or the establishment of an absolute despotism.

We have witnessed for more than a quarter of a century the struggles of the two great political parties for power and plunder, while grievous wrongs have been inflicted upon the suffering people. We charge that the controlling influences dominating both these parties have permitted the existing dreadful conditions to develop without serious effort to prevent or restrain them. Neither do they now promise us any substantial reform. They have agreed together to ignore, in the coming campaign, ever issue but one. They propose to drown the outcries of a plundered people with the uproar of a sham battle over the tariff, so that capitalists, corporations, national banks, rings, trusts, watered stock, the demonetization of silver and the oppressions of the usurers may all be lost sight of. They propose to sacrifice our homes, lives, and children on the altar of mammon; to destroy the multitude in order to secure corruption funds from the millionaires.

Assembled on the anniversary of the birthday of the nation, and filled with the spirit of the grand general and chief who established our independence, we seek to restore the government of the Republic to the hands of the "plain people," with which class it originated. We assert our purposes to be identical with the purposes of the National Constitution; to form a more perfect union and establish justice, insure domestic tranquillity, provide for the common defense, promote the general welfare, and secure the blessings of liberty for ourselves and our posterity…

Our country finds itself confronted by conditions for which there is not precedent in the history of the world; our annual agricultural productions amount to billions of dollars in value, which must, within a few weeks or months, be exchanged for billions of dollars' worth of commodities consumed in their production; the existing currency supply is wholly inadequate to make this exchange; the results are falling prices, the formation of combines and rings, the impoverishment of the producing class. We pledge ourselves that if given power we will labor to correct these evils by wise and reasonable legislation, in accordance with the terms of our platform. We believe that the power of government—in other words, of the people—should be expanded (as in the case of the postal service) as rapidly and as far as the good sense of an intelligent people and the teaching of experience shall justify, to the end that oppression, injustice, and poverty shall eventually cease in the land…

Platform

We declare, therefore—

First.—That the union of the labor forces of the United States this day consummated shall be permanent and perpetual; may its spirit enter into all hearts for the salvation of the republic and the uplifting of mankind.

Second.—Wealth belongs to him who creates it, and every dollar taken from industry without an equivalent is robbery. "If any will not work, neither shall he eat." The interests of rural and civil labor are the same; their enemies are identical.

Third.—We believe that the time has come when the railroad corporations will either own the people or the people must own the railroads; and should the government enter upon the work of owning and managing all railroads, we should favor an amendment to the constitution by which all persons engaged in the government service shall be placed under a civil-service regulation of the most rigid character, so as to prevent the increase of the power of the national administration by the use of such additional government employees.

FINANCE.—We demand a national currency, safe, sound, and flexible issued by the general government only, a full legal tender for all debts, public and private, and that without the use of banking corporations; a just, equitable, and efficient means of distribution direct to the people, at a tax not to exceed 2 per cent, per annum, to be provided as set forth in the sub-treasury plan of the Farmers' Alliance, or a better system; also by payments in discharge of its obligations for public improvements.

We demand free and unlimited coinage of silver and gold at the present legal ratio of 16 to 1.

1. We demand that the amount of circulating medium[2] be speedily increased to not less than $50 per capita.

2. We demand a graduated income tax.

3. We believe that the money of the country should be kept as much as possible in the hands of the people, and hence we demand that all State and national revenues shall be limited to the necessary expenses of the government, economically and honestly administered. We demand that postal savings banks be established by the government for the safe deposit of the earnings of the people and to facilitate exchange.

TRANSPORTATION.—Transportation being a means of exchange and a public necessity, the government should own and operate the railroads in the interest of the people. The telegraph and telephone, like the post-office system, being a necessity for the transmission of news, should be owned and operated by the government in the interest of the people.

LAND.—The land, including all the natural sources of wealth, is the heritage of the people, and should not be monopolized for speculative purposes, and alien ownership of land should be prohibited. All land now held by railroads and other corporations in excess of their actual needs, and all lands now owned by aliens should be reclaimed by the government and held for actual settlers only.

Expressions of Sentiments

Your Committee on Platform and Resolutions beg leave unanimously to report the following: Whereas, Other questions have been presented for our consideration, we hereby submit the following, not as a part of the Platform of the People's Party, but as resolutions expressive of the sentiment of this Convention.

RESOLVED, That we demand a free ballot and a fair count in all elections and pledge ourselves to secure it to every legal voter without Federal Intervention, through the adoption by the States of the unperverted Australian or secret ballot system.

1. RESOLVED, That the revenue derived from a graduated income tax should be applied to the reduction of the burden of taxation now levied upon the domestic industries of this country.

2. RESOLVED, That we pledge our support to fair and liberal pensions to ex-Union soldiers and sailors.

3. RESOLVED, That we condemn the fallacy of protecting American labor under the present system, which opens our ports to the pauper and criminal classes of the world and crowds out our wage-earners; and we denounce the present ineffective laws against contract labor, and demand the further restriction of undesirable emigration.

4. RESOLVED, That we cordially sympathize with the efforts of organized workingmen to shorten the hours of labor, and demand a rigid enforcement of the existing eight-hour law on Government work, and ask that a penalty clause be added to the said law.

5. RESOLVED, That we regard the maintenance of a large standing army of mercenaries, known as the Pinkerton system, as a menace to our liberties, and we demand its abolition. . . .

6. RESOLVED, That we commend to the favorable consideration of the people and the reform press the legislative system known as the initiative and referendum.

7. RESOLVED, That we favor a constitutional provision limiting the office of President and Vice-President to one term, and providing for the election of Senators of the United States by a direct vote of the people.

8. RESOLVED, That we oppose any subsidy or national aid to any private corporation for any purpose.

9. RESOLVED, That this convention sympathizes with the Knights of Labor and their righteous contest with the tyrannical combine of clothing manufacturers of Rochester, and declare it to be a duty of all who hate tyranny and oppression to refuse to purchase the goods made by the said manufacturers, or to patronize any merchants who sell such goods.

[1]A valuable white fur adorning the robes of some judges.
[2]Currency and/or coin.

[From "People's Party Platform," *Omaha Morning World-Herald* , 5 July 1892.]

Imperialism and "Isolationism": Contrasting Approaches to U.S. Foreign Policy

by Jeff Taylor

Imperialists believe that the American government should be very active in protecting the "national interest" regardless of geographic location. They believe our government has a responsibility to be involved in many conflicts around the globe. They believe our government has a duty to spread our political and economic systems to other countries, by force if necessary. In other words, they believe in American leadership of the world. The Federalists were the original American imperialists. Being Anglophiles, they looked to Great Britain as the role model for American foreign policy. Federalists desired strong financial and commercial ties to Europe and an economy based on overseas trade. Power needed to be concentrated in a strong federal government in order to speak with one voice to the governments of other nations. A strong military was needed to protect the interests of American bankers and businessmen.

An admirer of Caesar and Napoleon, Alexander Hamilton desired an imperialistic foreign policy for the new nation. In 1799, Major General Hamilton "was a man who dreamed dreams, and in his imagination he was already leading his army into Louisiana, the Floridas and points south. 'We ought,' he said, 'to squint at South America.'" The ideological division in early American public policy is clear: "Hamilton longs for empire, opulence, and glory for the nation, whereas Jefferson seeks virtue, freedom, and happiness for the social individual." Hamilton was "very opportunistic about international diplomacy" and distrusted "moralizing in foreign policy."

"Isolationists" believe that the American government should be predominantly concerned about the needs and desires of its own citizens. They do not believe our government should be potentially involved in every conflict around the globe. They do not believe our government should attempt to control the governments of other nations. In other words, they believe in national self-determination. The Anti-Federalists and Democratic-Republicans were the original American isolationists. They believed in decentralized politics, agrarian-based economics, no standing army, staying out of Europe's continual bloodshed, and friendship with the people of other nations but non-alliance with those people's governments.

Isolationists are often characterized as provincial bumpkins. This characterization hardly fits the nation's premier isolationist. Jefferson was a diplomat and a student of language, science, and philosophy. Cosmopolitan in outlook, he nonetheless opposed national involvement in overseas political and military conflicts. Referring to a controversy about the West Indies, in a 1791 letter to an American diplomat, he stated, "If there be one principle more deeply rooted than any other in the mind of every American, it is, that we should have nothing to do with conquest. In 1799, Jefferson wrote, "I am for free commerce with all nations; political connection with none; and little or no diplomatic establishment. And I am not for linking ourselves by new treaties with the quarrels of Europe; entering that field of slaughter to preserve their balance…"

Democratic-Republicans criticized Federalists for establishing "Quixotish embassies to the Turks, the Russians, Prussians, and Portuguese" rather than following George Washington's maxim "Not to intermeddle with European politics." In his first inaugural address (1801), President Jefferson urged "peace, commerce, and honest friendship with all nations, entangling alliances with none." He held this view throughout his life. Jefferson's support for the Monroe Doctrine was expressed in an 1823 letter to the president: "Our first and fundamental maxim should be, never to entangle ourselves in the broils of Europe. Our second, never to suffer Europe to intermeddle with cis-Atlantic affairs."

Right after using the famous phrase "empire for liberty," in an 1809 letter, Jefferson wrote, "It will be objected to our receiving Cuba, that no limit can then be drawn to our future acquisitions. Cuba can be defended by us without a navy, and this develops the principle which ought to limit our views. Nothing should ever be accepted which would require a navy to defend it." This was a clear, preemptive rejection of imperialism *à la* the 1890s. Cuba sí, but Guam, the Philippines, and Hawaii no.

Using the word *isolationism* to describe Jefferson's foreign policy is an oversimplification. Setting aside the negative images with which it is saddled due to 70 years of imperial propaganda, the term is still problematic because it does not express the full range of Jefferson's thought. In addition to the obvious forswearing of entangling alliances, Jeffersonian isolationism involved support for a republic rather than an empire, for national sovereignty, for ethical conduct, for human rights, and for popular control of foreign policy. These five beliefs could be thought of as causes, components, or concomitants of isolationism.

Jefferson "vigorously rejected the view that only individuals are bound by a moral code, and that nations are free to act in accordance with self-interest without any restraints." Writing to James Madison in 1789, he remarked, "I know but one code of morality for men, whether acting singly or collectively. He who says I will be a rogue when I act in company with a hundred others, but an honest man when I act alone, will be believed in the former assertion but not in the latter."

Despite his belief in the importance of moral conduct in foreign relations, Jefferson was not naive in his view of the world. He had, for example, a realistic assessment of foreign governments. In 1812, Jefferson condemned both the French and British governments for trying to "draw to themselves the power, the wealth and the resources of other nations." Three years later, he called Napoleon "the wretch… who has been the author of more misery and suffering to the world, than any being who ever lived before him. After destroying the liberties of his country, he has exhausted all its resources, physical and moral, to indulge his own maniac ambition, his own tyrannical and overbearing spirit." He did not, however, have a favorable view of the British government and other opponents of Napoleon. Jefferson condemned the imperialism of all the leading countries of Europe: "The will of the allies? There is no more moderation, forbearance, or even honesty in theirs, than in that of Bonaparte. They have proved that their object, like his, is plunder."

Isolationism is a problematic word. It is an epithet, it is anachronistic when applied to Jefferson, and it fails to indicate the full range of thought involved. Admittedly, it is a flawed term, but it may be the best term available. Non-interventionism is a non-definition that merely calls attention to another undefined term, the word continentalism never caught on after being proposed by scholar Charles Beard, and neutrality is too vague.

To some, "isolationism" may imply ostrich-like, willful ignorance of the rest of the world, but this was never the case with its most famous practitioners. The isolation is not one of intellect, trade, or travel, but one of entangling alliances, military conflict, and imperial domination. For isolationists, national self-determination for colonies and national sovereignty for America are closely-related principles emanating from a common source: a commitment to democracy, freedom, and decentralization. Isolationism is the foreign policy of traditional liberals. As Robert Morss Lovett noted in 1924,

> *It is historically characteristic of governments devoted to conservative measures and the maintenance of the status quo in domestic affairs to develop an aggressive policy in foreign affairs, and similarly for governments whose chief outlook is toward the progressive improvement of existing conditions to seek to disembarrass themselves from the complications of foreign policy.*

This progressive tradition was first manifested in power through the presidency of Thomas Jefferson.

"Isolationism" may be an unfortunate term in some ways, but it describes a real, deep, and honorable tradition in American politics. Prior to the 1930s, the ideological underpinning of our approach to the world lacked a distinct label because it was simply accepted as traditional U.S. foreign policy. In his 1776 pamphlet *Common Sense,* Thomas Paine wrote, "As Europe is our market for trade, we ought to form no partial connection with any part of it. It is the true interest of America to steer clear of European contentions…" In 1796, George Washington's Farewell Address noted, "The great rule of conduct for us, in regard to foreign nations, is in extending our commercial relations, to have with them as little political connection as possible…It is our true policy to steer clear of permanent alliances with any portion of the foreign world…"

The Independence Day speech of Secretary of State John Quincy Adams in 1821 indicated that isolationism was still taken for granted 25 years later. Referring to America, he reminded the House of Representatives, "She has abstained from interference in the concerns of others, even when conflict has been for principles to which she clings…She goes not abroad, in search of monsters to destroy. She is the well-wisher to the freedom and independence of all. She is the champion and vindicator only of her own."

The Monroe Doctrine acted as an isolationist bulwark for many years, until it was corrupted by the Theodore Roosevelt Corollary (1904) and virtually set aside by Woodrow Wilson and Franklin Roosevelt. The Doctrine asserted,

> *In the wars of the European powers in matters relating to themselves we have never taken any part, nor does it comport with our policy to do so....It is impossible that the allied powers [of Europe] should extend their political system to any portion of either [American] continent without endangering our peace and happiness; nor can anyone believe that our southern brethren, if left to themselves, would adopt it of their own accord....It is still the true policy of the United States to leave the [Latin American] parties to themselves, in hope that other powers will pursue the same course.*

In opposing the annexation of Santo Domingo (Dominican Republic) in 1870, Senate Foreign Relations Committee chairman Charles Sumner (R-MA) argued that Caribbean islands "should not be absorbed by the United States, but should remain as independent powers, and should try for themselves to make the experiment of self-government...To the African belongs the equatorial belt and he should enjoy it undisturbed." Things began to change dramatically in 1898. With the annexation of Hawaii and the Spanish-American War, we were well on our way to becoming an empire with extensive political and military ties to the rest of the world. As a result, traditional foreign policy fell into disfavor among U.S. elites and was eventually disparaged by the dismissive term "isolationism."

Excerpted from "Where Did the Party Go?" (© 2006 University of Missouri Press); originally appeared on Antiwar League website, November 2006.

The Christian Conservative Who Opposed the Vietnam War

David T. Beito

Power, a group blog at the History News Network

To the extent a religious right of any kind existed in 1964, Eugene Siler easily qualified as a platinum card member. In his nine years in the U.S. House, he was unrivaled in his zeal to implement "Christianism and Americanism." Yet forty-two years ago this month, on August 7, 1964, he did something that would be extremely rare for a modern counterpart on the religious right. He dissented from a president's urgent request to authorize military action in a foreign war. It was Siler who cast the lone vote in the U.S. House against the Gulf of Tonkin Resolution. Because he "paired against" the bill (meaning he was absent during the vote), however, most historical accounts do not mention him.

A self-described "Kentucky hillbilly," Siler was born in 1900 in Williamsburg, a town nestled in the mountains in the southeastern part of the state. Unlike most Kentuckians, he, like his neighbors, was a rock-ribbed Republican. The people of this impoverished area had backed the Union during the Civil War and had stood by the GOP in good times and bad ever since. Siler served in the Navy in World War I and two decades later as an Army captain during World War II. His experiences with the realities of war left him cold to most proposals to send American troops into harm's way.

After graduating from Columbia University, Siler returned to Williamsburg to be a small town lawyer. A devout Baptist, he gained local renown as a lay preacher, eventually serving as moderator of the General Association of Baptists in Kentucky. He abstained from alcohol, tobacco, and profanity. As a lawyer, he turned away all clients seeking divorces or who were accused of whiskey-related crimes.

He began service as an elected judge of the Court of Appeals of Kentucky in 1945 and promptly refused his regular monthly allotment of 150 dollars for expenses. Instead, he gave the money to a special fund he set up for scholarships. Not surprisingly, Siler often quoted the scriptures from the bench. He did the same in his speeches as the unsuccessful Republican candidate for governor in 1951 earning him a statewide reputation as a "Bible Crusader."

Siler consistently stressed social conservatism during his tenure in the U.S. House which began in 1955. He sponsored a bill to ban liquor and beer advertising in all interstate media. He said that permitting these ads was akin to allowing the "harsh hussy" to advertise in "the open door of her place of business for the allurement of our school children." Of course, he was "100 percent for Bible reading and the Lord's Prayer in our public schools."

Like his good friend, and fellow Republican, from Iowa, Rep. H. R. Gross, Siler considered himself to be a fiscal watchdog. He disdained all junkets and railed against government debt and high spending. Siler made exceptions for the homefolks, however, by supporting flood control and other federal measures that aided his district.

As with Gross, Siler was a Robert A. Taft Republican who was averse to entangling alliances and foreign quagmires. A consistent opponent of foreign aid, he was just one of two congressmen to vote against Kennedy's call up of reserves during the Berlin crisis. He favored Goldwater in 1964, but never shared his hawkish views. The people back home did not seem to mind. Sometimes, the Democrats failed to even put up a candidate.

Siler was an early, and prescient, critic of U.S. involvement in Vietnam. In June 1964, shortly after deciding not to run again, he quipped, half in jest, that he was running for president as an antiwar candidate. He pledged to resign after one day in office, staying just long enough to bring the troops home. He characterized the Gulf of Tonkin Resolution, which authorized Johnson to take "all necessary steps" in Vietnam as a "buck-passing" pretext to "seal the lips of Congress against future criticism."

The worsening situation in Vietnam prompted Siler to come out of retirement in 1968 to unsuccesfully run for the U.S. Senate nomination on a platform calling for withdrawal of all U.S. troops by Christmas. Ernest Gruening of Alaska and Wayne Morse of Oregon, the only two U.S. Senators who voted against the Gulf of Tonkin Resolution, also went down to defeat that year.

Although Siler lived on until 1987, few remembered his early stand against the Vietnam War. It is doubtful that this particularly bothered him. He knew that his reputation was secure among the plain Baptist Republican mountain folk of southeastern Kentucky who had sent him to Congress for nearly a decade.

David T. Beito is professor of history at the University of Alabama. He is writing a book on the history of the "New Deal Witch Hunt" and is a member of the Liberty and Power Group Blog at the History News Network.

Vietnamese Crucible, in Containment and Change

By Carl Oglesby, 1967

Submitted by Bill Kauffman

It would be a piece of great good fortune for America and the world if the libertarian right could be reminded that besides the debased Republicanism of the Knowlands and the Judds there is another tradition available to them—their own: the tradition of Congressman Howard Buffett, Senator Taft's midwestern campaign manager in 1952, who attacked the Truman Doctrine with the words: "Our Christian ideals cannot be exported to other lands by dollars and guns…We cannot practice might and force abroad and retain freedom at home. We cannot talk world cooperation and practice power politics." There is the right of Frank Chodorov, whose response to the domestic Red Menace was abruptly to the point: "The way to get rid of communists in government jobs is to abolish the jobs." And of Dean Russell, who wrote in 1955: "Those who advocate the 'temporary loss' of our freedom in order to preserve it permanently are advocating only one thing: the abolition of liberty… We are rapidly becoming a caricature of the thing we profess to hate." Most engaging, there is the right of the tough-minded Garet Garrett, who produced in 1952 a short analysis of the totalitarian impulse of imperialism which the events of the intervening years have reverified over and again. Beginning with the words, "We have crossed the boundary that lies between Republic and Empire," Garrett's pamphlet unerringly names the features of the imperial pathology: dominance of the national executive over Congress, court, and Constitution; subordination of domestic policy to foreign policy; ascendency of the military influence; the creation of political and military satellites; a complex of arrogance and fearfulness toward the "barbarian"; and, most insidiously, casting off the national identity—the republic is free; the empire is history's hostage.

This style of political thought, rootedly American, is carried forward today by the Negro freedom movement and the student movement against Great Society-Free World imperialism. That these movements are called leftist means nothing. They are of the grain of American humanist individualism and voluntaristic associational action; and it is only through them that the libertarian tradition is activated and kept alive. In a strong sense, the Old Right and the New Left are morally and politically coordinate.

Yet their intersection can be missed. Their potentially redemptive union can go unattempted and unmade. On both sides, vision can be cut off by habituated responses to passé labels. The New Left can lose itself in the imported left-wing debates of the thirties, wondering what it ought to say about technocracy and Stalin. The libertarian right can remain hypnotically charmed by the authoritarian imperialists whose only ultimate love is the subhuman brownshirted power of the jingo state militant, the state rampant, the iron state possessed of its own clanking glory.

McGovern Beats Nixon How the South Dakota Senator Remade the Right

Daniel McCarthy

George McGovern is enjoying a renaissance. The 86-year-old ex-senator best known for losing the 1972 presidential election in an avalanche—he carried only one state, Massachusetts—won new friends among libertarians last spring with two startlingly laissez-faire op-eds in the *Wall Street Journal*. He'll receive further attention in January when Times Books publishes his Abraham Lincoln, the latest installment in the Sean Wilentz-edited American Presidents series. But sweetest of all for the senator from Mitchell, South Dakota, in November he finally came back to win the White House—or so you might think.

Republicans had a hard time distinguishing Barack Obama from the Democrat Nixon trounced 36 years earlier. Writing at National Review Online, Victor Davis Hanson christened the Illinois senator, "the Second Coming of McGovern." In Commentary, Joshua Muravchik warned that Obama "comes to us from a background farther to the Left than any presidential nominee since McGovern, or perhaps ever." His associates certainly seemed to come straight out of the McGovern bestiary: conservatives pounced on the opportunity to tie Obama to the New Left (via Bill Ayers) and black radicalism (via Rev. Jeremiah Wright). Among liberals, Hillary Clinton supporter Harold Ickes and the *New Republic's* John Judis also ventured comparisons between the 1972 and 2008 Democratic nominees.

And not without reason: Obama's primary base of students, blacks, and cultural leftists bore a striking resemblance to the McGovern coalition of yesteryear. But for conservative Republicans, the demographic parallels were merely lagniappe—since for them every Democratic leader, no matter how Southern, how pro-war, how middle-of-the-road, is really a McGovernite. Indeed, for nearly 40 years the conservative movement has defined itself in opposition to the Democratic standard-bearer of 1972. Anti-McGovernism has come to play for the Right the unifying role that anticommunism once played, much to the detriment of older principles such as limited government, fiscal continence, and prudence in foreign policy.

That Republicans prefer to run against McGovern no matter whom the Democrats nominate is understandable enough. Nixon's victory against the South Dakotan was a blowout of historic proportions. The Democrat received just 37.5 percent of the popular vote to Nixon's 60.7 percent. The only electors McGovern won, besides those of Massachusetts, came from Washington, D.C. Even Walter Mondale performed better against Reagan in 1984. (Though not by much.) What's more, McGovern's nomination confirmed, in fact and symbolically, the hard Left's takeover of the Democratic Party and the shattering of the New Deal coalition of Southern conservatives, blacks, and working-class whites. The Republican playbook ever since has relied on securing the South while making whatever inroads are possible among blue-collar workers—the "hardhats" of the Nixon era, the Reagan Democrats, and of course Joe the Plumber.

On the other side of the ledger are Democratic "elites" with a small but radical base of "college-educated suburbanites, blacks, and liberated women, in addition to young people," in the words of *Why the Democrats Are Blue* author Mark Stricherz. McGovern, a minister's son, a World War II combat veteran—he flew 35 B-24 missions over enemy territory, earning the Distinguished Flying Cross—and scandal-free family man might have seemed an unlikely paladin for hippies and feminists, even if, as George Will notes, he is one of only two major-party presidential nominees to hold a Ph.D. (The other was Woodrow Wilson.) But what drove the countercultural Left to this unprepossessing South Dakotan was his unflinching opposition to the Vietnam War. He voted against sending U.S. troops to Indochina as early as 1963. In 1970, he sponsored an amendment with Republican Mark Hatfield to bring home all U.S. troops from Vietnam within a year. Quoting Edmund Burke—"A conscientious man would be cautious how he dealt in blood"—he told his colleagues the day of the vote:

> *Every Senator in this chamber is partly responsible for sending 50,000 young Americans to an early grave. This chamber reeks of blood. Every Senator here is partly responsible for that human wreckage at Walter Reed and Bethesda Naval and all across our land—young men without legs, or arms, or genitals, or faces*

> *or hopes...[W]e are responsible for those young men and their lives and their hopes. And if we do not end this damnable war those young men will some day curse us for our pitiful willingness to let the Executive carry the burden that the Constitution places on us.*

Little more than a year later, he was running for president on a platform of ending the war, slashing the military budget, reforming the tax code, and offering Americans a federally guaranteed annual income. (A bad idea, to be sure—but not so different from Milton Friedman's "negative income tax," a notion favored by Nixon.) To conservatives like *National Review* publisher Bill Rusher, "His original foreign policy was essentially a global bug-out, belatedly modified to provide for the all-out defense of Israel." As McGovern explained, "I don't like communism, but I don't think we have any great obligation to save the world from it."

This was sharp break with the Cold War liberalism of Harry Truman, John F. Kennedy, and Lyndon Johnson. Yet the McGovern revolution—as it seemed—never remade the Left as thoroughly as the reaction against him reshaped the Right. Famously, the most ardent supporters of Washington Sen. Scoop Jackson, one of McGovern's many rivals for the 1972 nomination, deserted the party to become the original neoconservatives. McGovern's victory, Irving Kristol recalled, "sent us...a message that we were now off the liberal spectrum and that the Democratic party no longer had room for the likes of us." Kristol and company were anti-Left and anti-peacenik, but they never embraced the old Goldwaterite goals of curbing the welfare state. They supplied the Right with a new intelligentsia, in the process transforming conservatism.

The neoconservatives were chiefs without braves. But the McGovern revolution also gave Republicans a new grassroots base. In '72, Senate Minority Leader Hugh Scott (R-Tenn.) described McGovern as the "triple-A candidate—acid, amnesty, and abortion." The "culture war" had begun before that. Until McGovern, however, that war had been fought within the Democratic Party—literally, in the case of the bloody clashes between Mayor Daley's police and New Left protestors at the 1968 Chicago convention. McGovern's nomination finally made the culture war a partisan issue, which Republican activists such as Paul Weyrich and Richard Viguerie were quick to capitalize upon. Their efforts to mobilize evangelicals for the culture war gave rise to the modern Religious Right. Weyrich, in fact, inadvertently named what became the most prominent Christian conservative group when he told a Lynchburg-based televangelist, "Out there is what one might call a moral majority."

Rev. Jerry Falwell liked the ring of that. His Moral Majority was by no means the only grassroots organization Weyrich, Viguerie, and their allies had a hand in creating, however. Another, the National Conservative Political Action Committee, took aim at liberal senators and congressmen from conservative districts. One of the first scalps NCPAC collected in November 1980 was that of George McGovern.

At first, the elite neoconservatives and the grassroots New Right had little in common with one another or with the older Goldwaterite conservatives. Irving Kristol acknowledged as much in a 1995 essay, "America's 'Exceptional Conservatism,'" which contrasted the "antisocialist, anti-Communist, antistatist" conservatives of old with the neoconservatives and Religious Right. All were anticommunist, but anticommunism was no longer the binding force that it had been at the height of the Cold War in the 1950s and 1960s. Anti-McGovernism, however, would do the trick. The politics of sex, drugs, and war—if not exactly acid, amnesty, and abortion—would define the new conservatism.

The Republican establishment was slow to adopt these issues. Gerald Ford and George H.W. Bush had no passion for them. Even Ronald Reagan paid more lip service than fealty to the new priorities of the Right: he had come of age with an earlier anticommunist and libertarian brand of conservatism. But in the 1990s, Republicans embraced anti-McGovernism with ardor. Bill Clinton, an unremarkable Southern governor and keen militarist, looked to the 1990s Right like another McGovern. "From a chicken in every pot," joked right-wing radio talkers, "to a chicken on pot"—a reference to Clinton's draft-dodging and drug-using. Republican House Speaker Newt Gingrich tagged administration officials "countercultural McGoverniks."

There were McGoverniks aplenty in the Clinton White House, including the president himself, who in his law-school days had campaigned for McGovern in Texas. And the Clintonites were every bit as beholden to the social Left as their critics maintained—as shown by the president's commitment to abortion rights and early attempt to end the ban on homosexuals serving in the military. Yet the Republicans' anti-McGovernite rhetoric disguised a retrenchment on the Right: with the influx of neoconservative intellectuals, official conservatism began honoring pre-McGovern liberal Democrats as heroes. In 1956, *National Review* considered Republican Dwight Eisenhower insufficiently conservative to merit endorsement. By 2008, National Review Online thought Harry S. Truman a model for George W. Bush—and meant that as a compliment. "Hopeful conservatives keep comparing Bush to Truman," wrote Fred Schwartz, the magazine's deputy managing editor.

If modern Democrats—Zell Miller and Joseph Lieberman aside—were countercultural McGoverniks, old liberals like Franklin Roosevelt, Harry Truman, and John F. Kennedy were now conservatives. And if this adjustment entailed conservatives making peace with the welfare state and Cold War liberalism, so much the better for right-wing social democrats like Irving Kristol, whose "chosen enemy," he avowed, "was contemporary [McGovern-style] liberalism, not socialism or statism." As for the social conservatives who flocked to the GOP, Kristol noted that economics and limited government were not their foremost concerns. They came to the conservative movement innocent of economics and political philosophy—and untutored in foreign policy as well. "Only neoconservatives can really speak to them in the language of moral values," Kristol insisted.

Throughout the 1990s, McGovern remained a touchstone for the culture war. After 9/11, he again became a symbol in a real war. "The Dems are still the party of George McGovern, and for them it's still 1968," Jed Babbin wrote in a 2003 column about the Iraq War. Notably, although McGovern was not the most prominent antiwar Democrat in '68—that distinction belonged to Minnesota Sen. Eugene McCarthy—Babbin still chose him as the benchmark of the antiwar Left. McCarthy, after all, had fallen short of his party's nomination and could hardly serve as synecdoche for all Democrats.

For 30 years, Republicans, neoconservatives, and liberal hawks have cultivated the myth of the McGovern Party: weak on defense, ineluctably opposed to Middle American values, the party of peaceniks and perverts. Not only has this narrative distorted the Right by allowing anyone starboard of McGovern to set himself up as a conservative, it has also led Republicans to misunderstand their enemy. Paula and Monica notwithstanding, Bill Clinton was less interested in sex than in NAFTA-style managed trade. And far from being a peacenik, Clinton led the country into military actions in Haiti, Somalia, Sudan, Afghanistan, Iraq, Kosovo, Serbia, and a plethora of other places. Clinton was no more a McGovern-style left-winger than George W. Bush was a Goldwater-style right-winger.

The Democrats have not nominated a McGovernite since McGovern himself. The senator's understudy and 1972 campaign manager, Gary Hart, lost the 1984 nomination to Hubert Humphrey's protégé, Walter Mondale. Left-wingers such as Jerry Brown and Dennis Kucinich have not fared as well in today's Democratic Party as Eugene McCarthy did in the Johnson-Humphrey party of '68. Both Jimmy Carter and Michael Dukakis were, by the standards of their party, moderate governors. Even John Kerry, a celebrity of the Vietnam-era antiwar movement, voted for the Iraq War in the Senate and didn't dare run as a McGovernite in 2004.

Though the party's social liberals—feminists, abortion supporters, and gay-rights activists—have indeed consolidated their power, they often did so in alliance with the party's right wing: the pro-business, Southern-accented Democratic Leadership Council. It was a DLC-run party that denied antiabortion Gov. Robert Casey of Pennsylvania a speaking slot at the 1992 Democratic convention. McGovern, on the other hand, was the last Democratic presidential nominee to select a pro-life running mate. (In fact, he chose two: Missouri Sen. Thomas Eagleton, who withdrew from the ticket when his history of psychiatric treatment came to light, and Peace Corps founder Sargent Shriver. McGovern's own position was that abortion was a matter properly left to the states.) While the social Left worked out a modus vivendi with the DLC, the antiwar Left steadily lost out to humanitarian interventionists. Madeleine Albright, not George McGovern, remains the face of the Democratic Party's foreign policy.

All indications are that this won't change under Barack Obama, even if his campaign had similarities to McGovern's. He ran on an anti-Iraq War platform and inspired hope among many of the same groups that McGovern did. And like the South Dakotan, he had trouble with white working-class voters during the primaries—indeed, both McGovern and Obama won the Democratic nomination with less than a majority of the votes cast in the primaries and caucuses.

McGovern received approximately 68,000 fewer votes than Hubert H. Humphrey; Obama, by the widest possible count, received about 176,000 fewer votes than Hillary Clinton. (Appropriately enough, the protracted Democratic nominating battle of 2008 was itself a legacy of electoral reforms McGovern had helped craft.) When John McCain added Miss Middle America—Alaska Gov. Sarah Palin—to his ticket, pundits Left and Right for a time thought Obama's fate was sealed. The McGovern coalition couldn't prevail in a rematch against Nixon's silent majority.

Yet it did. In the intervening decades, the McGovern coalition had grown. And perhaps more importantly, Middle Americans faced with a choice between the semicompetent socialism of the Left and the spectacularly incompetent socialism of the Republican Right split three ways—between McCain, Obama, and staying home. Mideast war, torture, and national bankruptcy turned out to be even less popular than social liberalism.

If Republicans and liberal hawks were correct in calling Obama a new McGovern, they only succeeded in proving how repellent most Americans, including many conservatives, find today's GOP. The trouble is, instead of the country getting George McGovern—a temperamental conservative, an anti-militarist, and a committed decentralist—we're getting Barack Obama, who dreams of another New Deal and picked Hillary Clinton as his chief diplomat. Somehow the neoconservatives and liberal interventionists prevailed again.

DEBATE ON CURRENT WARS

Battling the Bipartisan Consensus for War

By Doug Bandow/Campaign for Liberty 03/14/2010

The U.S. is rarely at peace. It doesn't matter which party or which politician is in power: American military forces will be on the move, invading a Third World nation here and threatening an emerging power there.

In January 2009 Republican George W. Bush yielded to Democrat Barack Obama, and the U.S. government increased military spending and expanded the war in Afghanistan. If a Republican is elected in 2012, recent history suggests that defense outlays will grow further, as Washington attacks another nation or two.

Enthusiasm for war crosses party lines—Robert Kagan recently wrote approvingly of the militaristic alliance between "liberal interventionist Democrats" and "hawkish internationalist Republicans"—both groups which have never met a war they didn't want to fight. However, support for peace also is transpartisan. Such sentiments are perhaps strongest on the Democratic left, which increasingly feels disenfranchised by President Obama. A smaller contingent of libertarians, traditional conservatives, and paleo-conservatives has resisted the conservative movement's adoption of war-mongering intervention as a basic tenet.

Right and Left recently came together for a day-long conference in Washington. Participants included this writer, editors from the *Nation, Progressive Review* online, *American Conservative, Reason,* and other publications; leftish anti-war activists reaching back to the Vietnam era and a professor at the Naval Postgraduate School; Ralph Nader; a supporter of Patrick Buchanan's 1992 presidential bid; a former campaign aide to Internet sensation Rep. Ron Paul (R-Tex.) and three members of the Paul-inspired group Young Americans for Liberty; representatives of several activist organizations, including Voters for Peace and Veterans for Peace; and writers, think tankers, academics, and organizers from across the political spectrum.

The moment economics, domestic policy, or election law came up, participants disagreed. But on the central issue of war and peace the group united. While war might sometimes be unavoidable—pacifism was not on the agenda, though some of the participants might have been pacifists—it should be a last resort, a tragic necessity to protect a free American society. While war sometimes brings out the finest and most sublime human values such as courage and honor, more often it looses the basest passions and destroys what we most hold dear. Despite today's constant celebration of all things military, Americans are best served by peace, allowing them to enjoy the pleasures and surmount the challenges of daily life.

Yet today the U.S. is one of the world's most militarized states, accounting for nearly half of the globe's military outlays. The U.S. government maintains hundreds of military installations and hundreds of thousands of troops abroad. No other country, democratic or authoritarian, comes close to matching America's aggressive military record in recent decades: nations and territories invaded or bombed include Iraq (twice), Serbia, Bosnian Serbs, Afghanistan, Haiti, Somalia, Panama, and Grenada. Threats have come fast and furious against North Korea, Iran, Pakistan, and most recently Yemen.

It is bad enough that Washington policymakers see war as a first resort, a convenient tool for conducting social engineering abroad. They seem to treat the resulting death and destruction as incidental and unimportant, especially if concentrated on others.

Even worse, many U.S. policymakers appear to enjoy wielding military force safely out of harm's way from their Washington offices. Rather than feel reluctant at loosing the dogs of war, some American leaders, almost always ones who have never put on a military uniform let alone served in combat, joyously add new targets. "Real men go to Tehran," ran the neoconservative mantra in the aftermath of the Iraq invasion, when otherwise sober analysts were filled with hubris at America's ability to remake the world at will. Never mind those who would be killed along the way.

It is this world which brought representatives from Right to Left together. Participants discussed rhetoric: criticizing "imperialism," for instance, resonates far better with the Left than the Right. But there was broad agreement on policy. Washington today has a strategy of "empire." The U.S. isn't the same as the Roman or British empires, to be sure. But American foreign and military policy could hardly be further from those one would expect from a constitutional republic with a government of limited powers intended to concentrate on protecting the safety and liberty of its citizens.

Thus, Americans need real change, not the faux variety offered by the Obama administration. The military should be configured to defend America, not client states around the globe. U.S. taxpayers should not be fleeced to subsidize wealthy allies. Washington should not use patriotic 18-year-olds to occupy Third World states, treating them like American satrapies, governed by U.S. ambassadors. Uncle Sam should stop trying to micro-manage the globe, treating every conflict or controversy as America's own, exaggerating foreign threats and inflating Washington's abilities.

The price of today's policy of empire is high. Far from being the costless adventure imagined by members of Washington's ubiquitous sofa samurai, war is the ultimate big government program, a threat to Americans' life, prosperity, and liberty.

So far the Iraqi "cakewalk" has resulted in the death of roughly 4,400 Americans and 300 other coalition soldiers. Then there are tens of thousands of maimed and injured Americans, others suffering from PSD, and numerous broken families and communities. At least 100,000 and probably many more Iraqis have died. Some estimates run up to a million, a truly astonishing number. America's ivory tower warriors seem particularly unconcerned about dead foreigners. However many Iraqis die, it is treated as a small price to pay for the privilege of being liberated by Washington.

Another cost is financial. Direct military outlays this year will run over $700 billion. Iraq is ultimately likely cost $2 or $3 trillion. Washington spends more on "defense," adjusted for inflation, today than at any point during the Cold War, Korean War, and Vietnam War. The U.S. accounts for nearly half of the globe's military expenditures.

American taxpayers pay to defend prosperous and populous European states. Japan devotes about a fourth as much of its economic strength to the military as does the U.S. The NATO member which makes the most military effort is crisis-prone Greece—in response to nominal ally Turkey. For years American taxpayers spent as much as South Koreans to defend the Republic of Korea.

Such generosity might have made sense in the aftermath of World War II, when so many Asian and European states had been ruined by war and faced Stalin's Soviet Union and Mao's China. No longer, however. Especially with the U.S. budget deficit expected to run nearly $1.6 trillion this year alone. Over the next decade Uncle Sam likely will rack up another $10 trillion in red ink. In effect, Washington is borrowing every penny which it is spending to defend other nations.

Liberty also suffers from a policy of empire. "War is the health of the state," intoned Randolph Bourne, and it certainly is the health of the national security state. The constitutional deformations of the Bush years were legendary, yet President Barack Obama has done little to rein in his predecessor's lawless conduct. Executive aggrandizement, government secrecy, privacy violations, military arrests and trials, and constitutional violations. The U.S. is in danger of losing its republican soul.

Of course, one could imagine a truly necessary war which would have to be fought almost irrespective of cost—World War II, perhaps. However, while jihadist terrorists are ugly and murderous, they are a poor substitute for Adolf Hitler with armored divisions and Joseph Stalin with nuclear weapons. We aren't fighting World War III. We aren't fighting anything close to World War III.

And if we were in such a conflict, a policy of empire, of meddling around the globe, of engaging in international social engineering, would be about the most foolish strategy possible. Most of what the U.S. military does has nothing to do with American security: protecting European states threatened by no one, aiding a South Korea which vastly outranges its northern antagonist, attempting to turn decrepit Third World states into liberal democracies and Western allies.

The problem of terrorism is real, but is best met by sophisticated, targeted countermeasures rather than promiscuous blunt-force intervention. The war in Iraq has enhanced Iran's strategic position, weakened America's reputation, stretched U.S. military forces, spurred terrorist recruitment, and confirmed the radical terrorist narrative. A lengthy occupation of Afghanistan and overflow combat into Pakistan risk doing much the same—potentially for years. Expanded American intervention in Somalia, Yemen, and elsewhere would have a similar effect.

Militaristic sloganeering, patriotic preening, and demagogic ranting are no substitute for making a realistic assessment both of threats and capabilities. Meeting participants agreed that pro-peace activists must seize back the patriotic mantle. Patriotism should no longer be the last refuge of the scoundrel, used to shield from scrutiny policies drafted by those personally unwilling to serve which have wreaked death and destruction abroad and increased debt and insecurity at home. And any antiwar movement should welcome those who have worn the nation's uniforms, whose courage has been misused by self-serving politicians.

This is not the first time that people from across the political spectrum have joined in an attempt to stop imperialist adventures. Various groups opposed the Spanish-American War and especially the brutal occupation of the Philippines. Woodrow Wilson's bloody crusade for democracy was resisted by conservatives and progressives; socialist Eugene Debs went to prison for criticizing that conflict. Left and Right even opposed Franklin Delano Roosevelt's surreptitious push for war, though the Japanese attack on Pearl Harbor and German declaration of war ultimately made involvement inevitable.

Indeed, mainstream American concern about international adventurism goes back to George Washington's famed farewell address warning against "foreign entanglements" and consequent "overgrown military establishments." Secretary of State John Quincy Adams warned against going abroad "in search of monsters to destroy." Future Civil War generals Ulysses S. Grant and Robert E. Lee expressed disquiet at America's rapacious war with Mexico even while serving their nation in that very conflict. "The commercial interests" angered war-hawk Teddy Roosevelt for opposing his campaign for war against Spain. Middle America resisted demands that the U.S. join both great European wars of the 20th century. President Dwight D. Eisenhower left office warning about the military-industrial complex.

Unfortunately, politicians have proved extraordinarily adept at rousing, at least temporarily, public support for foreign military adventures. Resisting the ivory tower warmongers will be no easier today. But those who believe in peace have no choice but to try, and try again.

Peace should be America's natural condition. Unfortunately, it will not be so as long as today's unnatural alliance of liberal and neoconservative hawks runs U.S. foreign policy. And only the American people can take back control. The future of the American people and republic is at stake.

Bombs Away: Conservatives Embrace War

By Doug Bandow 02/10/2010

Leading Democrats and Republicans alike agree on the need for action against Iran. At least some liberal Democrats seem reluctant to use military force; in contrast, many conservative Republicans are eager to start bombing. While the latter say they oppose Big Government, these days they spend much of their time proposing new wars.

Conservatives once resisted the imperial tendencies of government. The Founders opposed creating a standing army. Even when the nation went to war—against Great Britain, Mexico, and Spain in the 19th century, for instance—Washington quickly demobilized afterward. Conservatives recognized the threat to individual liberty and budget economy posed by an imperial foreign policy. The Right opposed Woodrow Wilson, who pushed the U.S. into the murderous slugfest of World War I to satisfy his own messianic pretensions. Conservatives led the fight against Franklin Delano Roosevelt's surreptitious campaign to take the U.S. into war against Germany while promising the American people that their husbands and sons would not be sent to die on foreign battlefields. Conservatives then were reluctant warriors who insisted on following the Constitution.

Republican President Dwight D. Eisenhower refused to expand the Korean War to the Chinese mainland: he settled for compromise rather than risk triggering World War III. And it was Eisenhower who both warned of the malign influence of the military-industrial complex and insisted that congressional approval was necessary to go to war. He may have been the last president to take the latter provision of the Constitution seriously.

Ronald Reagan belied his cowboy reputation, using the military only sparingly and modestly, intervening in Lebanon—which even he later implicitly acknowledged to be a mistake—invading Grenada, and bombing Libya. George H.W. Bush invaded Panama and attacked Iraq, but sharply limited U.S. objectives in the latter. Many Republicans were generally unenthused when President Bill Clinton turned American foreign policy into social work. Yet most GOP leaders, like 1996 presidential nominee Sen. Robert Dole, supported the Clinton administration's bombing of Serbia, a campaign based on hypocritical humanitarian claims and no recognizable security objectives.

Then President George W. Bush launched grand nation-building crusades in both Afghanistan and Iraq; in justifying the latter he sounded like he was channeling liberal Woodrow Wilson. The administration also intervened to stage regime change in Haiti. The president, along with his officials and conservative allies, threatened military action against Iran, North Korea, and Syria. The administration apparently even considered intervening militarily against nuclear-armed Russia in Georgia—another conflict with no relevance to American security.

After sanctimoniously triggering a disastrous conflict which has killed at least 100,000, and perhaps many more, in Iraq, leading conservatives advocate doing the same to Iran. Republican Presidential nominee John McCain gaily sang what he termed the old Beach Boys' classic "Bomb, bomb, bomb, bomb Iran" when asked about the issue. Today the Right takes for granted America's unilateral right to unleash death and destruction upon whatever people in whatever nation for whatever reason. Like Iraq, Iran has neither attacked nor threatened America. "Bombs away!" appears to be the new conservative mantra. Lest some on the Right be uncomfortable with the results of the Iraqi war, the hawks say: Don't worry, be happy. This time everything will work out. This time America will be received with love.

Moreover, argues Daniel Pipes of the Middle East Forum, Barack Obama would benefit politically as well. The president, writes Pipes, "needs a dramatic gesture to change the public perception of him as a light-weight, bumbling ideologue, preferably in an arena where the stakes are high, where he can take charge, and where he can trump expectations." So President Obama should send in the bombers over Tehran.

But President Obama should be skeptical of the argument that war with Iran would be win-win for America and his presidency.

First, war advocates say bombing would end Iran's threat to the U.S. What threat is that, however? Iran doesn't have nuclear weapons. It isn't even certain that Tehran is developing weapons. War enthusiasts who confidently claimed that Iraq possessed a fearsome nuclear capability now ridicule the 2007 National Intelligence

Estimate that Iran had halted its program. However, the latter conclusion, though controversial, was supported by evidence—far better evidence than that indicating Baghdad possessed nuclear weapons. There are good reasons to be suspicious of Iran's intentions, especially after the revelation of the uranium-enrichment plant near the holy city of Qum. But hard evidence of a weapons program remains elusive. Some analysts suspect that Iran desires to establish a "turn-key" capability, like that presently possessed by Japan, rather than an arsenal.

Even assuming the worst intent, Tehran appears to remain far away from actually building nuclear weapons, let alone deploying deliverable nuclear weapons. Even possessing the latter wouldn't be enough to endanger the U.S. Some analysts worry about the impact of an electromagnetic pulse attack more than a traditional nuclear strike. But in either case Washington could effectively wipe Iran off of the map as retaliation. The authoritarian regime in Tehran appears to be evil, not suicidal. It surely is undesirable that Iran develop a nuclear weapon, just as it was undesirable that Stalin's Soviet Union and Mao's China built nuclear weapons. That is, however, very different from saying that America would be at risk.

Second, Pipes worries that the Iranians "might deploy these weapons in the [Middle East], leading to massive death and destruction." Deploy them against whom? While many Arab states are understandably uneasy about the prospect of a more powerful regime in Tehran, Israel is the only nation which publicly worries about being attacked. And it is the only nation most U.S. policy-makers worry about being attacked. Yet Israel has upwards of 150 nuclear weapons. The reason Israel developed nuclear weapons was to deter aggression by countries such as Iran. The Tehran government would have to be suicidal to attack Israel. Again, the fact that current Iranian leaders are malevolent doesn't mean they are crazy.

Obviously, it would ease minds in Washington and throughout the Middle East if Iran was prevented from developing nuclear weapons. But then, minds also would have been eased if the Soviet Union, China, India, and Pakistan had never developed nukes. Some minds in the Middle East likely feel the same way about Israel. That doesn't mean preventive war would have been a better response than wary accommodation in these cases, however. Loosing the bombers would not be the slam-dunk that most conservative crusaders seem to assume. Not all Iranian nuclear facilities may be identified and known works are dispersed and underground. The result of a U.S. strike, then, might only be to delay rather than forestall an Iranian weapon—at most a modest benefit not worth war.

An American bombing run also would reinforce the message sent by the attacks on Serbia and Iraq: only the speedy and secret acquisition of nuclear weapons can protect other states from unilateral U.S. military action. Tehran probably would redouble its effort; the already de minimis chance of North Korea abandoning its program would shrink still further.

Ironically, even a democratic Iran might choose to develop nuclear weapons. America's long-time ally, the Shah, began Iran's nuclear program before the Islamic Revolution. Any Iranian government might like the assurance of a weapons capability if not actual weapons.

Moreover, if the U.S. strikes Tehran, all bets would be off on a democratic revolution in Iran. The situation in Tehran appears to be explosive and the regime looks unstable. But how the Iranian public would respond to a U.S. attack, despite the growing popular estrangement from the government, is unclear. Certainly the regime would use any strike as an excuse to justify a further crackdown on the opposition. Despite dissatisfaction among the public and internal conflicts among the ruling elite, the regime might benefit from a "rally around the flag" effect. Nor would war be costless for the U.S. Retaliation would be certain. The degree of Tehran's reach and potential for harm are disputed, but Iran is larger and more populous than Iraq. Iran might launch terrorist attacks against the U.S. and encourage proxy forces in the occupied territories and Lebanon to strike at Israel.

U.S. troops in Iraq would be especially vulnerable to attack by Iranian agents as well as Iraqi citizens sympathetic to their co-religionists next door. Tehran might not be able to close the Persian Gulf, but it could disrupt oil shipments and push up insurance rates. Washington's gaggle of authoritarian Islamic allies—Egypt, Jordan, Saudi Arabia, and the Gulf States—could find themselves under popular assault from populations angered by yet another U.S. government attack on a Muslim nation. Political tremors even could reach already unstable Pakistan. Overall, it would not be as easy to end as start war with Iran.

A bombing run by Washington also would reinforce the meme that animates many terrorists, that the U.S. is at war with Islam. While U.S. officials debate how to improve Washington's PR efforts abroad, the substance of American foreign policy continues to send a far more dramatic and powerful message. Although U.S. foreign policy does not justify attacks on civilians, U.S. policymakers must consider all of the consequences of their decisions.

The substantive arguments for striking Iran are dubious enough. Worse is Pipes' contention that war would be good presidential politics. He points out, correctly, that opinion polls show popular support for military action. Moreover, he figures "Americans will presumably rally around the flag, sending that number much higher." This is no argument for war, however. Presidents should not mete out death and destruction to boost their poll ratings.

Pipes also underestimates the political downsides of war. He writes: "Just as 9/11 caused voters to forget George W. Bush's meandering early months, a strike on Iranian facilities would dispatch Obama's feckless first year down the memory hole and transform the domestic political scene. It would sideline health care, prompt Republicans to work with Democrats, and make the netroots squeal, independents reconsider, and conservatives swoon."

In fact, the Bush experience demonstrates that popular support for war can be temporary at best. Conservatives swoon all too easily at the sight of blood, since so few of the hawkish elites advocating promiscuous war-making actually serve in the military and risk their own lives. They leave that to the brave men and women who actually join the armed services. Independents and liberals usually are less impressed with aggressive war-making. Anyway, George Bush quickly turned the public against a war incompetently waged based on false premises resulting in disastrous consequences. Perhaps Iran would be a quick victory, resulting in regime change and democratic triumph, with statues of Barack Obama sprouting across ancient Persia. But then, Iraq was supposed to be a cakewalk, yielding a pro-American government willing to host U.S. troops and join the Bush administration in enforcing U.S. dictates elsewhere in the region. Something went wrong along the way. Counting on votes from a successful war against Iran might result in a trip to the unemployment line for President Obama in 2012.

There are no good solutions in Iran. The world will be a better place if Iran becomes democratic and abandons any nuclear weapons program. But initiating war likely would inhibit reform in Iran while making the world a more dangerous place. The disastrous experience of Iraq should teach us many lessons, the most important of which is that war always should be a last resort. That standard is no where close to being met in Iran.

Time for a Defense Policy that Defends America

Doug Bandow

The American empire is in shambles. U.S. soldiers and Marines who expected flowers and candies in Iraq were cut down by bombs and bullets instead. Afghanistan is spinning ever further out of Washington's control. Russia, China, and even Europe increasingly resist U.S. demands.

At the same time, America stands on an economic precipice. The national debt is currently $10.6 trillion, almost $35,000 per person. The deficit for 2009 will exceed $1 trillion. Congress is preparing to spend almost another trillion dollars to "stimulate" the economy. And America's long-term unfunded liabilities for Social Security and Medicare exceed $100 trillion.

In other words, the U.S. is effectively broke at home and increasingly unable to control events abroad.

Yet the new administration looks almost identical to the old one when it comes to foreign policy. Secretary of State Hillary Clinton promised to use "smart power" to achieve the administration's ends, but her objectives looked little different from those of her predecessor. The U.S. must micro-manage affairs around the world, only more competently and sensitively. Wars must still be waged in Afghanistan and Iraq, NATO must still be expanded into Georgia and Ukraine, countries like Iran and North Korea must still be threatened, and allies must still be protected around the globe.

It doesn't take a rocket scientist to recognize that promiscuously intervening in countries and initiating conflicts is dangerous. After fighting bloody insurgencies in Vietnam, Iraq, and Afghanistan, it should be obvious to all that there are few easy victories in such Third World battles. After confronting Russia over Georgia and threatening to challenge China over Taiwan, it should be obvious that small wars risk turning into big wars. After suffering terrorist attacks on America's homeland, it should be apparent even to the most enthusiastic international meddlers that there is a price to be paid for making endless enemies overseas.

Attempting to play global policeman, protecting prosperous and populous allies as well as remaking failed states, also is extraordinarily expensive. As then Chairman of the Joint Chiefs of Staff Colin Powell observed after the collapse of the Soviet Union, he was running out of enemies—down to just Fidel Castro and Kim Il-Sung. Even adding Osama bin Laden, America's opponents are a pitiful few. Toss in China and Russia, and America still outspends all its potential adversaries on defense by three or four times.

Indeed, the U.S., which is allied with most every other advanced industrial state, accounts for roughly half of the world's military spending. No other nation compares. Some hawks worry about China's military build-up. Yet this year Washington will spend upwards of six times as much on "defense." And America starts with a far larger base force: for instance, Washington deploys 11 carrier groups, while China has none.

In short, Beijing doesn't threaten the U.S. Rather, the U.S. threatens China. What China is doing now is attempting to create a military sufficient to deter American intervention. But even Beijing's modest increases in defense outlays lead to calls from hawks in America for yet higher military expenditures here.

What do Americans receive in return for their government's constant meddling abroad? The satisfaction of having taken sides in conflicts in which no participant has clean hands. The pleasure of having created grievances which cause terrorists to target Americans at home and abroad. The joy of subsidizing well-heeled trading partners, which then can invest their resources in economic development rather than bigger and more weapons.

Advocates of promiscuous intervention abroad talk as if Washington has no choice but to police the globe. That's nonsense, of course. America's very power and influence allow it to react with benign detachment to most events overseas. That doesn't mean Americans need be indifferent to tragedy overseas; ordinary people have been organizing and contributing to help the hungry, sick, and victims of war for decades. But the U.S. government's duty is far narrower: providing for the common defense, as authorized by the Constitution.

This isn't "isolationism," the usual swear word tossed by those who demand that Washington routinely visit death and destruction upon one country or another. Rather, it is non-intervention, a policy that limits the U.S. government's political demands and military assaults on other nations while encouraging Americans to interact peacefully with the rest of the world. It is a policy that rests on the belief that war is always a last resort and never a matter of choice.

Such a strategy would not be a radical jump into the unknown. After all, this was the Founders' foreign policy, continued by the early Americans. At the Constitutional Convention delegates rejected proposals to replicate the British king, who could unilaterally take the country into war. When leaving office George Washington warned of foreign entanglements and permanent attachments in his famous Farewell Address. Secretary of State John Quincy Adams later rejected proposals to aid Greek freedom fighters against the Ottoman Empire. The mere fact that the U.S. is more powerful today does not mean that it should be more warlike.

It has long been obvious that America's pretense to empire costs far more than any benefits which result. Now it should also be obvious that the U.S. can no longer afford to play global policeman.

Only a change in foreign policy can match America's capabilities with its objectives. Washington should adopt a policy of nonintervention, dedicated to keeping America free, prosperous, and at peace. This is, in fact, the only approach consistent with remaining a republic dedicated to limited government and individual liberty.

You Know It's Time to Leave Iraq When...

Doug Bandow

You need 1900 guards for your embassy more than six years after the invasion. Reports the *Washington Post*:

The U.S. Embassy has 88 special agents who supervise about 1,300 security contractors and 1,900 perimeter guards. The Iraqi government is expanding access to the Green Zone, where the embassy is located, and two large U.S. military bases near the embassy will close over the next couple of years. American military officers are training Iraqi soldiers who patrol the Green Zone.

You have to spend almost $2 billion annually to maintain your embassy. Reports the Post:

Although the United States is reducing the scope of its diplomatic engagements in Iraq, U.S. officials anticipate that security expenses will contribute to the higher cost of running the embassy over the next couple of years. American officials project that the embassy will need more than $1.8 billion each year in 2010 and 2011, compared with this year's estimated $1.5 billion budget, according to the inspector general.

Iraq was a tragic mistake from the start. The U.S. should never have invaded. Having invaded, the U.S. never should have sent over a bevy of 20-year-olds to try to run Iraq's economy, recreate Iraq's government, and rewrite Iraq's legal code.

Having sent kids in to run Iraq, the U.S. should not have attempted to create permanent bases for use to intervene elsewhere in the region. Having failed in all these ways, the U.S. should have embraced the Iraqi determination to ensure an American exit.

Will Iraq "fail" if America leaves? Perhaps so: violence, punctuated by renewed bombing, remains high; the political environment remains more authoritarian than liberal; the gulf between religious and other factions remains huge; both sides in an incipient civil war, Sunni and Shia, remain well-armed (by the U.S.); minorities, such as Christians, remain at risk.

But there's no reason to believe that a continued U.S. presence can prevent failure. To the contrary, Washington's involvement relieves

Iraqis of responsibility for their own affairs and creates another source of antagonism while turning American military personnel into targets. And U.S. officials have demonstrated little ability in the nation-building department. In Iraq it is Washington's multiple mistakes that have yielded today's explosive situation. In this regard, at least, the U.S. government has demonstrated a reverse "Midas touch" of sorts.

The future of Iraq is up to the Iraqis. It's time to bring home U.S. forces.

The First Black President Defeats the Anti-War Movement

Glen Ford

In the streets, on the campuses and on Capitol Hill, the anti-war movement is no longer moving anywhere. It has been crippled by the Obama Effect, the deep and wide delusion that imperialism with a Black face is somehow—something else. When a movement disbands itself without coming even close to achieving its objective, that is a defeat. We can now definitively state that, for the time being, the U.S. anti-war movement has been defeated—not by Republicans, but by Barack Obama's Democratic Party.

A recent article in *The Hill,* a newspaper that covers Congress, relates a meeting among staffers for Out of Iraq caucus leaders Barbara Lee, Maxine Waters and Lynn Woolsey. They were supposed to come up with a response to President Obama's announcement that he would immediately send 4,000 additional troops to Afghanistan, with lots more to come. Obama is determined to leave at least 50,000 troops in Iraq for an open-ended period of time under the guise of "training" the Iraqis, and is rapidly merging Afghanistan and Pakistan into one theater of war, called Af-Pak. Clearly, the Obama administration is expanding its war in Af-Pak, and has no intention of ending the U.S. military presence in Iraq—ever. The staffers for the Out of Iraq caucus leaders spent two hours trying to come up with a position. They failed.

For all intents and purposes, the Out of Iraq caucus has ceased to function. Black Congresswomen Barbara Lee and Maxine Waters have at times shown great courage in the face of stupendous odds. But they will not confront Barack Obama, even when he expands the arenas of war, claims that combat soldiers are merely trainers and advisers, and pushes through a war budget that is bigger than any of George Bush's war budgets. Obama pretends he wants peace, and anti-war members of Congress pretend to believe him.

"The anti-war movement has hit rock-bottom because of its failure to challenge this particular president."

Another Capitol Hill publication, the *Congressional Quarterly*, recently ran an article on the low demonstration turn-out and money woes of the anti-war movement. A March 21st rally at the Pentagon drew pitiful numbers of demonstrators, only 3,000 according to police. Organizers claim they can't raise money these days, and have been forced to cut staff. A spokesperson for ANSWER, the Act Now to Stop War and End Racism Coalition, said the peace movement is seeing the impact of the "promises the Obama campaign made." Outgoing United for Peace and Justice leader Leslie Cagan says her money people aren't giving because "It's enough for many of them that Obama has a plan to end the war and that things are moving in the right direction."

But Obama has no plans or intention to end his wars except on imperialism's own terms—which means never-ending war, just like under Bush—a basic truth that United for Peace and Justice refuses to recognize or admit. ANSWER organizers also fail to confront the Obama White House head-on. The *Congressional Quarterly* article concludes that the anti-war movement is suffering from the results of "its own success." That's absolute nonsense. The anti-war movement has hit rock-bottom because of its failure to challenge this particular president, an imperialist with charm, a warmonger with a winning smile. Obama has whipped them, but good. And they will stay whipped, until they stand up like men, like women, like leaders. For Black Agenda Radio, I'm Glen Ford.

Obama's Af-Pak is as Whack as Bush's Iraq

Glen Ford

Black Agenda Report
December 2, 2009

"More occupation means less occupation."

Barack Obama's oratorical skills have turned on him, revealing, as George Bush's low-grade delivery never could, the perfect incoherence of the current American imperial project in South Asia. Bush's verbal eccentricities served to muddy his entire message, leaving the observer wondering what was more ridiculous, the speechmaker or the speech. There is no such confusion when Obama is on the mic. His flawless delivery of superbly structured sentences provides no distractions, requiring the brain to examine the content—the policy in question—on its actual merits. The conclusion comes quickly: the U.S. imperial enterprise in Afghanistan and Pakistan is doomed, as well as evil.

The president's speech to West Point cadets was a stream of non sequiturs so devoid of logic as to cast doubt on the sanity of the authors. "[T]hese additional American and international troops," said the president, "will allow us to accelerate handing over responsibility to Afghan forces, and allow us to begin the transfer of our forces out of Afghanistan in July of 2011."

Obama claims that, the faster an additional 30,000 Americans pour into Afghanistan, the quicker will come the time when they will leave. More occupation means less occupation, you see? This breakneck intensification of the U.S. occupation is necessary, Obama explains, because "We have no interest in occupying your country."

"The U.S. imperial enterprise in Afghanistan and Pakistan is doomed, as well as evil."

If the Americans were truly interested in occupying Afghanistan, the logic goes, they would slow down and stretch out the process over many years, rather than mount an 18-month surge of Taliban-hunting. The Afghans are advised to hold still—the pulsating surge will be over before they know it.

At present, of course, the Americans have assumed all "responsibility" for Afghanistan—so much so that President Hamid Karzai only learned about Obama's plans earlier on Tuesday during a one-hour tele-briefing. This is consistent with Obama's detailed plans for Afghan liberation, under U.S. tutelage. The president is as wedded to high stakes testing of occupied peoples as he is for American public school children. "This effort must be based on performance. The days of providing a blank check are over," said the Occupier-in-Chief. He continued:

"And going forward, we will be clear about what we expect from those who receive our assistance. We will support Afghan Ministries, Governors, and local leaders that combat corruption and deliver for the people. We expect those who are ineffective or corrupt to be held accountable."

Such rigorous oversight of their country's affairs should keep Afghan minds off the fact that they have been fighting to remain independent of foreign rule for centuries, if not millennia. If Obama is right, Afghans might also be distracted from dwelling on the question of who their "Ministries, Governors, and local leaders" are answerable to—the Afghan people or the Americans?

"Obama advises Afghans to be patient and trusting regarding their sovereignty."

Although President Obama is anxious to bring U.S. troop levels above 100,000 as quickly as possible, he advises Afghans to be patient and trusting regarding their sovereignty. "It will be clear to the Afghan government, and, more importantly, to the Afghan people, that they will ultimately be responsible for their own country." That is, it will become clear in the fullness of time, but hopefully no later than 18 months after the planned surge begins. If all goes well, the Taliban will be dead or nearly so, and the non-Taliban Afghans will be prepared to begin assuming "responsibility for their own country." If not, then the Americans will be forced to continue as occupiers—reluctantly, of course, since, as the whole world and the more intelligent class of Afghans know, the Americans "have no interest in occupying your country"—unless they have to.

Should the Afghans become confused about American intentions, they might consult with their Pakistani neighbors, for whom President Obama also has plans.

"[We] have made it clear that we cannot tolerate a safe-haven for terrorists whose location is known, and whose intentions are clear," the president declared. "America is also providing substantial resources to support Pakistan's democracy and development. We are the largest international supporter for those Pakistanis displaced by the fighting."

Obama did not mention that it was the Americans that coerced and bribed the Pakistani military into launching the attacks that displaced over a million people in the Swat region and hundreds of thousands more in border areas. How nice of them to join in humanitarian assistance to the homeless.

The Pakistanis, like the Afghans, were assured the Americans will not abandon them to their own, independent devices. Said Obama: "And going forward, the Pakistani people must know: America will remain a strong supporter of Pakistan's security and prosperity long after the guns have fallen silent, so that the great potential of its people can be unleashed."

Some Pakistanis might consider that a threat. According to polling by the Pew Global Attitudes Project, only 16 percent of Pakistanis held a favorable view of the United States in 2009. Actually, that's a point or two higher than U.S. popularity in Occupied Palestine (15 percent) and Turkey (14 percent), the only other Muslim countries on the Pew list.

Not to worry. Obama knows things that escape the rest of us. For example, the fact that "we have forged a new beginning between America and the Muslim World—one that recognizes our mutual interest in breaking a cycle of conflict, and that promises a future in which those who kill innocents are isolated by those who stand up for peace and prosperity and human dignity."

Which means, we can expect those polling numbers to start going up, soon.

"Only 16 percent of Pakistanis held a favorable view of the United States in 2009."

When Obama isn't launching bold initiatives and "new beginnings," he's busy taking care of U.S. imperial business as usual.

Obama is most proud that the U.S. spends more on its military than all the rest of the nations of the planet, combined.

"[T]he United States of America has underwritten global security for over six decades," he told the cadets, "a time that, for all its problems, has seen walls come down, markets open, billions lifted from poverty, unparalleled scientific progress, and advancing frontiers of human liberty." Others might not view the rise of U.S. hegemony in such a positive light. But they are wrong, said the president. "For unlike the great powers of old, we have not sought world domination. Our union was founded in resistance to oppression. We do not seek to occupy other nations. We will not claim another nation's resources or target other peoples because their faith or ethnicity is different from ours."

In Obama's worldview, it's the thought that counts. Americans don't seek world domination; it just comes to them. "We do not seek to occupy other nations," they leave us no choice. If it were not for American concern for the welfare of all the world's people, the U.S. would not maintain 780 military bases in other people's countries.

Obama has certainly matured as an American-style statesman in his nine and a half months in office. As a TV Native American might say, "Black man in white house speak like forked tongued white man." Only better.

House War Vote: Answer Remains No for Now

Bruce Gagnon Thursday, March 11, 2010

The House of Representatives voted yesterday to deny the resolution put forward by Rep. Dennis Kucinich (D-OH) that called for Obama to bring the troops home from Afghanistan. The vote was 356 against the resolution, 65 in favor, with nine not voting.

It was clearly a vote that showed that there is one key issue in Washington where the Republicans and Democrats largely agree and that is on endless war. Out of the 356 votes to shoot down the resolution 189 of them were Democrats and 167 were Republican. Only five Republicans voted in favor of the Kucinich resolution.

I watched most of the three-hour debate via C-SPAN and it was quite interesting to see that the two leaders on the House floor managing the anti-Kucinich resolution effort were liberal Rep. Howard Berman (D-CA) and right-wing Cuban-American Rep. Ileana Ros-Lehtinen from Miami, Florida.

Our two representatives from Maine (Mike Michaud and Chellie Pingree) both voted to support the Kucinich resolution. Very good. Now we have to see if they vote against the next war funding supplemental of $33 billion expected to come up late next month and will they become leaders in the House to help bring others in their party around on this issue? It's nice to have their support on this resolution but by looking at the vote totals it is clear that unless the Democratic Party comes around on this issue soon we will have no $$$ back home for jobs, education, health care, bridge and road repair and a whole lot more!

Some of the language from those who spoke during yesterday's debate was of particular note. Rep. Berman called the recent U.S. attacks on the rural hamlet of Marjah in Afghanistan a great success, calling it a "city" and justified the surge in Afghanistan as revenge against "those who attacked us on 9-11".

Rep. Ros-Lehtinen said we can't "pull out now" or we'd lose face around the world. This debate, she claimed, will "demoralize our troops."

Several Democrats expressed disappointment and outrage that

the Kucinich resolution was even allowed to come to the House floor. Gary Ackerman (D-NY) said House members "should not be allowed to waste three hours of our time on a resolution that should fail." Rep. Janet Harmon (D-CA) also spoke against the resolution and made the case that "We now have a better strategy from our president." Rep. John Tanner (D-TN) also called for defeat of the Kucinich resolution and said, "NATO is becoming a global military alliance that will help us fund and supply troops [for our wars] around the world."

Kucinich and Rep. Ron Paul (R-TX) responded saying that this was really the first time since the war on Afghanistan began that the House was allowed to really debate the war.

Not one person I heard, including Rep. Kucinich, mentioned a mumbling word about oil/natural gas pipeline routes through Afghanistan and Pakistan.

Rep. Patrick Kennedy (D-RI) called it "despicable" that only two members of the media were covering the debate. When I looked on the web site of the *Washington Post* I could find nothing about the Kucinich resolution.

As I said above five Republicans voted with Kucinich on his resolution. John Duncan (R-TN) said, "There is nothing conservative about the war in Afghanistan. Fiscal conservatives should be horrified about the hundreds of billions of dollars that have been wasted over there."

Former civil rights leader Rep. John Lewis (D-GA) made an emotional appeal for support for the anti-war resolution and asked the question, "How much more debt must we bare?"

Immediately after Lewis spoke, Rep. Hank Johnson (D-GA) came to the podium. I recognized Johnson because he was the business community candidate put up to run against former Rep. Cynthia McKinney for her seat. Johnson called the resolution an "usurpation of the power of the Commander in Chief....our policy is bringing promising results....the resolution is ill-timed and ill-conceived.... let the president implement his strategy." His corporate funders in Atlanta were likely pleased that their investment in his House seat was already paying dividends.

We must thank Rep. Kucinich but in the end the whole three-hour affair really showed just how bankrupt the Congress really is.

Here is the full list of those who voted in favor of the

Kucinich resolution to bring our troops (and war $$) home from Afghanistan.

---- YEAS 65 ---
Baldwin
Campbell (Republican)
Capuano
Chu
Clarke
Clay
Cleaver
Crowley
Davis (IL)
DeFazio
Doyle
Duncan (Republican)
Edwards (MD)
Ellison
Farr
Filner
Frank (MA)
Grayson
Grijalva
Gutierrez
Hastings (FL)
Jackson (IL)
Jackson Lee (TX)
Johnson (IL) (Republican)
Johnson, E. B.
Jones (Republican)
Kagen
Kucinich
Larson (CT)
Lee (CA)
Lewis (GA)
Maffei
Maloney
Markey (MA)
McDermott
McGovern
Michaud (Maine)
Miller, George
Nadler (NY)

Napolitano
Neal (MA)
Obey
Olver
Paul (Republican)
Payne
Pingree (Maine)
Polis (CO)
Quigley
Rangel
Richardson
Sánchez, Linda T.
Sanchez, Loretta
Schakowsky
Serrano
Speier
Stark
Stupak
Tierney
Towns
Tsongas
Velázquez
Waters
Watson
Welch
Woolsey

---- NOT VOTING 9 ----

Barrett (SC)
Camp
Conyers
Davis (AL)
Deal (GA)
Diaz-Balart, L.
Hoekstra
Wasserman Schultz
Young (FL)

Prediction: When the vote comes in late April on the next $33 billion war supplemental I would bet my bottom dollar that half those on the Democrat party list above will turn around and vote for the money. That vote will be the true test of who is for real on this issue.

Bruce Gagnon Location: Bath, Maine, United States

Check out the revised version of my book *Come Together Right Now: Organizing Stories from a Fading Empire*—updated thru the end of 2008

Strategic Defense Initiative: Distance from Disorder Is the Key to Winning the Terror War

By William S. Lind

In the cacophony of an election year, one matter of prime importance seemed to be agreed by all parties: in the so-called War on Terror, America must remain on the offensive. Immediately before George W. Bush's State of the Union speech, the White House released as an excerpt, "America is on the offensive against the terrorists." Speaking to the Congress of Tomorrow in Philadelphia later the same month, Bush said, "No question, we will win the war on terror by staying on the offensive. This administration and this leadership is committed to making sure we stay on the offensive against the terrorists." He told the American Legion, "We're on the offensive against terror, and we will stay on the offensive against terror." Following the Madrid railway bombings, the *Washington Post* reported, "Bush's aides said he began talking to other world leaders about his determination to remain on the offensive in the war on terrorism." It sounded as if the ghost of von Schlieffen prowled the halls of the Bush White House.

The offensive strategic orientation of John Kerry was subtler but present nonetheless. In March 2004, speaking to the International Association of Firefighters, Kerry said, "I do not fault George Bush for doing too much in the War on Terror; I believe he's done too little." And in a speech at Drake University in December 2003, where he laid out a broad foreign-policy vision, Kerry said, "From the Battle of Belleau Wood to the Battle of the Bulge, from Korea to Kosovo, the story of the last century is of an America that accepted the heavy responsibility of its historic obligation—to serve as not just a beacon of hope, but to work with allies across the world to defend and extend the frontiers of freedom…To provide responsible leadership, we need…a bold, progressive internationalism—backed by undoubted military might—that commits America to lead in the cause of human liberty and prosperity." This is strong Wilsonianism, which by its nature puts America on the strategic offensive.

There is little doubt that "being on the offensive" sounded good to most voters. But if the objective is to design a strategy that brings victory in the War on Terror, a different approach may have much to recommend it. That oft-quoted if seldom read Prussian, Carl von Clausewitz, believed that the defensive was the stronger form of war.

Early in his book *On War* (a German friend has a first edition; he notes, "It is in perfect condition. It was in a regimental library, so it was never touched."), Clausewitz writes, "defense is simply the stronger form of war, the one that makes the enemy's defeat more certain…We maintain unequivocally that the form of warfare that we call defense not only offers greater probability of victory than attack, but that its victories can attain the same proportions and results." In a direct swipe at most of what is being said and written at present, he perorates, "So in order to state the relationship precisely, we must say that *the defensive form of warfare is intrinsically stronger than the offensive* [emphasis in original]. This is the point that we have been trying to make, for although it is implicit in the nature of the matter and experience has confirmed it again and again, it is at odds with prevalent opinion, which proves how ideas can be confused by superficial writers." And, perhaps, by candidates for high political office.

What might a defensive strategy in America's War on Terror look like? Before we can approach that question, we must address two other points. First, the threat America faces is not merely terrorism, which is only a technique. The threat is Fourth Generation warfare, which is a vastly broader phenomenon. Fourth Generation war marks the greatest dialectically qualitative change in the conduct of war since the Peace of Westphalia that ended the Thirty Years War in 1648. It has three central characteristics:

- *The loss of the state's monopoly on war and on the first loyalty of its citizens and the rise of non-state entities that command people's primary loyalty and that wage war. These entities may be gangs, religions, races and ethnic groups within races, localities, tribes, business enterprises, ideologies—the variety is almost limitless;*
- *A return to a world of cultures, not merely states, in conflict; and*
- *The manifestation of both developments—the*

decline of the state and the rise of alternate, often cultural, primary loyalties—not only "over there," but in America itself.

Second, no state armed forces know how to defeat Fourth Generation opponents militarily, and thus far none have been able to do so. Politically, the most fundamental characteristic of the Fourth Generation, a crisis of legitimacy of the state, is not recognized in any national capital. Combined, these two facts render many states extraordinarily vulnerable to Fourth Generation opponents.

Col. John Boyd, USAF, America's greatest military theorist, defined grand strategy as the art of connecting to as many other independent power centers as possible, while isolating the enemy from as many independent power centers as possible. The grand strategic question facing the U.S. is how to do that in a 21st century that will increasingly be dominated by non-state, Fourth Generation forces.

The answer begins by considering why the state first arose toward the end of the 15th century. Medieval Europe was a highly ordered, cultured, and successful society. It was brought down primarily by the plague, a point of more than historical interest in a world where many non-state forces may be able to carry out biological attacks. After the medieval order fell, it was succeeded by disorder, which led naturally to a strong desire for order, which in time was supplied by the state.

As we already see in those parts of the world such as West Africa where the state is disappearing, the state, like the medieval world, is followed by disorder. A Fourth Generation world will be one where disorder spreads like mold in a damp bathroom.

What does Colonel Boyd's definition of grand strategy mean in such a world? It means America's grand strategy should seek to connect our country with as many centers and sources of order as possible while isolating us from as many centers and sources of disorder as possible. This is the only reasonable chance of preserving something called the "United States" in a 21st century dominated by Fourth Generation war. And, as we will see, it leads toward a defensive, not offensive, military strategy.

What do we mean by centers and sources of order? First, places where the state still stands. The state arose to bring order, and in portions of the world it continues to do so. While the crisis of legitimacy of the state is universal, that does not mean it will everywhere reach catastrophic proportions. Those places where the state endures not simply as an empty form will remain centers of (relative) order. America is already connected to those places in a wide variety of ways and should strive to remain so. Actions such as the war in Iraq that tend to isolate us from successful states run counter to our interests.

In a Fourth Generation world, surviving states will not be the only centers of order. One of the central characteristics of the Fourth Generation is a return to a world where culture will often be more significant than statehood, and some cultures tend toward order. An example is Chinese culture, which extends well beyond the borders of the Chinese state. Order is the highest Chinese virtue; so, at least, Confucianism would suggest.

As people around the world transfer their primary loyalty from the state to a wide variety of other entities, some of these entities may also emerge as sources of order. Religions may become sources of order; we see that happening today as Christianity grows in places of chronic disorder such as Africa. Ideologies may be centers of order, depending on the ideology. Businesses and other commercial undertakings may be sources of order. So might mercenary armies. Because some, perhaps many, sources of order in the 21st century will not be states and may even appear strange or disreputable, the people who run foreign ministries may find it difficult to imagine building connectivity to them. But that is one of the novel actions the Fourth Generation will require.

One of the primary centers of disorder in the 21st century will be failed states—areas where the state has either disappeared or become simply one more criminal gang among many. Current examples include much of Africa, Somalia, Mesopotamia (following America's destruction of the Iraqi state), Afghanistan, parts of the former Soviet Union, and the West Bank of the Jordan River. These areas represent the future for much of the world.

Just as some cultures are likely to be centers of order, others will be centers or sources of disorder. One culture provides an example of the fact that centers and sources of disorder may not be identical—Islam. Because Islam is a religion of rules, it is capable of providing internal order in Islamic societies. As Robert Kaplan has noted, a stranger with a fat wallet can walk safely through some of the poorest Islamic slums. Islam, however, is likely to be one of the principal sources of disorder in a Fourth Generation world, even while some parts of the Islamic world may be centers of order. The reason is that Islam demands its believers wage endless jihad in the dar al harb, the non-Islamic world (literally the "world of war"), and a world where the state is weakening will be a happy hunting ground. The long-standing Arab military tradition of irregular light cavalry warfare is especially well suited when adapted with modern technologies and carried out at operational and strategic levels. Indeed, that is much of what Washington now calls terrorism.

One important way in which centers of disorder will also act as sources of disorder will be by producing hordes of refugees and emigrants. It is natural to flee disorder. But as some European countries have already discovered, accepting refugees from centers of disorder imports disorder. Just as people from highly ordered cultures, such as Germans or Scandinavians, take order with them wherever they go, so people from disordered places are bearers of chaos. The ways of life necessary for survival in centers of disorder—lying, cheating, stealing, and killing—become habits, and they are not easily left behind.

Other centers and sources of disorder will to some extent mirror centers of order: religions, ideologies, commercial enterprises (the drug trade is already a powerful example), mercenaries, and so on. One source of disorder that will not have a mirror image is disease. Centers of disorder will become breeding grounds for plagues and diseases of every sort, and some of them will travel well. West Nile virus is already a growing concern in the U.S. and it is merely the forerunner of a vast Pandora's box. The fact that some diseases may be genetically engineered as weapons of war will make the danger all the greater.

The Bush administration appears to recognize dimly that the fundamental fault line of the 21st century will be that between order and disorder. In his Sept. 25, 2003 speech to the United Nations, Bush declared, "Events during the past two years have set before us the clearest of divides, between those who seek order and those who spread chaos." The administration errs in assuming that the forces of order are the stronger party, and this assumption underlies its offensive strategy. But because the root of Fourth Generation war lies in a crisis of legitimacy of the state, and the state is still the main agent of order in the world, the forces of order in the 21st century will be weaker than the forces of disorder. When the Bush administration decided to invade Iraq, it assumed order would be easy to maintain or restore because the Iraqi state would endure. The actual effect of the invasion was to destroy the Iraqi state and replace it with chaos.

This brings us to the next question: what do we mean by "connect" and "isolate"? Connection is easy enough to understand. Goods, money, people, and ideas all flow freely with minimal barriers. Americans view those to whom we are connected as friends, extending help in times of need and also asking for and receiving assistance, including in war. Commercially, we buy their products and sometimes they even buy ours.

"Isolate" is more difficult to understand, in part because in the lexicon of the present foreign-policy establishment, "isolationism" is a term of opprobrium. But as America learned on Sept. 11, a Fourth Generation world will be a place where our physical security will depend on our ability and willingness to isolate ourselves from certain forces.

What isolation means will vary from case to case, but in some situations it will require actions that appear harsh by current standards. For example, we may find it necessary to prohibit people from certain places from entering the U.S. We may need to profile on a variety of bases, including religious belief and ethnic origin. Isolation may also inflict hardships on Americans, as when we must avoid becoming dependent on imports such as Middle Eastern oil.

In general, isolation will mean minimizing contacts that involve flows of people, money, materials, and new primary loyalties, such as religions and ideologies, into the United States. Flows in the other direction will generally be less dangerous, except for the fact that one-way relationships are difficult to sustain. They tend to become reciprocal, which means importing danger. Americans will require a newfound self-discipline in a Fourth Generation world, realizing they cannot have it all (and have it cheaply) without creating serious threats to America's homeland security.

In terms of foreign relations, isolation will more often apply to regions where the state is weak or has vanished. But it will sometimes be necessary for us to isolate ourselves from other states, especially states that exist in form but not in reality. Unfortunately, friendly relations will leave open the door to the non-state elements that are the real powers within the hollow form of the other state, and those powers may be threats to us. Saudi Arabia may soon be a state that falls in this category.

How does this isolate the enemy, which in our strategy means centers and sources of disorder, from other independent power centers? Here, our proposed grand strategy works indirectly, in a way John Boyd might appreciate. To use one of his favorite expressions, it folds the enemy back on himself.

As the offensive strategy of the Bush administration has demonstrated, when we choose to engage centers and sources of disorder, attacking them militarily or demanding reforms inconsistent with their cultures, we provide an external threat against which they can unite. Conversely, if we isolate ourselves from them, we will help them focus on and thus accentuate their internal contradictions. This is a classic case of inaction being a form of action.

The Islamic world offers an example. Islam mandates jihad against all non-Islamics, which means Islam will always be a threat to the U.S. But Islam itself is also riven with internal conflicts. Those internal conflicts are now minimized because Islamics can call for unity against an external threat. Even so, internal conflicts persist: many Shi'ite Iraqis blame car bombings in Shi'ite areas on Wahhabi Muslims. *In Terror's Mask: Insurgency Within Islam,* Michael Vlahos argues that what we are seeing in the Islamic world today follows an age-old pattern. Purist elements arise that accuse existing Islamic governments of straying from Islam; they triumph, only to find that pure Islam cannot govern; attempting to make things work, they also become corrupt; and new purist elements gather to bring about their overthrow. This cycle could work to America's advantage if she isolated herself from it, because it focuses Islamic energies inward. As Boyd would say, it tends to fold Islam back on itself.

What are the implications for the conduct of strategy, the military component of grand strategy?

First, note that no strategy is a hard and fast rule that can be applied mechanically. Strategy is an art; its conduct, as Helmuth von Moltke said, is a matter of expedients. In the conduct of strategy, the engineering approach to problems favored by Americans is not useful. Past attempts along engineering lines, such as the Weinberger

Doctrine and the Powell Doctrine, resulted only in pseudo-strategies that were useless in the real world. Real strategies do not seek to create templates but rather inform and shape specific actions, harmonizing them and giving them a coherence that will often be visible only in retrospect.

Within this context, one of the first implications of our recommended grand strategy is that America's current military strategy—a strong strategic offensive coupled with a weak tactical offensive—is wrong. Strategically, we are launching military attacks on perceived opponents worldwide, or at least threatening to do so, under a doctrine of preventive war. But tactically, our attacks are weak because it is relatively easy for our real enemies, non-state forces, to sidestep them.

Both Afghanistan and Iraq provide examples. America took the strategic military offensive, invading both countries. But in Afghanistan, on the tactical level, both al-Qaeda and the Taliban survived our attempts to destroy them and are now coming back. The reason they could do so is that our Second Generation armed forces fight by putting firepower on targets, and Fourth Generation forces are very good at making themselves untargetable. Even in Operation Anaconda, when al-Qaeda stood and fought, the inability of the Second Generation American Army to fight a battle of encirclement (something that is central to Third Generation tactics) allowed the enemy to escape with small losses.

The situation in Iraq is similar. For the most part, the Iraqi armed forces did not contest our advance to Baghdad. Whether that was part of their strategy is not yet known. But the result was to leave those forces alive and armed to serve as a basis for a guerrilla war. The non-state forces that are emerging from the wreckage of the Iraqi state are proving to be as untargetable as those in Afghanistan.

Instead of a strategic military offensive coupled with a weak tactical offensive, our grand strategy would urge a strategic military defensive coupled with a powerful strategic and tactical counter-offensive. In simple terms, this means we would leave centers and sources of disorder alone militarily (and in other ways) unless they attacked us. But if they attacked us, our response would be Roman, which is to say annihilating.

The logic of a defensive strategy is almost self-evident. If our grand strategic goal is to connect ourselves to order while isolating ourselves from disorder, we will not want to undertake military offensives aimed at other states that are themselves centers of (again, relative) order. If successful, such offensives will usually result in the destruction of the opposing state and its reduction to a new center of stateless disorder. Offensives against centers and sources of disorder run directly contrary to the goal of isolating ourselves from them. As we see both in Afghanistan and in Iraq, the most thorough way to enmesh ourselves in a center of disorder is to invade and occupy it. A strategically defensive military posture is a necessary outgrowth from our recommended grand strategy.

The second part of our prescription, an annihilating counteroffensive, needs some elaboration. Here again, Clausewitz is helpful:

> *What is the concept of defense? The parrying of a blow. What is its characteristic feature? Awaiting the blow. It is this feature that turns any action into a defensive one; it is the only test by which defense can be distinguished from attack in war. Pure defense, however, would be completely contrary to the idea of war, since it would mean that only one side was waging it. Therefore, defense in war can only be relative, and the characteristic feature of waiting should be applied only to the basic concept, not to all of its components.*

The challenge facing an annihilating counterstroke is not theoretical but practical: how do we accomplish it? There may be some instances in which our Second Generation armed forces can do it, for example by carpet bombing from B-52s. Should we ever succeed in transitioning the American armed services to the Third Generation, more options would open up, such as large-scale battles of encirclement. But in some cases, unconventional weapons will have to be employed.

When that is the case, it will be imperative that the employment of unconventional weapons follows instantly after a successful attack on the United States. As Machiavelli would understand, such a reaction must appear to be a "spasm" on our part, not a calculated act. In 1914, had Austria-Hungary declared war on Serbia within 48 hours of the assassination of the Archduke Franz Ferdinand, she might well have gotten away with it. While the world, in shock over the 9/11 attack, might have accepted an apparent American spasm with unconventional weapons, it also might have objected that any first use of such weapons would be the end of efforts to stop the proliferation of weapons of mass destruction.

But in fact, from a Fourth Generation perspective, the genie of WMD is already out of the bottle. The Fourth Generation threat is not states delivering nuclear weapons by ballistic missile but non-state actors developing genetically engineered plagues that can be delivered anonymously by shipping container (small nuclear weapons, bought or stolen, may come the same way). The technology already exists, and unlike that required to build nuclear weapons, it does not require much in the way of facilities. It is knowledge based, and the knowledge is or soon will be universally available. Such plagues can be more, not less, devastating than nuclear weapons.

A defensive military strategy that includes an annihilating counterattack is consistent with our grand strategy of isolating centers and sources of disorder while folding them back on themselves, yet it runs no danger of being perceived as weakness on our part. On the contrary, it both demonstrates and demands more strength of will than is currently evident in the Washington establishment, in either political party.

The next implication, or perhaps precondition, of our grand strategy is one that is very difficult, yet essential, to grasp. America itself may not remain a center of order in a Fourth Generation world. As dangerous as the importation of Fourth Generation war into America is, more dangerous still is the Fourth Generation war that America may develop from within.

To survive the crisis of legitimacy of the state that lies at the heart of Fourth Generation war, a state needs two qualities: an open political system and a unitary culture. At present, America has a closed political system, dominated by an establishment that is in essence a single political party, and she is pursuing a policy of multiculturalism that enhances and exacerbates cultural frictions. While an open political system and a unitary culture are to some degree fungible—Japan's unitary culture will probably allow the Japanese state to survive despite its closed political system, while Switzerland's open political system preserves legitimacy despite three distinct cultures—any state that has neither is likely to experience a crisis of legitimacy. At the least, we cannot assume that the United

States will not experience such a crisis, to the point where self-generated Fourth Generation war is not even a possibility. Police departments in some large American cities would be quick to note that they are already facing Fourth Generation opponents on the streets.

There are, of course, steps the American state could take to minimize the chance of Fourth Generation war developing here. The most urgent is to end the current de facto policy of open immigration. Because multiculturalism works against acculturation of immigrants, mass immigration from other cultures is a clear and present danger in a Fourth Generation world. When large numbers of immigrants retain a primary loyalty to their own cultures rather than to the American state, they provide an ideal base for Fourth Generation war.

More broadly, if America is to avoid Fourth Generation war on her own soil, she needs to address the two origins of the crisis of legitimacy of the state. That means opening up the political system and abandoning multiculturalism for a policy of encouraging what used to be called Americanization (and is in fact the adoption of Anglo-Saxon norms, at least in the public square). Americanization means actions such as restoring America's public schools as primary centers of acculturation, a role they played effectively a century ago, and making English the only legal language in public business. Opening the political system means actions such as giving third parties a real chance against the two major parties, term limits, putting "none of the above" on the ballots, reducing the power of money in politics (what American politicians call "campaign contributions" are recognized in the rest of the world as bribes), making much more use of ballot initiatives and referenda, and restraining the judiciary from legislating.

On the grand strategic level, where foreign and domestic policy unite, avoiding Fourth Generation war on America's own soil (regardless of its source) means recognizing that in a Fourth Generation world, the enemy is disorder itself. This does not mean that the answer to the Fourth Generation threat is to increase the raw power of the state through ill-considered legislation such as the Patriot Act. On the contrary, giving the state extraconstitutional powers will exacerbate its crisis of legitimacy. The American Constitution, as it was created and understood by the founders, is a means to a new legitimacy, not an obstacle to it.

America's ability to prevent the spread of Fourth Generation war elsewhere in the world will be small. Overt American military support to states facing Fourth Generation threats will most often be counterproductive because it will undermine the legitimacy of the government the United States is fighting to uphold. The more relevant question is how an America that has succeeded in avoiding the Fourth Generation at home might relate to a world where the state is generally in decline.

The Islamic world, as noted, may not everywhere be a center of disorder, but it is likely to be a vast source of disorder. Isolating ourselves from it will mean weaning ourselves from dependence on Arab oil (Russian oil could substitute, at least for a while). Because China may be a major center of order in the 21st century, those voices in Washington that see war with China as inevitable represent folly. From a Fourth Generation perspective, America and China are united by the most powerful of all strategic common interests, an interest in the preservation of order. China should be viewed as a strategic ally of the first importance, under any government that can maintain China's internal unity.

Latin America is likely to be an area where the crisis of legitimacy of the state sharpens and Fourth Generation forces grow more powerful. Isolating the United States from the resulting disorder will above all mean effective immigration control. Africa is already being devoured by Fourth Generation war, which is not surprising in a region where states were never real and most governments are kleptocracies. The rapid spread of Christianity could provide a countervailing force, but Africa's future is probably war, plague, famine, and death. Isolating America from Africa will be necessary but should not be difficult, barring pure imbecility on the part of American politicians. India's future is uncertain; her national unity depends on maintaining the veneer of the Raj, which is wearing a bit thin. Isolating America from a disordered India, should India crumble, would not be difficult.

Europe's future, like that of the United States, is not so assured as some may assume. Europe has imported an enormous source of disorder in the form of immigrants from other cultures, many of them Islamic. It is by no means impossible that the 21st century will see Europe compelled to undertake a second expulsion of the Moors. If Europe is to survive, it will have to bring its birthrate up substantially. Russia is an important part of Europe, and regrettably it is a part where the state is now fragile. The U.S. missed a golden opportunity to forge an enduring, strategic alliance with Russia when Communism fell; to the degree that opportunity has not been lost—largely through inane American actions such as going to war with Serbia on behalf of Islam—it should be pursued.

One theme shines through this brief circumnavigation: the requirement that America not be dependent on any part of the world that is a center or source of disorder. Here, the implication is less for American foreign policy than for American economic policy. While the United States need not pursue a policy of autarky, it does require what might best be termed full economic independence. That is to say, we need to be able to manage on what we've got if we have to, in terms both of natural resources and manufacturing capability.

By now, one point should be clear: a defensive strategy oriented toward a Fourth Generation threat leaves us with an entirely different frame of reference from the one that now prevails in Washington. Everything changes, in what would be the greatest alterations in American grand strategy, military strategy, and force structure since 1917. Nothing illustrates better the magnitude of the challenge than the response a defensive strategy and its logical outgrowths would surely elicit from those in power. "Is such a transformation even imaginable politically?" they will ask. Their answer, stated or implied, will be, "Certainly not." At the same time, the question that the decline of the state, the state's loss of its monopoly on war, and the rise of the Fourth Generation poses is, "Would even these changes be sufficient to enable the United States to protect itself in a world dominated by Fourth Generation war?" The distance between those two questions measures the likelihood that the American state will survive the 21st century.

The Afghan Quagmire

By Ralph Nader

Thursday, December 3, 2009
In the Public Interest

Misusing professional cadets at West Point as a political prop, President Barack Obama delivered his speech on the Afghanistan war forcefully but with fearful undertones. He chose to escalate this undeclared war with at least 30,000 more soldiers plus an even larger number of corporate contractors.

He chose the path the military-industrial complex wanted. The "military" planners, whatever their earlier doubts about the quagmire, once in, want to prevail. The "industrial" barons because their sales and profits rise with larger military budgets.

A majority of Americans are opposed or skeptical about getting deeper into a bloody, costly fight in the mountains of central Asia while facing recession, unemployment, foreclosures, debt and deficits at home. Congressman Dennis Kucinich (D-OH), after hearing Mr. Obama's speech said, "Why is it that war is a priority but the basic needs of people in this country are not?"

Let's say needs like waking up to do something about 60,000 fatalities a year in our country related to workplace diseases and trauma. Or 250 fatalities a day due to hospital induced infections, or 100,000 fatalities a year due to hospital malpractice, or 45,000 fatalities a year due to the absence of health insurance to pay for treatment, or, or, or, even before we get into the economic poverty and deprivation. Any Obama national speeches on these casualties?

Back to the West Point teleprompter speech. If this is the product of a robust internal Administration debate, the result was the same cookie-cutter, Vietnam approach of throwing more soldiers at a poorly analyzed situation. In September, the chair of the Joint Chiefs of Staff, Admiral Mike Mullen told an American Legion Convention, "I've seen the public opinion polls saying that a majority of Americans don't support the effort at all. I say, good. Let's have the debate, let's have that discussion."

Where? Not in Congress. There were only rubberstamps and

grumbles; certainly nothing like the Fulbright Senate hearings on the Vietnam War.

Where else? Not in the influential commercial media. Forget jingoistic television and radio other than the satire of Jon Stewart plus an occasional non-commercial Bill Moyers show or rare public radio commentary. Not in the op-ed pages of the *New York Times* and the *Washington Post*.

A FAIR study published in the organization's monthly newsletter EXTRA reports that of all opinion columns in the *New York Times* and the *Washington Post* over the first 10 months of 2009, thirty-six out of forty-three columns on the Afghanistan War in the *Times* supported the war while sixty-one of the sixty-seven *Post* columns supported a continued war.

So what would a rigorous public and internal administration debate have highlighted? First, the more occupation forces there are, the more they fuel the insurgency against the occupation, especially since so many more civilians than fighters lose their lives. Witness the wedding parties, villagers, and innocent bystanders blown up by the U.S. military's superior weaponry.

Second, there was a remarkable absence in Obama's speech about the tribal conflicts and the diversity of motivations of those he lumped under the name of "Taliban." Some are protecting their valleys, others are in the drug trade, others want to drive out the occupiers, others are struggling for supremacy between the Pashtuns on one side and the Tajiks and Uzbeks on the other (roughly the south against the north). The latter has been the substance of a continuing civil war for many years.

Third, how can Obama's plan begin to work, requiring a stable, functioning Afghan government—which now is largely a collection of illicit businesses milking the graft, which grows larger in proportion to what the American taxpayers have to spend there—and the disorganized, untrained Afghan army—mainly composed of Tajiks and Uzbeks loathed by the Pashtuns.

Fourth, destroying or capturing al Qaeda attackers in Afghanistan ignores Obama's own intelligence estimates. Many observers believe al Qaeda has gone to Pakistan or elsewhere. The *New York Times* reports that "quietly, Mr. Obama has authorized an expansion of the war in Pakistan as well—if only he can get a weak, divided, suspicious Pakistani government to agree to the terms."

Hello! Congress did not authorize a war in Pakistan, so does Obama, like Bush, just decree what the Constitution requires to be authorized by the legislative branch? Can we expect another speech at the Air Force Academy on the Pakistan war?

Fifth, as is known, al Qaeda is a transnational movement. Highly mobile, when it is squeezed. As Rolf Mowatt-Larssen, the former CIA officer operating in Pakistan, said: "There is no direct impact on stopping terrorists around the world because we are or are not in Afghanistan." He argues that safe havens can be moved to different countries, as has indeed happened since 9/11.

Sixth, the audacity of hope in Obama's speech was illustrated by his unconvincing date of mid-2011 for beginning the withdrawal of U.S. soldiers from Afghanistan. The tendered exit strategy, tied to unspecified conditions, was a bone he tossed to his shaky liberal base.

The White House recently said it costs $1 million a year to keep each single soldier in Afghanistan. Take one fifth of that sum and connect with the tribal chiefs to build public facilities in transportation, agriculture, schools, clinics, public health, and safe drinking water.

Thus strengthened, these tribal leaders know how to establish order. This is partly what Ashraf Ghani, the former respected Afghan finance minister and former American anthropology professor, called concrete "justice" as the way to undermine insurgency.

Withdraw the occupation, which now is pouring gasoline on the fire. Bring back the saved four-fifths of that million dollars per soldier to America and provide these and other soldiers with tuition for their education and training.

The principal authority in Afghanistan is tribal. Provide the assistance, based on stage-by-stage performance, and the tribal leaders obtain a stake in stability. Blown apart by so many foreign invaders—British, Soviet, American—and internally riven, the people in the countryside look to tribal security as the best hope for a nation that has not known unity for decades.

Lifting the fog of war allows other wiser policies urged by experienced people to be considered for peace and security.

Rather than expanding a boomeranging war, this alternative has some probability of modest success unlike the sure, mounting loss of American and Afghani lives and resources.

Left Behind
Liberals Get a War President of Their Very Own

by Murray Polner

> *With his Nobel Peace Prize acceptance speech, Barack Obama signaled that the world had better get ready for a tougher, less forgiving, more quintessentially American approach from a man who certainly gave the soft touch a try.*
> *—Robert Kagan,* Washington Post, *Dec. 13, 2009*

Suddenly and surprisingly, we have a Bush-like Obama Doctrine. To the applause of liberal hawks and formerly critical neocons, the president declared in his Nobel Peace Prize speech that the U.S. will continue to wage war—though naturally, only "just" war—anywhere and against anyone it chooses in a never-ending struggle against the forces of evil. His antiwar supporters can take seats on the sidelines. It's all reminiscent of John F. Kennedy and the prescient George Ball, and afterward Ball and Lyndon Johnson. In the early '60s, JFK—reluctantly, we are told by his admirers—decided to send 16,000 "trainers" to Vietnam to teach the South Vietnamese how to play soldier and to stop the Communists from sweeping over Southeast Asia. Vast quantities of money and assorted advisers were shipped without accountability to the corrupt gang of thugs running and ruining that country. Ball, the one dissenter in Kennedy's entourage, pleaded with JFK to recall France's devastating defeat in 1954 at Dien Bien Phu and throughout Indochina. "Within five years we'll have 300,000 men in the paddies and jungles and never find them again," he warned the liberal icon in the White House. But JFK thought he knew better, caustically answering, "George, you're crazier than hell. That just isn't going to happen." Ball would also press Lyndon Johnson to stand down in Vietnam before he destroyed his presidency, domestic agenda, and more importantly the lives of tens of thousands of American soldiers and their families, not to mention a few million Southeast Asians. But LBJ wasn't going to be the first president to lose a war and be blasted by pugnacious home-front warriors. Failing to stop the North Vietnamese would sooner or later have us fighting them on Waikiki Beach, or so the Cold War line went. Ever since then, we have continued to hear about regional menaces that supposedly, if left unchecked, will threaten vital U.S. interests or even Americans at home. Ronald Reagan employed that rationale in defending the proxy war in Central America waged by U.S.-backed Contras. George H.W. Bush and Bill Clinton extended the tradition of intervention, sending troops to theaters of combat as far-flung as Panama, Kuwait, and the Balkans, while the second Bush launched invasions of Iraq and Afghanistan. They have all been war presidents.

But Barack Obama was going to be different, or so my fellow antiwar liberals—and a few antiwar conservatives—hoped. He was to herald the end of that uncompromising and unilateral era of preventive war. The hundreds of thousands who joyously greeted the president-elect in Grant Park or the 1.5 million at his inauguration were ecstatic with anticipation. Left-wing pundits wrote excitedly about FDR's One Hundred Days and projected great plans onto the new Man From Illinois. In countless articles, Republicans were declared brain dead, and the Bush-Cheney policies that got us into Iraq, Afghanistan, and the torture business were buried. One year after those celebrations, it's the neocons cheering, seeing in Obama's policies a vindication of the late administration. Who would have dreamed that following Obama's West Point speech announcing 30,000 more troops destined for Afghanistan, William Kristol would laud Obama in the pages of the *Washington Post,* writing, "the rationale for this surge is identical to Bush's," and praise the Democratic president for having "embraced the use of military force as a key instrument of national power"? War makes strange bedfellows. Michèle Flournoy, Obama's under secretary of defense for policy, has been invited to speak about the president's hopes for a new Afghanistan on a panel led by Frederick W. Kagan at the American Enterprise Institute, the heart of neoconservatism. Why did Obama buy what the hawks sold him? What if he had leveled with the nation and acknowledged that, however obnoxious and cruel the Taliban may be, they pose no danger to the United States? What if he had vowed that we would not dispatch tens of thousands of additional troops to a civil war in an agrarian, impoverished, largely illiterate country divided by tribal loyalties? It was not to be. Instead, as *New York Times* columnist David Brooks stated approvingly, "With his two surges, Obama will more than double the number of American troops in Afghanistan." Charles Krauthammer was direct and sharp: "most supporters of the Afghanistan war were satisfied. They got the policy; the liberals got the speech"—and no say in the construction of that policy. After West Point and Oslo, neocons saw Obama as a more coherent Bush, an electrifying orator who had dazzled antiwar Democrats and independents and then promptly dumped them. When the *New York Times* printed a photo of the men and women who helped Obama reach his decision to escalate, not one dove was present. Were there no alternatives? In this huge country, could he not find a handful of realists, whether Left or Right, to supply some workable ideas for eliminating third and fourth tours for our overextended troops and the resulting suicides, amputations, epidemics of post-traumatic stress disorder, and legions of weeping relatives at gravesides? Hold on, Obama's loyal liberal defenders counter, shuddering at the memory of Bush. Why blame him for the miserable decisions he has to make based on impossible situations he did not create? They would prefer not to explain why they and their allies in the think tanks and Congress have so little influence. Granted, some of Obama's base reacted negatively. In December, MoveOn.org sent its millions of members a scorching email denouncing Obama's troop escalation for "deepen[ing] our involvement in a quagmire." Anti-Vietnam War rebel Tom Hayden removed the Obama sticker from his car. United for Peace and Justice, the main organizer of mass peace rallies around the country, announced, "It's Obama's War, and We Will Stop it." The widely read liberal TomDispatch.com dubbed its former champion the "Commanded-in-Chief" for giving way to the hardball pressures exerted by the generals. Matthew Rothschild of The Progressive, founded by the fabled anti-militarist Robert M. LaFollette Sr. in 1909, compared Bush and Obama's rhetoric and wrote an article called "Obama Steals Bush's Speechwriters." But these protests notwithstanding, we remain—and will throughout Obama's presidency—an empire of military colonization, the goal for decades of neoconservatives and assorted liberal hawks.

In anthropologist Hugh Gusterson's wonderfully evocative words, "The U.S. is to military bases as Heinz is to ketchup." American forces are stationed at approximately 1,000 military bases in 120 countries at a cost topping $100 billion annually. Diego Garcia, a remote island in the Indian Ocean midway between Africa and Indonesia, is apparently so essential a base that 5,000 locals were thrown out of their homes so the U.S. could have yet another top-secret facility from which to conduct its perpetual wars. Far from being a consensus-seeking peacenik, Obama would not even sign the Landmine Ban Treaty, which Bush also refused to endorse, thus leaving the U.S. the only NATO nation unwilling to participate. Said Steve Goose of Human Rights Watch's Arms Division, "they have simply decided to allow the Pentagon to dictate terms." A shocked Bill Moyers pointed out that 5,000 people died from mine explosions in 2008, noting the disconnect between Obama's refusal to enlist the support of the government he leads and the Oslo speech in which he maintained, "I am convinced that adhering to standards, international standards, strengthens those who do and isolates and weakens those who don't." In another instance of history repeating, the first Obama defense budget has been virtually the same as Bush's military appropriations. Obama has reduced spending on Cold War weapons such as the F-22 fighter, but he reportedly plans to ask Congress for an extra $33 billion for the ongoing wars in the Middle East and Central Asia. To his credit, the president is trying to negotiate a new nuclear-arms reduction pact with Russia and close a few of the CIA's clandestine prisons. But in many other vital areas of defense and national security, like warrantless wiretaps and renewal of much of the Patriot Act, he persists in activities that violate fundamental freedoms. He has also refused to hold anyone from the Bush-Cheney era accountable. There's more: his administration has just signed an accord with Colombia granting the U.S. a ten-year right to use seven of its bases, including the centerpiece of the agreement, Palanquero AFB. Take heed, any leftist South American government that dares defy Uncle Sam. At the same time, Obama blinked at the coup d'état in Honduras. "They really thought he was different," said Julia Sweig of the Council on Foreign Relations, referring to Latin America's opinion of Obama. "But those hopes were dashed over the course of the summer." It was not to be. So what happened? Barack Obama happened. More eloquence than substance happened. More time-honored political caution than audacity or hope. Liberal and conservative Cold Warriors as key advisers. A reluctance to cross wartime profiteers. A recognition by his poll counters that, with future elections in mind, it was best to govern from some ill-defined center, acting tough abroad to keep the neocons off his back while throwing an occasional bone to his left.

That strategy may buy him a second term as fruitless as his first—or it could render him indistinguishable from his deservedly maligned predecessor and cost him re-election in 2012. The Left howls now, but from the very start, Obama signaled his lack of interest in McGovernite ideas of change in foreign policy. There was a time when he talked about pressing Israel to dismantle its settlements. But thus far he has been cowed by Netanyahu and his American backers, betraying any hope for a genuinely independent Palestinian state. There was that stirring speech in Cairo and then silence. There was talk about closing Guantanamo but no mention of the much larger Bagram prison in Afghanistan. The sad truth is everything we are seeing we have already seen. Despite presidents who come and go, permanent war is a hallowed American institution. Start if you will with the War of 1812, the invasion of Mexico, and the carnage of a Civil War. Move to the mass murder of Native Americans and theft of their property, the killing, torture, and prison camps in the Philippines, then the blood-drenched 20th century. The 21st likewise dawns red. It never changes. Doves protest, hawks rule, ordinary people pay the penalty. All wars are "just." As surely as the bloodletting persists, so does the opposition. The old chestnut that liberals have always stood for peace and conservatives for war is historically false. In fact, our past is rich with anti-militarist heroes of surprisingly varied political colors. Daniel Webster opposed the War Hawks and the draft they proposed in 1812. Abolitionist Theodore Parker denounced the Mexican War and called on his fellow Bostonians in 1847 "to protest against this most infamous war." Henry Van Dyke, a Presbyterian minister and ardent foe of the annexation of the Philippines, told his congregation in 1898, "If we enter the course of foreign conquest, the day is not far distant when we must spend in annual preparation for wars more than the $180,000,000 that we now spend every year in the education of our children for peace." Socialist and labor leader Eugene Debs received a ten-year prison sentence for daring to tell potential draftees in 1918 that it was "the working class who fight all the battles, the working class who make the supreme sacrifices, the working class who freely shed their blood and furnish the corpses." Against U.S. Entry into World War I, Republican Sen. George Norris of Nebraska asked, "To whom does this war bring prosperity? Not to the soldier…not to the brokenhearted widow…not to the mother who weeps at the death of her baby boy…War brings no prosperity to the great mass of common and patriotic citizens…War brings prosperity to the stock gambler on Wall Street." Rep. Barbara Lee (D-Calif.), the only member of Congress in 2001 who voted against George W. Bush's decision to invade Afghanistan, warned her colleagues to be "careful not to embark on an open-ended war with neither an exit strategy nor a focused target." Conservative Russell Kirk laid out a post-World War II program for conservatives by reminding them, "A handful of individuals, some of them quite unused to moral responsibilities on such a scale, made it their business to extirpate the populations of Nagasaki and Hiroshima; we must make it our business to curtail the possibility of such snap decisions." Anti-militarism is very much an American tradition, but it has never been a majority position. Who now reads Finley Peter Dunne, the Chicago newspaperman who invented the brogish bartender Mr. Dooley speaking to his customer, Mr. Hennessey, while deriding American excesses and the national passion for imperial expansion? He wondered why many leaders and everyday Americans passively embraced, without much knowledge, our devotion to world hegemony—specifically in his time, the decision to invade and occupy the Philippines. "'Tis not more than two months," he told his pro-annexation readers, "ye larned whether they were islands or canned goods." Yet just as certain as opposition to foreign adventuring arises, again it goes unheeded. As we begin President Obama's second year in office, of this we can be certain: in global affairs, but for a few crumbs here and there, antiwar views will rarely be welcomed by this White House. And when these marginalized voters complain, all the president's men will remind them that they were told Afghanistan was a "necessary war" and "national security" is everything. I can imagine Obama's advisers confidently telling him that however many troops he ships to these and future wars, however much money he spends on military hardware, his anguished allies have no place else to go.

Murray Polner is the author of *No Victory Parades: The Return of the Vietnam Veteran* and is co-editor, with Thomas E. Woods Jr., of *We Who Dared Say No to War.*

March 2010, *The American Conservative*

The Abolition of War

Sam Smith

Progressive Review 2007

Could the end of war be the abolition movement of the 21st century?

Even leaving morality aside, it would make a lot of sense. The United States, for example, hasn't won a war—in the sense of gaining something significant other than the symbolism of "victory"—in over sixty years.

America's defense expenditures are more than double those of all the other top ten militaries combined. Yet we continue to drastically shortchange healthcare, retirement and education on behalf of purported military readiness.

One reason we are so willing to do so is because we consider war inevitable. In fact, war is not the product of human nature but of the organized state, a fairly recent invention in human history. Further, the nature of this invention has drastically changed over time. What general today would order his troops to fight in the manner of Henry VIII or even General Grant or Lee? And what did the American Revolution, the Civil War and Vietnam have in common, how were they different and which list is longer? Why do we use the same term to describe conflict that a hundred years ago claimed civilians as only 20% of its casualties but today results in 80% of its victims being civilians?

A logical review of America's own wars since WWII would lead almost inevitably to the conclusion that wars are no longer—if they ever were—an effective way of handling foreign affairs. They are excessively costly, environmentally disastrous, kill too many people and don't produced the sought-after results.

We avoid such questions because they seem almost unpatriotic. But what if war is another form of behavior—like slavery in the 19th century—that we now—if we so will it—have the potential of declaring extinct as part of our moral and social evolution?

We rarely ask this question not only because it seems too hard, but because we routinely accept accustomed approaches that are reasonable in the short run—such demanding the end to a particular war—but which avoid the larger issue.

In other words, we remain peace activists instead of becoming war abolitionists.

We call ourselves anti-war protestors but are really only talking about Iraq. And so forth.

The alternative would be a serious war abolition movement that would help others understand the futility of the military approach, its masochistic costs and the techniques and advantages of peace and mediation.

If this all sounds too radical, consider the following:

"I know war as few other men now living know it, and nothing to me is more revolting. I have long advocated its complete abolition, as its very destructiveness on both friend and foe has rendered it useless as a means of settling international disputes..."

And this:

"Men since the beginning of time have sought peace. Various methods through the ages have been attempted to devise an international process to prevent or settle disputes between nations. From the very start workable methods were found in so far as individual citizens were concerned, but the mechanics of an instrumentality of larger international scope have never been successful.

"Military alliances, balances of power, leagues of nations, all in turn failed, leaving the only path to be by way of the crucible of war. The utter destructiveness of war now blocks out this alternative. We have had our last chance. If we will not devise some greater and more equitable system, our Armageddon will be at our door."

The first words were spoken by General Douglas MacArthur during his farewell address to Congress. The second was from his statement soon after the surrender of the Japanese aboard the battleship Missouri.

A couple of years later, Japan approved a constitution with this provision:

"Aspiring sincerely to an international peace based on justice and order, the Japanese people forever renounce war as a sovereign right of the nation and the threat or use of force as means of settling international disputes."

Essays on War

From the writings of Sam Smith

The one place where the modern American military has been successful is right here in the US, where it has long occupied much of the budget and captured many of the politicians.

I sometimes fantasize that war will be the slavery of the 21st century, which is to say a concept once widely accepted is turned into the pariah practice it should always have been. For this to happen abolitionism will have to replace pacifism; it is not the good of the resister that is important but rather the evil of the practitioner. We need to demystify the military, pointing out not just its moral weaknesses but its logical fallacies. We should sensibly regard people who walk around with pins on their chests celebrating their life as, at best, somewhat unstable. And we need to remind the media that it can not call itself objective and repeatedly rebuff the voices of peace.

Empires and cultures are not permanent and while thinking about the possibility that ours is collapsing may seem a dismal exercise it is far less so than enduring the dangerous frustrations and failures involved in having one's contrary myth constantly butt up against reality like a boozer who insists he is not drunk attempting to drive home. Instead of defending the non-existent we could turn our energies instead towards devising a new and saner existence.

Places like Harvard and Oxford—and their after-school programs such as the Washington think tanks—teach the few how to control the many. It is impossible to do this without various forms of abuse ranging from sophism to corporate control systems to napalm. It is no accident that a large number of advocates of this war—in government and the media—are the products of elite educations where they were taught both the inevitability of their hegemony and the tools with which to enforce it. It will be some time before places such as Harvard and the Council on Foreign Relations are seen for what they are: the White Citizens Councils of state violence.

From two speeches during the Bosnian War National Mall Rally, 1999

I am a native of this place. You might even call me an ethnic Washingtonian. For two centuries, this little colony of America has been denied the rights called for in the Declaration of Independence and the Constitution, and more recently in the Charter of the United Nations.

At no time during this 200 years, however, has a single bomb been dropped on our behalf. In fact President Clinton and the Congress, now busy saving the Kosovars—whether they survive to thank us or not—conspired to remove what little self-government we had on the grounds of a budget deficit worth about the cost of four nights' Belgrade bombing runs. It was the greatest disenfranchisement of African-Americans since the end of post-reconstruction in the 19th century.

You will excuse me, therefore, if I am a bit skeptical about current professions of interest in democracy in distant places…

At what point does the constant reiteration of failed and fatal policy become a war crime and reckless incompetence become grotesque cruelty and tactics of death become—to use a term used casually these days—become genocide?

Well, consider this. The Holocaust resulted in some six million deaths. Now here are some other figures:

There were nearly two million killed during the Vietnam war, most by air attacks that dropped twice as many bombs as we did in all of World War II—nearly one 500-pound bomb per person. One million civilians were killed by our strategic bombing in Japan even before we got to Hiroshima and Nagasaki. More than two million civilians were killed in our bombing runs over North Korea. And one million Iraqi have died as a result of our sanctions.

Add these up and you come to the same figure as the Holocaust. Which is shocking enough until you realize that together, the Holocaust and our bombing raids of the past fifty years represent less than ten percent of all the deaths by warfare in our century.

Trace the American role in this extraordinary violence to its source and you come not upon political extremes, but to the heart of this country's establishment. Contrary to all myths the most deadly place on the American political spectrum is in the center. It is there that a fatal combination of power, machismo, incompetence, avarice and delusions of adequacy has time and again caused murder, mayhem and suffering for those who want only to live their lives in peace and decency.

It is this violent, extremist center of American politics and culture that was responsible for the weapons, the ignorance, and the anger that helped kill 15 young people in Columbine, Colorado. Mass murder is not genetic, it is a skill learned from other adults like other skills. Consider this. The boy killer in the shootings in Paducuh had never fired a real gun before, yet hit his target eight times with eight shots. Trained police officers are lucky to hit fifty percent of the time. The boy had learned his skill by playing video games. The free market taught him how to kill. Today, NATO is teaching others.

We have, of course, been trained to think of our own leaders as normal, sane people. That these destroyers of land, lives, and the ecological balance of the earth are wise and honorable men and women engaged in noble and difficult tasks.

But ask yourself this:

Is it normal to kill millions of innocent people in the name of a freedom they will never live to know?

Is it normal to let the young and the ill suffer so you can support a military budget so huge that $30 billion a year simply can't be accounted for?

Is it normal to lock up nearly two million citizens—the most of any country ever—many of them for simply preferring marijuana over such legal drugs as vodka and cigarettes?

Is it normal, because of one's draconian penal system, to remove the franchise from one out of every seven black men?

Is it normal to damage the health of a planet for better 4th quarter profits?

When I was a child in this town, the cruelties of segregation were considered normal. An elite not unlike the one in charge today insisted it was so, just as they later told us that if we crawled under our school desks we would be safe from the atom bomb.

Few in power dared tell us that what was said to be normal was actually madness. We had to find out for ourselves. And when we did, and when we discovered that others had as well, things began to get better.

Today we must make this same self-discovery, and learn from those on either side of us, in front of us and behind us, that we are not alone. The elite, including its media, will try to keep us from this news. They will not tell us the biggest secret of our age—that the widest political, cultural and moral division on earth is not between right and left, east and west, or black and white, but between the peoples of the world and their own reckless leaders. . .

At the end of the Second World War, Albert Camus wrote an imaginary letter to a German friend in which he said,

> *"This is what separated us from you; we made demands. You were satisfied to serve the power of your nation and we dreamed of giving ours her truth."*

That is our business today, and every day, until those who lead us make it theirs as well—and no longer hide behind barricades celebrating mindless power, deadly weapons, and corrupt intentions. Until they turn instead to their proper business which is to join us in giving all the lands of this fragile earth their truth.

Dupont Circle Rally 1999

I want to tell you about a nightmare I had. At first, it was pretty much your ordinary nightmare—dragons, wraiths, witches, pterodactyls, poltergeists, Stygian swamps, Bill Clinton, Madeleine Albright, that sort of thing.

Then the dragons, wraiths, witches, pterodactyls and poltergeists faded away. Clinton and Albright were still there but they had been transformed into doctors and the Stygian swamps had become the emergency room of a hospital…

Then an ambulance drove up and deposited a man in terrible pain from some bad food he had eaten. And Dr. Clinton walked up and said to the man, "We must strike in the name of freedom and gastronomy against the criminally heartless restaurant that did this foul deed to you" and he drove his scalpel into the man's stomach. Which of course, didn't help much and after a few more such blows the patient died.

Then a man came in who had suffered a heart attack and Dr. Albright stood over him and declared loudly, "You are a victim of a evil disease; we shall not sleep until it is exorcised. It is clear, though, that you must be partitioned before we can reconstruct you" and so Dr. Albright took a hatchet and cut off the man's arms and legs and instructed a nurse to Fedex them to the far corners of the country. The man, of course, died.

Finally a young woman arrived at the cusp of childbirth but before Dr. Blair would attend to her he demanded that a commission of nurses determine whether any sex crimes had been committed against the woman and when he found that the child was the consequence of a rape, he delivered the baby but promptly threw it out the window declaring that democracy had triumphed again.

Just then I awoke and realized that it was just a dream and that all along I had been listening to the home service of the Voice of America, better known as NPR. The words were coming not from Doctors Clinton, Blair and Albright but from Cokie Roberts and I realized that, in fact, all was once again well with the world.

There is a name for this sort of medicine. It is called iatrogenic—in which the disease is caused by the physician. Doctors who cause diseases or ruin the health of the patient through arrogance, incompetence, and mindless machismo have large insurance policies because people sue them for something we call malpractice. In medicine this is considered a bad thing.

We have just gone through yet another iatrogenic war, in which our elites have argued falsely that their stated intentions outweigh any actual consequences…

We, of course, have had other iatrogenic wars. This is what happened in Vietnam when we declared that it was necessary to destroy villages in order to save them. This is what happened in Iraq when in the name defeating a modern Hitler we caused the post-war death by disease and malnutrition of far more people than Hussein himself had killed…

In fact, every moral act in the face of mental or physical injury carries twin responsibilities: to mend the injury and to avoid replacing it with another. This twin burden is faced every day by doctors. Every police officer faces it. Every firefighter. It was what I was taught as a Coast Guard officer. It's well past time for our politicians do so as well.

The point of speaking of the evils of a Milosovec or a Hussein is to raise the alarm. But once that has been successfully done, this alarm may not rightfully be used as a perpetual excuse for our own misdeeds. From the moment we commence a moral intervention we become a part of the story, and part of the good and evil. We are no longer the innocent bystander but a full participant whose acts will either help or make things worse. Our intentions become irrelevant; they are overwhelmed by the character of our response to them. The morality of the disease is supplanted by the morality of the cure. Any other course amounts to reckless and negligent political malpractice.

9/11: Not Pearl Harbor but Dien Bien Phu

2001: The media and politicians call what happened terrorism. This is a propagandistic rather than a descriptive term and replaces the more useful traditional phrases, guerilla action or guerilla warfare. The former places a mythical shroud around the event while the latter depicts its true nature. Guerillas do not play by the rules of state organization or military tactics. This does not make them cowardly, as some have suggested, but can make them fiendishly clever. The essence of guerilla warfare is to attack at times and places unsuspected and return to places unknown. You can not invade the land of guerillas, you can not bomb them out of existence, you can not overwhelm them with your technological wonders.

This was a lesson we were supposed to have learned in Vietnam but appear to have forgotten. The journalist Bernard Fall early noted that the French, after Dien Bien Phu, had no choice but to leave Southeast Asia. America, with its vast military, financial, and technological resources, was able to stay because it had the capacity to keep making the same mistakes over and over. Our war against "terrorism" has been in many ways a domestic version of our Vietnam strategy. We keep making the same mistakes over and over because, until now, we could afford to. One of these has been to define the problem by its manifestations rather than its causes. This turns a resolvable political problem into a irresolvable technical problem, because while, for example, there are clearly solutions to the Middle East crisis, there are no other solutions to the guerilla violence that grows from the failure to end it.

In other words, if you define the problem as "a struggle against terrorism" you have already admitted defeat because the guerilla will always have the upper hand against a centralized, technology-dependent society such as ours. We will always be blindsided, just as Bernard Fall said the French were under much simpler circumstances: "What surprised the French completely was the Viet-Minh's ability to transport a considerable mass of heavy artillery pieces across roadless mountains to Dien Bien Phu and to keep it supplied with a sufficient amount of ammunition to make the huge effort worthwhile."

There is one way to deal with guerilla warfare and that is to resolve the problems that allow it to thrive. The trick is to undermine the violence of the most bitter by dealing honestly with the complaints of the most rational. As we have demonstrated in the Middle East, one need not even reach a final solution as long as incremental progress is being made. But once that ceases, as has happened in the past year, the case for freelance violence is quickly strengthened and people simply forget that peace is possible.

The trouble with moats

2002: So here we are a year later, $37 billion out of pocket and still scared as hell someone's going to attack us. We're not the first with the problem. Many years ago some people built castles and walled cities and moats to keep the bad guys away. It worked for a while, but sooner or later spies and assassins figured out how to get across the moats and climb the walls and send balls of fire into protected compounds. The Florentines even catapulted dead donkeys and feces during their siege of Siena.

The people who built castles and walled cities and moats are all dead now and their efforts at security seem puny and ultimately futile as we visit their unintended monuments to the vanity of human presumption.

Like the castle-dwellers behind the moat, we are now spending huge sums to put ourselves inside a prison of our own making. It is unlikely to provide either security for our bodies nor solace for our souls, for we are simply attacking ourselves before others get a chance.

This is not the way to peace and safety. Peace is a state without violence, interrogations, and moats. Peace is a state of reciprocity, of trust, of empirically based confidence that no one is about to do you in. It exists not because of intrinsic goodness or rampant naiveté but because of a common, implicit understanding that it works for everyone.

This discovery is often hard to come by, but it is still cheaper, less deadly, and ultimately far more effective than the alternative we seem to have chosen, which is to imprison ourselves in our castle and hope the moat keeps the others out.

Repelling the Martian Invasion: The Religious Right is Wrong on War

by Jeff Taylor

Christmas celebrates the birth of the Prince of Peace. With all of the clerical cheering on behalf of recent wars, the intertwining of cross and flag, and the blessings bestowed on every Commander in Chief by the leading evangelists of the day, it can be difficult to discern the testimony for peace by theologically conservative Christianity. It can be found with a little searching.

Just as professing Christians cannot follow Christ while serving Mammon, they are not being faithful to the Prince of Peace while glorifying Mars. It's nothing new. The worldly principles of violence and war entered the church within its first three centuries of existence.

The invasion was largely triggered by Constantine's supposed vision of a Chi-Rho cross in the sky encouraging him, in Greek, with the words "In this Sign, Conquer." (ἐυ τούτῳ υίκα or, translated into Latin, In hoc signo vinces.) He then proceeded to win the Battle of Milvian Bridge (312). Emperor Constantine may have been a sincere believer, but the vision sounds apocryphal. The accounts of the vision or dream by church fathers Lactantius and Eusebius are contradictory. In addition to being church leaders, the two were court historians who had a tendency to flatter Constantine.

If the story is not apocryphal, it was either wishful thinking or satanic deception. To borrow an analogy from an earlier Greek tale, Constantine went on to serve as a Trojan Horse inside Christianity. The linking of Christ and Caesar brought some short-term benefits but the long-term harm has been immense. The facilitation of war by the chaplains of power has been one sad effect.

Turning to the U.S.A.: With all of the clerical and pewful cheering on behalf of recent wars, the intertwining of cross and flag, and the blessings bestowed on every Commander in Chief by the leading evangelists of the day, it can be difficult to discern the testimony for peace by theologically conservative Christianity. This testimony can be found primarily, but not only, among the historic peace churches: the Amish, Mennonites, Hutterites, Schwenkfelders, Quakers, Moravians, and German Baptist Brethren. Roman Catholicism places some limits on the martial spirit with its doctrine of just war, derived from Augustine and Aquinas. Dispensationalism—one of two main sources for fundamentalism—was traditionally apolitical and encouraged neutrality in fallen, worldly activities such as warfare. This influence can be seen in figures from A.C. Gaebelein to Watchman Nee. As a young man, evangelist D.L. Moody refused to enlist in the Civil War because he was a conscientious objector. He recalled, "There has never been a time in my life when I felt I could take a gun and shoot down a fellow human being. In this respect I am a Quaker."

Faced with the prospect of war between England and Russia, in 1885, William Booth publicly declared that every true soldier of the Salvation Army should "shut his ears to all the worldly, unscriptural, unchristian talk about war being a necessity." He warned, "Oh, what vice, what blasphemies, what cursing, what devilries of every kind accompany and follow in the train of war." In a subsequent *War Cry* editorial, Booth looked forward to the day when the Prince of Peace would abolish "this inhuman and fiendish system of wholesale murder." The focus of the conflict between the English and Russian empires? Afghanistan. Some things never change.

The Christian statesman William Jennings Bryan was directly influenced by the great writer Leo Tolstoy. The two talked for twelve straight hours at Tolstoy's home during Bryan's international trip in 1903. As a result of this visit, and earlier writings, Tolstoy's nonviolent views were spread to American Christians who were far more culturally provincial, theologically conservative, and politically mainstream than the Russian anarcho-pacifist himself. A decade later, when Secretary of State Bryan broke with Woodrow Wilson because the president was pushing the nation into World War I, he became the first holder of that high position to resign over a matter of political principle. He was also the last. In accepting the Democratic presidential nomination in 1900, Bryan said, "If true Christianity consists in carrying out in our daily lives the teachings of Christ, who will say that we are commanded to civilize with dynamite and proselyte with the sword? Imperialism finds no warrant in the Bible.

The command, 'Go ye into all the world and preach the gospel to every creature,' has no Gatling gun attachment.…Compare, if you will, the swaggering, bullying, brutal doctrine of imperialism with the golden rule and the commandment, 'Thou shalt love thy neighbor as thyself.'"

On the eve of U.S. entry into World War II, in 1940, the Southern Baptist Convention issued a resolution expressing its "utter abhorrence of war as an instrument of International policy." The nine-point statement concluded, "Because war is contrary to the mind and spirit of Christ, we believe that no war should be identified with the will of Christ. Our churches should not be made agents of war propaganda or recruiting stations. War thrives on and is perpetuated by hysteria, falsehood, and hate and the church has a solemn responsibility to make sure there is no black out of love in time of war." There was not a single resolution issued by the Southern Baptists during World War II or Vietnam expressing support for the president or the troops, but there were resolutions in support of conscientious objectors. The bold 1940 resolution can be found even today on the SBC website but the Southern Baptists have changed their tune…and their lyrics…perhaps even their hymnal.

As late as 1970, Francis Schaeffer, an orthodox Presbyterian, was warning, "In the United States many churches display the American flag. The Christian flag is usually put on one side and the American flag on the other. Does having two flags in your church mean that Christianity and the American Establishment are equal? If it does, you are really in trouble.…Equating of any other loyalty with our loyalty to God is sin." Ironically, Schaeffer's later writings helped give rise to the Moral Majority, with its endorsement of Constantinianism and the Mush God of American civil religion.

To their credit, Pope John Paul II and Cardinal Joseph Ratzinger (the future Pope Benedict XVI) condemned the Iraq War as unjust in 2002-03. Unfortunately, there was no teeth to their pronouncements. I am not a Roman Catholic, but if I were, I would want my pope armed with anathemas and bulls of excommunication. What is the point of having an episcopal form of government headed by the "vicar of Christ" if he does not wield at least one of the two swords of Gelasius?

The "holy father" ought to have disciplined disobedient children like Senators Tom Daschle, Joe Biden, John Kerry, Pete Dominici,

Susan Collins, and Sam Brownback, who supported waging an unjust war against Iraq. When it comes to peace, the Catholic hierarchy if often politely correct, but it is no Erasmus of Rotterdam, Dorothy Day, or Thomas Merton in denouncing militarism and the perfidy of its practitioners. Too much diffidence and compromise.

Without jargon or hedging, the French Catholic mathematician-scientist-philosopher-mystic Blaise Pascal put it simply centuries ago: "[Q:] Why do you kill me? [A:] What! Do you not live on the other side of the water? If you lived on this side, my friend, I should be an assassin, and it would be unjust to slay you in this manner. But since you live on the other side, I am a hero, and it is just.... Can anything be more ridiculous than that a man should have the right to kill me because he lives on the other side of the water, and because his ruler has a quarrel with mine, though I have none with him?" (Pensées, V: 293-94)

Still, the peace rhetoric of the papacy is much to be preferred to the refined war mongering of Richard Land, President of the Ethics and Religious Liberty Commission of the Southern Baptist Convention. As Congress was preparing to give President Bush a blank check to wage war against Iraq, in October 2002, Land organized an open letter to Bush, signed by prominent evangelical Protestants, that began, "In this decisive hour of our nation's history we are writing to express our deep appreciation for your bold, courageous, and visionary leadership. Americans everywhere have been inspired by your eloquent and clear articulation of our nation's highest ideals of freedom and of our resolve to defend that freedom both here and across the globe. We believe that your policies concerning the ongoing international terrorist campaign against America are both right and just." Specifically, the planned attack on Iraq was sanctified as a just war. After the bombing and invasion, Land remained confident of God's blessing on the undertaking, writing, "I believe we are seeing in Iraq an illustration of waging a war of defense and liberation according to the criteria of just war."

Of course, you do not have to be a Bible-believing Christian to care about humanity and peace. Scores of atheists, agnostics, and adherents of other religions share these concerns. But the theologically orthodox Christian should have an even deeper commitment to such values. The book by Laurence M. Vance entitled *Christianity and War, and Other Essays Against the Warfare State* (Vance Publications,

2nd ed., 2008) is an excellent overview of organized violence from a conservative Christian perspective. Vance writes regularly for LewRockwell.com. You may be a Christian who does not embrace pacifism. That's okay. The perfect need not be the enemy of the good. Most of us can agree that most of the wars in which we have been involved during the past century have been unjustified wars of aggression and greed, having more to do with empire and monopoly than with national defense or humanitarian crusades.

Moralists, populists, and libertarians–regardless of religion–can often come together when it comes to society and politics. We don't have to sacrifice our theology to work together on some common causes. Whether you're (1) a complete pacifist; (2) a Just War advocate; (3) a national-defense, patriotic Jacksonian; (4) an anarchosocialist, anti-imperialist Chomskyite; or (5) a non-coercive libertarian, is there any overriding justification, let alone glorification, of the Iraq War? The war in Afghanistan, as it has been waged? What do these wars have to do with peace, with justice, with national defense, with human rights, or with freedom? Let's not lose sight of our common aims even though we may irritate one another on occasion. Socially and politically speaking, we may end up at the same place by different routes. That's a good thing. That's how coalitions are built.

In 1761, William Law, the Anglican divine who helped lead John Wesley to evangelicalism and eventually flowered as a Christian mystic, wrote about war in his final book, *An Address to the Clergy*. He did so with truth and eloquence. Sadly, but predictably, his condemnation of Christian war was deleted when the book was reprinted by evangelical publishers in the 1890s and 1970s. Not uplifting, too discomforting, I suppose. Law wrote,

> *Look now at warring Christendom, what smallest drop of pity towards sinners is to be found in it? Or how could a spirit all hellish more fully contrive and hasten their destruction? It stirs up and kindles every passion of fallen nature that is contrary to the all-humble, all-meek, all-loving, all-forgiving, all-saving Spirit of Christ. It unites, it drives and compels nameless numbers of unconverted sinners to fall, murdering and murdered among flashes of fire with the wrath and swiftness of lightning, into a fire infinitely worse*

than that in which they died.... Here, my pen trembles in my hand. But when, O when, will one single Christian Church, people, or language, tremble at the share they have in this death of sinners?

...Again, would you further see the fall of the universal Church, from being led by the Spirit of Christ to be guided by the inspiration of the great fiery Dragon, look at all European Christendom sailing round the globe with fire and sword and every murdering art of war, to seize the possessions and kill the inhabitants of both the Indies.... To this day what wars of Christians against Christians, blended with scalping heathens, still keep staining the earth and the seas with human blood, for a miserable share in the spoils of a plundered heathen world!—a world, which should have heard or seen or felt nothing from the followers of Christ, but a divine love, that had forced them from distant lands and through the perils of long seas to visit strangers with those glad tidings of peace and salvation to all the world, which angels from heaven and shepherds on earth proclaimed at the birth of Christ.

The Christmas story of incarnation and rejoicing is not only about personal salvation, about God and sinners reconciled. It is also about social reconciliation, about temporal peace and justice. As Mary said to her cousin Elizabeth "He has scattered the proud in the imagination of their hearts, He has put down the mighty from their thrones, and exalted those of low degree. He has filled the hungry with good things, and the rich he has sent empty away." As the angels sang after the birth of the Babe in Bethlehem, "Glory to God in the highest, and on Earth peace, good will toward men!"

Originally appeared on Front Porch Republic website, December 2009.

The Wages of Peace

By Robert Pollin & Heidi Garrett-Peltier

Submitted by Katrina vanden Heuvel
This article appeared in the March 31, 2008 edition of *The Nation.*

There is no longer any doubt that the Iraq War is a moral and strategic disaster for the United States. But what has not yet been fully recognized is that it has also been an economic disaster. To date, the government has spent more than $522 billion on the war, with another $70 billion already allocated for 2008.

With just the amount of the Iraq budget of 2007, $138 billion, the government could instead have provided Medicaid-level health insurance for all 45 million Americans who are uninsured. What's more, we could have added 30,000 elementary and secondary schoolteachers and built 400 schools in which they could teach. And we could have provided basic home weatherization for about 1.6 million existing homes, reducing energy consumption in these homes by 30 percent.

But the economic consequences of Iraq run even deeper than the squandered opportunities for vital public investments. Spending on Iraq is also a job killer. Every $1 billion spent on a combination of education, healthcare, energy conservation and infrastructure investments creates between 50 and 100 percent more jobs than the same money going to Iraq. Taking the 2007 Iraq budget of $138 billion, this means that upward of 1 million jobs were lost because the Bush Administration chose the Iraq sinkhole over public investment.

Recognizing these costs of the Iraq War is even more crucial now that the economy is facing recession. While a recession is probably unavoidable, its length and severity will depend on the effectiveness of the government's stimulus initiatives. By a wide margin, the most effective stimulus is to expand public investment projects, especially at the state and local levels. The least effective fiscal stimulus is the one crafted by the Bush Administration and Congress--mostly to just send out rebate checks to all taxpayers. This is because a high proportion of the new spending encouraged by the rebates will purchase imports rather than financing new jobs in the United

States, whereas public investment would concentrate job expansion within the country. Combining this Bush stimulus initiative with the ongoing spending on Iraq will only deepen the severity of the recession.

Is Militarism Necessary for Prosperity?

The government spent an estimated $572 billion on the military in 2007. This amounts to about $1,800 for every resident of the country. That's more than the combined GDPs of Sweden and Thailand, and eight times federal spending on education.

The level of military spending has risen dramatically since 2001, with the increases beginning even before 9/11. As a share of GDP, the military budget rose from 3 percent to 4.4 percent during the first seven years of the Bush presidency. At the current size of the economy, a difference between a military budget at 4.4 rather than 3 percent of GDP amounts to $134 billion.

The largest increases in the military budget during the Bush presidency have been associated with the Iraq War. Indeed, the $138 billion spent on Iraq in 2007 was basically equal to the total increase in military spending that caused the military budget to rise to 4.4 percent of GDP. It is often argued that the military budget is a cornerstone of the economy—that the Pentagon is a major underwriter of important technical innovations as well as a source of millions of decent jobs. At one level these claims are true. When the government spends upward of $600 billion per year of taxpayers' money on anything, it cannot help but generate millions of jobs. Similarly, when it spends a large share of that budget on maintaining and strengthening the most powerful military force in the history of the world, this cannot fail to encourage technical innovations that are somehow connected to the instruments of warfare.

Yet it is also true that channeling hundreds of billions of dollars into areas such as renewable energy and mass transportation would create a hothouse environment supporting new technologies. For example, utilities in Arizona and Nevada are developing plans to build "concentrated" solar power plants, which use the sun to heat a liquid that can drive a turbine. It is estimated that this technology, operating on a large scale, could drive down the costs of solar electricity dramatically, from its current level of about $4 per watt of installed capacity to between $2.50 and $3 per watt in the sunniest regions of the country. At these prices, solar electricity becomes much cheaper than oil-driven power and within range of coal. These and related technologies could advance much more rapidly toward cost competitiveness with coal, oil and nuclear power if they were to receive even a fraction of the subsidies that now support weapons development (as well as the oil industry).

Swords, Plowshares and Jobs

How does it happen that government spending devoted to healthcare, education, environmental sustainability and infrastructure can generate up to twice as many jobs per dollar as spending on militarism?

Three factors play a role in determining the overall job effects of any target of government spending. Let's compare the construction of Camp Victory, the main US military base on the western outskirts of Baghdad, with weatherizing existing homes in New England to increase their energy efficiency. The first factor to consider is the jobs that get created directly by each project. The second is the job creation in the industries that supply products for building the camp or weatherizing the homes. These would include the steel, concrete, weapons and telecommunications industries for building Camp Victory; and lumber, insulation and trucking industries for home weatherization. Finally, new jobs will result when people who are paid to build Camp Victory or weatherize a house spend the money they have earned—a weapons engineer at Camp Victory buying a lawnmower during his vacation leave at home or a construction worker in New England buying a new car.

How does one spending target create more jobs for a given amount of dollars spent? Still considering Camp Victory construction versus New England home weatherization, there are, again, three factors:

1. *More jobs but lower-paying jobs.* Average pay is lower in the construction industry working on home weatherization in New England than in mounting weapons installations at Camp Victory. So a given pool of money is divided among more employed people.

2. *More spending on people, less on machines and supplies.* In weatherizing a home, the machinery and supplies costs are relatively low, while the need for construction workers is high. Building a high-tech military base in Baghdad entails enormous investments in steel

and sophisticated electronic equipment and relatively less spending for people on the job.

3. *More money stays within the US economy.* We roughly estimate that US military personnel spend only 43 percent of their income on domestic goods and services, while the overall population spends an average of 83 percent of their income on domestic products and 17 percent on imports.

It is important to know which of these three factors is relatively more important in generating the overall increase in jobs. In particular, it would not necessarily be a favorable development if the overall increase in employment opportunities is mainly just a byproduct of creating lots of low-paying jobs.

In fact, if we were simply to send a rebate to taxpayers for the full amount of the Iraq War budget—i.e., a measure similar to Bush's current stimulus plan—the increased spending on personal consumption would produce lots of what are now bad jobs, in areas such as retail, hotels, restaurants and personal services. Because of this, a transfer of funds from the military to tax rebates and personal consumption increases would produce a 25 percent increase in employment but an 11 percent decline in overall wages and benefits paid to working people.

The opposite is true with education as the spending target. Here, both the total number of jobs created and the average pay are higher than with the military. It's less clear-cut when it comes to healthcare, energy conservation and infrastructure investments. More jobs will be created than with military spending, and the total amount of wages and benefits going to workers will also be significantly higher than with military spending. But the average pay for a healthcare worker or those engaged in mass transit or construction is lower than in the military.

Is it better for overall economic welfare to generate more jobs, even if average wages and benefits are lower? There isn't a single correct answer to this question. It depends on the size of these differences: how many low-paying jobs are being generated, and how bad are these jobs? How many high-quality jobs would be sacrificed through a transition out of the military, where the average pay is relatively high? Indeed, by completely shutting off Iraq War-related spending and transferring the money in equal shares to education, healthcare, energy conservation and infrastructure, average salaries would decline. However, the majority of new jobs created by these peaceful alternatives would command salaries above a reasonable living-wage standard of $16 an hour.

Pushing Unemployment Down

As of January there were 7.6 million people unemployed in a labor force of 154 million, producing an official unemployment rate of 4.9 percent. This was a significant increase over the 4.5 percent unemployment rate in mid-2007, and thus one important sign of a weakening economy. Unemployment is likely to keep rising as the economic slowdown continues.

In our current context, what would be the overall job effects of transferring the entire 2007 Iraq War budget of $138 billion into healthcare, education, energy conservation and infrastructure investments? If we assume that all else would remain equal in the labor market, a net increase (i.e., the total expansion of jobs in public investments minus the reduction in military jobs) in the range of 1 million jobs would therefore reduce the total number of unemployed people to around 6.6 million. The unemployment rate would fall to about 4.3 percent.

This is still an unacceptably high unemployment rate. But if the public-investment-directed spending shift out of Iraq were combined with a stimulus package of roughly the same size as the Iraq War budget—i.e., in the range of the Bush Administration's $150 billion stimulus—the overall impact would be a strong program to fight recession and create decent jobs.

In particular, through this combination of a spending shift out of Iraq and a stimulus program focused on public investment, there is a good chance that unemployment would fall below 4 percent. When unemployment fell below 4 percent in the late 1960s and late 1990s, the high demand for workers led to rising wages and benefits, in particular at the low end of the job market. Poverty fell as a result. Near full employment in the late '60s also brought better working conditions and less job discrimination against minorities.

Of course, we cannot assume that everything about the labor market would stay unchanged after a huge job expansion in healthcare, education, energy conservation and infrastructure investments, while jobs connected with the military contracted. There would no doubt be skill shortages in some areas and labor gluts in others. There would also probably be an increase in inflation that would have to be managed carefully.

These concerns are real. But it is still true that large-scale job creation within the United States is possible as an outgrowth of ending the Iraq War, reallocating the entire Iraq budget to important domestic public investment projects and fighting the recession with further increases in public investments.

What if the Iraq War budget is transferred only partially to domestic public investments? Let's assume, optimistically, that a new Administration takes serious initiatives to end the Iraq War immediately after coming into office next January. This new Administration would almost certainly not have the wherewithal to shut down operations within one year. And even if it could completely end the war within a year, the government should still commit significant funds to war reparations for the Iraqi people.

The job expansion within the United States will decline to the extent that spending of any sort continues in Iraq rather than being transferred into domestic public investments. But even if the net transfer of funds is, say, $100 billion rather than $138 billion, several hundred thousand new domestic jobs would still be created. There is also no reason that the domestic public investment expansion has to mirror the decrease in the Iraq War budget. Any stimulus program initiated over the next few months--either a Bush-style program or one focused on public investment--would entail spending beyond the current Iraq budget levels.

Public Investment and Recession

There's also a strong argument for a stimulus program that emphasizes public investment at the state and local level. State and local government revenues--which primarily finance education, healthcare, public safety and infrastructure--are always badly hit by economic downturns and will be especially strapped as a result of the current recession. State and local government revenues decline when the incomes and property values of their residents fall. Property tax revenues will fall especially sharply as a result of the collapse of housing prices. Moreover, state and local governments, unlike the federal government, cannot run deficits and are forced to maintain balanced budgets, even in a recession. This means that unless the federal government injects new revenue into the state and local budgets, spending on public investments will decline.

Deficit Reduction: The Responsible Alternative?

The federal fiscal deficit in 2007 was $244 billion. Shutting down the Iraq War and using the fiscal savings to cut the deficit would mean a 57 percent deficit reduction.

Is this the best use of the funds released by the Iraq War? Of course, the government cannot run a reckless fiscal policy, no matter how pressing the country's social and environmental needs. But a $244 billion deficit in today's economy is not reckless. It amounts to about 1.8 percent of GDP. This is slightly below the average-sized deficit between 1960 and 2006 of 1.9 percent of GDP. The largest deviation from this long-term average occurred under Ronald Reagan's presidency, when the deficit averaged 4.2 percent of GDP—i.e., more than twice as large as the current deficit as a share of the economy.

The recession and stimulus program will of course produce a large increase in the deficit. Recessions are not the time to focus on deficit reduction. But even if we allowed the deficit to double from its 2007 level--to about $500 billion--its size, as a share of GDP, would still be below the average figure for the entire Reagan presidency, including both the boom and recession years.

We would certainly need to worry about the deficit today, and even more after the recession ends, if it were persistently running at Reagan-era levels. This is because the government would soon be consuming upward of 20 percent of the total federal budget in interest payments, as it did at the end of the Reagan era. This is opposed to the 10 percent of total government spending we now pay to the Japanese and Chinese bondholders, US banks and wealthy private citizens who own the bulk of US government debt. But because the deficit has been at a reasonable level coming into the recession, the primary problem with the Treasury's fiscal stance is not the size of the deficit per se but how the money is being spent—that we are using the money for Iraq and a private consumption-led stimulus rather than public investment.

There are many good reasons government policy should now initiate major commitments to investment in the areas of healthcare, education, environmental sustainability and infrastructure. All these spending areas stand on their own merits. But moving the $138 billion spent on the Iraq War in 2007 into public investments will also increase employment, adding up to 1 million jobs. On top of this, expanding public investment spending is the single most effective tool for fighting the recession.

A great deal is at stake here. The Iraq War has been about death and destruction. Ending the war could be a first serious step toward advancing a viable program for jobs, healthcare, education and a clean-energy economy.

Robert Pollin is a professor of economics and co-director of the Political Economy Research Institute (PERI) at the University of Massachusetts. His books include *Contours of Descent: U.S. Economic Fractures and the Landscape of Global Austerity.*

Heidi Garrett-Peltier is a PhD candidate in economics at the University of Massachusetts and a research assistant at PERI.

An Imperial Moment

By John Maxwell & Jonathan Schell

Submitted by Katrina vanden Heuvel
This article appeared in the December 23, 2002 edition of *The Nation.*

Long before Trent Lott and John Ashcroft accused Bush Administration opponents of aiding the enemy, McKinley's men shouted down the small group of Mugwumps and members of the Anti-Imperialist League, who were opposed to an America that projected its ideals abroad by force without considering the consequences. "If we ever come to nothing as a nation," Theodore Roosevelt wrote to his colleague-in-arms, Senator Henry Cabot Lodge, "it will be because the treachery of Carl Schurz, [Harvard] President Eliot, and the *Evening Post* and the futile sentimentalists of the international arbitration type, bears its legitimate fruit in producing a flabby, timid type of character, which eats away the great fighting features of our race."

Long before September 11, when Americans hung flags on mailboxes and highway overpasses and pasted them to the bumpers of their cars, audiences at theaters and music halls sang "The Star-Spangled Banner" after each performance. The conflict with Spain, John Hay said, would be "a splendid little war."

It is not the first time. And if those voices raised against imperialism were not adequately heard a hundred years ago, it is time to let them speak again.

On the Need to Follow Our Constitutional Principles

> *"It is not that we would hold America back from playing her full part in the world's affairs, but that we believe that her part could be better accomplished by close adherence to those high principles which are ideally embodied in her institutions—by the establishment of her own democracy in such wise as to make it a symbol of noble self-government, and by exercising the influence of a great, unarmed and*

peaceful power on the affairs and the moral temper of the world."
—Charles Eliot Norton, professor of fine arts, Harvard

"I would gladly pay twenty millions today to restore our republic to its first principles.
—Andrew Carnegie,explaining why he would buy the Philippines from the United States in order to give the islands their independence

On the Need to Address Our Own National Problems

"Nations and communities don't die from disorders external to them; dangerous decay is internal. The trouble with Rome wasn't in the colonies and the empire; it was in the Senate and the forum."
—Charles Francis Adams Jr., historian, industrialist

"The serious question for the people of this country to consider is what effect the imperial policy will have upon ourselves if we permit it to be established."
—Frederick Gookin

On the Power of Christian Fundamentalists

"The Kingdom of Heaven is to come as a grain of mustard seed, not as a thirteen-inch shell."
—The Rev. H. P. Faunce, Baptist minister

On the Evils of a Permanent Military Establishment

"A wretched fatuity that so-called patriotism which will not remember that we are the envy of the whole world for the priceless privilege of being exempt from the oppressive burden of warlike preparations."
—Carl Schurz, reform journalist and senator

On American Hypocrisy

"Extending the Blessings of Civilization to our Brother who Sits in Darkness has been a good trade and has paid well, on the whole; and there is money in it yet, if carefully worked—but not enough, in my judgment, to make any considerable risk advisable. The People that Sit in Darkness are getting to be too scarce—too scarce and too shy. And such darkness as is now left is really of but an indifferent quality, and not dark enough for the game. The most of those People that Sit in Darkness have been furnished with more light than was good for them or profitable for us. We have been injudicious...Is it, perhaps, possible that there are two kinds of Civilization—one for home consumption and one for the heathen market?"
—*Mark Twain,* "To the Person Sitting in Darkness"

On the Loss of National Virtue

"We had supposed ourselves (with all our crudity and barbarity in certain ways) a better nation morally than the rest, safe at home, and without the old savage ambition, destined to exert great international influence by throwing in our 'moral weight,' etc. Dreams! Human Nature is everywhere the same; and at least temptation all the old military passions rise, and sweep everything before them."
—*William James*

"God damn the U.S. for its vile conduct... We can destroy their [Filipino] ideals but we can't give them ours."
—*William James, on American annexation of the Philippines and the guerrilla war it engendered*

On the Failure to Lead by Example

"If we turn this war, which was heralded to the world as a war of humanity, in any sense into a war of conquest,

we shall forever forfeit the confidence of mankind."
—Carl Schurz

"The United States has lost her unique position as a leader in the progress of civilization and has taken up her place simply as one of the grasping and selfish nations of the present day."
—Charles Eliot Norton

On the Limitations of Free Speech

"He who, as a lover of his country, jealous of her liberty and mindful of the lessons of history, dares oppose these schemes of Colonial power, is in danger of being denounced as a traitor, and held up as an object of public contumely and scorn."
—Tennant Lommax, Democratic politician

"To be popular is easy; to be right when right is unpopular, is noble...I repudiate with scorn the immoral doctrine, 'Our country, right or wrong.'"
—Andrew Carnegie

On the Role of the Press

"They rely mostly on large sales, and for large sales on sensational news. Now nothing does so much to keep sensational news coming in over the considerable period of time as war....Next to war they welcome the Promise of war."
—E.L. Godkin, editor of The Nation

The Cost of a National Crime, The Hell of War and Its Penalties, Criminal Aggression*—titles of three pamphlets sent by Edward Atkinson, a founder of the Anti-Imperialist League, to American troops in the field in the Philippines, as a test of free speech.*

Postmaster Charles Smith declared the pamphlets "seditious" and had them removed from the mail.

On the Dangers of Success

"If all these imaginings are in vain, and our success is a rapid and bloodless one as the most sanguine can hope, such a victory is more dangerous than defeat. In the intoxication of such a success, we would reach out for fresh territory, and to our present difficulties would be added an agitation for the annexation of new regions which, unfit to govern themselves, would govern us. We would be fairly launched upon a policy of military aggression, of territorial expansion, of standing armies and growing navies, which is inconsistent with the continuance of our institutions. God grant that such calamities are not in store for us."

John Maxwell Hamilton is a fellow at the Shorenstein Center for the Press, Politics, and Public Policy at Harvard University.

Jonathan Schell is the Harold Willens Peace Fellow at The Nation Institute and teaches a course on the nuclear dilemma at Yale. He is the author of *The Seventh Decade: The New Shape of Nuclear Danger*.

An Open Letter to the Members of Congress, a *Nation* Editorial

Submitted by Katrina vanden Heuvel

Soon, you will be asked to vote on a resolution authorizing the United States to overthrow the government of Iraq by military force. Its passage, we read on all sides, is a foregone conclusion, as if what the country now faces is not a decision but the disclosure of a fate. The nation marches as if in a trance to war. In the House, twenty of your number, led by Dennis Kucinich, have announced their opposition to the war. In the Senate, Robert Byrd has mounted a campaign against the version of the resolution already proposed by the Bush Administration. He has said that the resolution's unconstitutionality will prevent him from voting for it. "But I am finding," he adds, "that the Constitution is irrelevant to people of this Administration." The Joint Chiefs of Staff, according to the *Washington Post,* oppose the war. Telephone calls and the mail to your offices run strongly against it.

Polls and news stories reveal a divided and uncertain public. Yet debate in your chambers is restricted to peripheral questions, such as the timing of the vote, or the resolution's precise scope. You are a deliberative body, but you do not deliberate. You are representatives, but you do not represent.

The silence of those of you in the Democratic Party is especially troubling. You are the opposition party, but you do not oppose. Raising the subject of the war, your political advisers tell you, will distract from the domestic issues that favor the party's chances in the forthcoming Congressional election. In the face of the Administration's pre-emptive war, your leaders have resorted to pre-emptive surrender. For the sake of staying in power, you are told, you must not exercise the power you have in the matter of the war. What, then, is the purpose of your re-election?

If you succeed, you will already have thrown away the power you supposedly have won. You will be members of Congress, but Congress will not be Congress. Even the fortunes of the domestic causes you favor will depend far more on the decision on the war than on the outcome of the election.

On April 4, 1967, as the war in Vietnam was reaching its full fury,

Martin Luther King Jr. said, "A time comes when silence is betrayal." And he said, "Some of us who have already begun to break the silence of the night have found that the calling to speak is often a vocation of agony, but we must speak. We must speak with all the humility that is appropriate to our limited vision, but we must speak."

Now the time to speak has come again. We urge you to speak—and, when the time comes, to vote—against the war on Iraq.

The case against the war is simple, clear and strong. The Administration calls it a chapter in the war on terror, but Iraq has no demonstrated ties either to the September 11 attack on the United States or to the Al Qaeda network that launched it. The aim of the war is to deprive President Saddam Hussein of weapons of mass destruction, but the extent of his program for building these weapons, if it still exists, is murky. Still less clear is any intention on his part to use such weapons. To do so would be suicide, as he well knows. Democratic Representative Anna Eshoo of California has reported that in closed session Administration officials have been asked several times whether they have evidence of an imminent threat from Saddam against the United States and have answered no. She elaborated, "Not 'no, but' or 'maybe,' but 'no.'" On the other hand, if he does have them, and faces his overthrow and possible death at the hands of US forces, he might well use them--or, more likely, give them to terrorist groups to use after his fall. He may be doing so even now.

Some observers have likened the resolution under discussion to the Gulf of Tonkin resolution of 1964 authorizing President Johnson to use force in Vietnam. But that was passed only after a report was received of two attacks on US naval forces. (We now know that the first attack was provoked by a prior secret American attack and the second was nonexistent.) The new resolution, which alleges no attack, not even a fictional one, goes a step further. It is a Tonkin Gulf resolution without a Tonkin Gulf incident.

Even if Saddam possesses weapons of mass destruction and wishes to use them, a policy of deterrence would appear perfectly adequate to stop him, just as it was adequate a half-century ago to stop a much more fearsome dictator, Joseph Stalin. It is not true that military force is the only means of preventing the proliferation of these weapons, whether to Iraq or other countries. An alternative path is clearly available. In the short run it passes through the United Nations and its system of inspections, now more promising than before because Iraq, responding to US pressure, has opened itself unconditionally to inspectors. At the very least, this path should be fully explored before military action—the traditional last resort—is even considered. Such a choice in favor of multilateralism, diplomacy and treaty agreements should be part of a much broader policy of nonproliferation and disarmament of the kind that has already enjoyed great success over the past several decades. Under the Treaty on the Non-Proliferation of Nuclear Weapons, for example, 182 nations have agreed to do without nuclear weapons. The larger issue is whether proliferation—not just to Iraq but to many other countries as well—is best addressed by military or political means.

But the decision to go to war has a significance that goes far beyond the war. The war is the product of a broader policy that has been spelled out in the clearest possible terms by the Bush Administration. Two other countries with nuclear programs—Iran and North Korea—have already been identified by the President as potential targets for military attack. The Administration's recently published "National Security Strategy of the United States" sets forth even larger ambitions. It declares a policy of military supremacy over the entire earth—an objective never before attained by any power. Military programs are meanwhile forbidden to other countries, all of whom are to be prevented from "surpassing or equaling" the United States. China is singled out for a warning that by "pursuing advanced military capabilities," it is following an "outdated path" that "threaten[s] its neighbors." The new policy reverses a long American tradition of contempt for unprovoked attacks. It gives the United States the unrestricted right to attack nations even when it has not been attacked by them and is not about to be attacked by them. It trades deterrence for pre-emption—in plain English, aggression. It accords the United States the right to overthrow any regime—like the one in Iraq—it decides should be overthrown. (The President would like international support and he would like Congressional support but asserts his right to wage war without either.) It declares that the defense of the United States and the world against nuclear proliferation is military force. It is an imperial policy—more ambitious than ancient Rome's, which, after all, extended only to the Mediterranean and European world. Nelson Mandela recently said of the Administration, "They think they're the only power in the world.…One country wants to bully the world."

A vote for the war in Iraq is a vote for this policy. The most important of the questions raised by the war, however, is larger still. It is what sort of country the United States wants to be in the twenty-first century. The genius of the American form of government was the creation of a system of institutions to check and balance government power and so render it accountable to the people. Today that system is threatened by a monster of unbalanced and unaccountable power—a new Leviathan—that is taking shape among us in the executive branch of the government. This Leviathan—concealed in an ever-deepening, self-created secrecy and fed by streams of money from corporations that, as scandal after scandal has shown, have themselves broken free of elementary accountability—menaces civil liberties even as it threatens endless, unprovoked war. As disrespectful of the Constitution as it is of the UN Charter, the Administration has turned away from law in all its manifestations and placed its reliance on overwhelming force to achieve its ends.

In pursuit of empire abroad, it endangers the Republic at home. The bully of the world threatens to become the bully of Americans, too. Already, the Justice Department claims the right to jail American citizens indefinitely on the sole ground that a bureaucrat in the Pentagon has labeled them something called an "enemy combatant." Even the domestic electoral system has been compromised by the debacle in Florida. Nor has the shadow cast on democracy by that election yet been lifted. Election reform has not occurred. Modest campaign reform designed to slow the flood of corporate cash into politics, even after passage in Congress, is being eviscerated by executive decisions. More important, this year's Congressional campaign, by shunning debate on the fundamental issue of war and peace, has signaled to the public that even in the most important matters facing the country neither it nor its representatives decide; only the executive does.

Members of Congress! Be faithful to your oaths of office and to the traditions of your branch of government. Think of the country, not of your re-election. Assert your power. Stand up for the prerogatives of Congress. Defend the Constitution. Reject the arrogance—and the ignorance—of power. Show respect for your constituents—they require your honest judgment, not capitulation to the executive. Say no to empire. Affirm the Republic. Preserve the peace. Vote against war in Iraq.

The Fog of Hubris: The Life and Afterlife of Robert McNamara

Published on *Reason* magazine's website at reason.com, July 9, 2009

By Jesse Walker

Robert Strange McNamara—secretary of defense under John F. Kennedy and Lyndon B. Johnson, president of the Ford Motor Company and the World Bank, co-architect of the Vietnam War—died Monday at age 93. Two days later, the *New York Times* published a column by the filmmaker Errol Morris, who once directed a documentary about McNamara. Morris noted, with more sympathy than I could ever muster, that McNamara did take some blame for the disaster that the Vietnam War turned out to be. "He said, 'We were wrong,'" wrote Morris. "He was reluctant to use the first person. It was always 'we,' not 'I.'"

By losing himself in the plural form, McNamara may have been evading responsibility for his personal role in the deaths of hundreds of thousands of people. But he was imparting an important truth as well. Vietnam was collective endeavor, and one way men like McNamara made it happen was by refusing to rock the boat even after they started to have their doubts about the project. McNamara was an Organization Man.

Indeed, he encapsulated the entire Organization Man era. After his work as an analyst for Gen. Curtis LeMay during World War II—"If we'd lost the war," he later quoted LeMay as saying, "we'd all have been prosecuted as war criminals"—he came to Ford, where he was one of a group of number-crunching ex-military men who applied the management control systems they'd developed at the Pentagon to the business of creating cars. If the individualists of mid-century America often found big business as alienating as big government, that surely had something to do with the culture at corporations like Ford, which drew on the same pool of technocrats who were running Washington. McNamara eventually became president of the company, and from there he slid back into the public sector, becoming Kennedy's secretary of defense in 1961.

At the Pentagon, McNamara oversaw the escalation of the Vietnam War as though the conflict were an industrial assembly line; he sent hundreds of thousands of soldiers into combat, and he killed countless civilians by bombing Vietnamese villages. In 1968, with growing doubts about the efficacy of those approaches, he jumped to the World Bank. He brought the same technocratic mentality to his duties there, with similarly destructive results: He sponsored vast white-elephant "development projects" whose most notable effect was to evict peasants from their land, and he doled out dollars to dictators from the right-wing regime in Argentina to the Stalinist state in Romania.

By this time you might expect McNamara to have been exiled from polite society. Instead, the worst sanction he suffered came one summer in the '60s when antiwar vacationers on Martha's Vinyard refused to play tennis with him, leaving his household with no partners but McGeorge Bundy's family. With time those old animosities faded, and through it all McNamara stayed atop the World Bank, a job he didn't leave until 1981. It's easy to fall out of favor in the circles of American power, much harder to be expelled from the establishment entirely.

McNamara even rearned the respect of some figures on the left, criticizing the arms race in the '80s and finally confessing in the '90s that "we" had been wrong in Vietnam. After Errol Morris' movie *The Fog of War* appeared at the end of 2003, McNamara had a brief impact on the public debate over the occupation of Iraq. Morris is a great filmmaker, but *The Fog of War* is an uneven, poorly organized picture. It attempts to draw 11 vague "lessons from the life of Robert S. McNamara" (among them: "There's something beyond one's self" and "Get the data") but it's often impossible to connect the material we're shown with the platitude the sequence is supposed to illustrate. Nonetheless, the film won high praise and an Oscar, in part because it was politically useful—and obviously accurate—to draw parallels between the hubris of McNamara's generation and the hubris of the Iraq hawks.

Since then, the wing of the establishment that invaded Iraq has been eclipsed by the wing of the establishment that invaded theaters to see *The Fog of War.* But if you think that means the old McNamara mentality has died, think again. Obama's best and brightest seem intent on retracing the dead man's footsteps, sending one passel of planners to run the auto industry and another to escalate a war in southern Asia. The Organization Man may belong to an earlier era, but hubris is alive and well.

Against All Flags

Published on *Reason* magazine's website at reason.com, April 17, 2009
Questions and answers about pirates and Somalia

By Jesse Walker

Looks like we're good at shooting pirates. Why not send in the Navy and root out the rest?

America's SEALs did an extraordinary job of rescuing Richard Phillips, the captain captured by pirates off the shores of Somalia, but there's a big difference between saving a hostage and putting a dent in hostage-taking. The Somali coastline is approximately 2,000 miles long, and the pirates there strike quickly in small boats. They pay close attention to naval activity and adjust their activities accordingly. The U.S. and its allies simply don't have the resources to cover all that water all the time.

There are more-modest suggestions floating around for international patrols, in which the region's coast guards pool their resources and the western powers merely offer technical expertise and the like. That's a more plausible approach in terms of the costs involved, but it will fall far short of "rooting out the rest."

But you don't have to patrol everywhere to be effective. Just raise the risks of doing business and the problem will decrease to manageable levels.

There's some truth to that. But in that case, the most important thing is to make it costlier to attack a ship in the first place, whether or not the navy is nearby. A decentralized threat demands a decentralized defense.

Do you mean arming the boats themselves?

Sometimes yes, sometimes no. There are risks to arming crews, just as there are risks to leaving crews unarmed. For each particular ship, the owners—and their insurers—are better able to assess those relative hazards than any pundit bloviating from afar. Some companies might prefer to give weapons to their employees; some might prefer to hire private security; some might prefer training their crews in vigilance and nonlethal defense. And given that training people to use weapons—or hiring people who are already trained—is expensive, some might prefer just to buy insurance. (Note, though, that insurance rates in the Gulf of Aden have risen sharply, by some reports more than tenfold, since the recent wave of ship seizures began. As the piracy problem increases, the market responds.)

In addition to all that, though, there are legal barriers to carrying arms onboard, and these may have distorted the ship owners' calculations. In the wake of the recent attacks, there's been some chatter about negotiating a new international agreement to ease or eliminate those restrictions. That's an excellent idea that would at least give the shippers more options.

Self-defense won't solve the problem entirely, though. The piracy problem off Somalia is driven not just by opportunity at sea but also by circumstances onshore.

So you want to attack the pirates' bases on the mainland?

No no no no no. The idea that we could sweep in, destroy the pirates' infrastructure, and consider the problem solved vastly overestimates both the extent and the importance of any particular organization's infrastructure. Let me say it again: The Somali coastline is 2,000 miles long. Pirates have shifted their bases of operation before—since 2007, for example, most of their activity has moved from the waters near Mogadishu towards the breakaway statelet of Puntland. They could easily pull up stakes again. And if you do eliminate one group of criminals, you still haven't eliminated or even, in the long run, reduced the crime. Think of the drug war: The authorities are sometimes able to break up particular gangs or cartels, but the profit motive that drives people into the drug business is still there, so other gangs and cartels take their place. At best, you'll be playing a game of whack-a-mole. At worst, you'll also be whacking a lot of civilians in the process.

Somali piracy is a nuisance, but it isn't a national security issue. Some hawks have tried to link the pirates to jihadist terrorism, but their arguments haven't held up: As Commander John Patch, a former director of the National Maritime Intelligence Watch at the Office of Naval Intelligence, pointed out in the December 2008 issue of *Proceedings,* a journal published by the U.S. Naval Institute, there isn't any credible evidence of such an alliance. He adds that "there is no great risk of terrorists posing as pirates or adopting their methods either to seize a ship for hostages or to use the vessel itself as a weapon by igniting volatile cargo. To be sure, maritime terrorism is clearly a proven method of al Qaeda and other terrorist groups, but piracy cannot be plausibly conflated with it."

Pirate activity might not be a threat to national security, but it's still costly.

Absolutely. But you have to keep your perspective. The cost of the fight would be far greater than the cost imposed by piracy itself.

So if you don't send the Marines, what do you send? Aid? Nation-building advisors?

The wise men in Washington are no better equipped at remolding Somali society than they are at remolding the auto industry. The aid we have sent there over the last few decades has almost invariably ended up boosting the power of one local faction or another.

Somalia is capable of producing for itself; it's just that poor governance and civil strife periodically get in the way. Unfortunately, the U.S. has done much more to foster that poor governance and fan that civil strife than to end them. The evidence of this goes all the way back to the 1970s, when, for reasons related to the Cold War, the Ford administration started sponsoring a brutal military regime run by a self-proclaimed Marxist, Siad Barre.

Hold on. If this was part of the Cold War, why were we siding with a Marxist?

Somalia's great rival was Ethiopia, and Ethiopia had just joined the Soviet bloc.

Did Barre change his ways when he started getting U.S. aid?

He and his representatives deployed a different set of platitudes when begging from their benefactors. But the basic structure of the Somali state stayed the same. It didn't have much to do with either socialism or capitalism as a set of principles: The regime was a kleptocracy in which those who had political pull stole from those who did not. The old tribal structure adjusted itself to the new political context. Now one subclan could expropriate a chunk of land from another, start a "project" on it, and present it to the international community as aid-worthy "economic development."

After Barre was overthrown in 1991, such interclan battles stopped being subsumed within the system and spilled out into the open. Figures once called bureaucrats were now called warlords. But the civil strife of the early 1990s was essentially the same process carried out in a bloodier way.

And that's when the United States and United Nations sent in soldiers?

Yes. As we all know, that didn't go well.

But when the troops pulled out, didn't everything go to pot?

You've got it backwards. The U.S./U.N. intervention made things worse: It undercut local farmers by dumping free food into circulation, herded self-reliant nomads into disease-ridden refugee camps, and disarmed civilians while leaving the warlords' stockpiles largely untouched. At every point during the country's crisis in the early to mid 1990s, the most constructive responses came from the Somalis themselves. (The local Red Crescent Society was responsible for more successful relief than all the foreign efforts combined.) When the outsiders left, the peacemaking elements of Somali society were able to reassert themselves, with elders arbitrating truces between the clans and entrepreneurs establishing a growing economy.

The results were hardly utopian—literacy rates were low, violence was down but was still fairly high, and the drinking water wasn't always clean—but conditions were improving, and by the region's standards they were pretty impressive. A 2004 study for the World Bank revealed that Somalia had as many roads per capita as its immediate neighbors, a better telecommunications infrastructure, and lower rates of extreme poverty; despite the absence of a central government, the country had reasonably effective systems of courts, credit, social insurance, and electric power. After 9/11, though, when the U.S. started channeling aid to the warlords, the fragile social peace started breaking down.

Wait. Back up. America aided the warlords?

Yes. The Bush administration worried that jihadists were seeking shelter in Somalia, so it allied itself with secular Somalis, who styled themselves the "Alliance for the Restoration of Peace and Counter-Terrorism." They included some of the very same figures the U.S. had battled in the early '90s.

How did that work out?

The warlords used the aid to pursue their own agendas, and the fighting ramped back up. The chaos pushed ordinary Somalis into the arms of the Islamic Courts Union, a confederation of sharia-based arbitrators that gradually took over roughly half the country, including the nominal capital, Mogadishu.

Displeased with this result, Washington backed an Ethiopean invasion and occupation of the country. This was supposed to establish a central government for once and for all. Instead it was a gory failure whose chief effect was to rip apart civil society and turn the country into a violent free-for-all. As Human Rights Watch reported in 2008, "the last two years are not just another typical chapter in Somalia's troubled history. The human rights and humanitarian catastrophe facing Somalia today threatens the lives and livelihoods of millions of Somalis on a scale not witnessed since the early 1990s."

One effect was to push more people into desperate and risky ways of making a living. Such as piracy.

That wasn't the beginning of the piracy, though.

No, pirates had been active off the Somali coast since the '90s. At first, to give the devil his due, this was a sort of self-defense, as fishermen fought off foreigners poaching in their waters and seized European boats illegally dumping nuclear waste. Such targets made the freebooters into folk-heroes, and it is one of the two main reasons the pirates have a fair amount of popular support onshore.

What's the other reason?

A wise thief learns to spread the wealth around.

The buccaneers still describe themselves with PR-savvy names like the "National Volunteer Coast Guard." But as it became clear that there were enormous profits in piracy, any innocent sailor on an inadequately defended boat became potential prey. Once the war wiped out many other means of making a living, the number of pirate attacks increased further.

Now Ethiopia has withdrawn and left the "transitional government" in charge, to the extent that anyone in Somalia is in charge. The newly elected president of the transitional government, incidentally, is Sheikh Sharif Sheikh Ahmed, whose previous job title was commander in chief of the Islamic Courts Union.

Let me get this straight. To combat communism in east Africa, the United States propped up a Marxist dictator. After sending troops to battle the warlords, it intervened again to assist the warlords. It did this about-face to stanch the growth of Islamism, but the effect was to put an Islamist group in charge of the country. And after Washington backed an invasion and occupation of the nation to end the Islamic Courts Union's control, the result was a government run by a former commander of the Islamic Courts Union?

You can see why I'm skeptical about a war on the pirates. It'll probably end with Obama dedicating a 60-foot statue of Blackbeard in the middle of Mogadishu.

So how do we fix the problems on the mainland, if we don't invade and don't send aid?

We butt out. If we can't solve Somalia's problems, we can at least refrain from making them worse. The closest the country has had to a period of optimism and growth came when the international community—with the ignoble exceptions of the fish thieves and waste dumpers—largely left the place to its own devices. Do that long enough, and the Somalis may develop institutions strong enough to help rein in the pirates. In the meantime, the best place for us outsiders to focus our efforts is in finding smarter, more effective ways to defend our ships.

That isn't a very optimistic conclusion.

Sorry, but the region isn't exactly bubbling over with reasons for hope. It's easy to call vaguely for humanitarian assistance or for military action. It's harder when you think through the likely consequences of such interventions, especially in light of the consequences of all the earlier aid and war.

Whether you're building a working society on the land or protecting ships at sea, real solutions are only going to come incrementally, experimentally, and at the initiative of the people directly affected. The best thing the world's governments can do is to figure out what they might be doing that blocks rather than facilitates such gradual, bottom-up change, and then to stop doing it.

Antiwarriors: Divided and Conquered Shame on All of Us

Counterpunch
February 12, 2008

By John V. Walsh

There is an enormous antiwar majority in this country—upwards of 70%. And yet the war goes on and on and on. Who is to blame? We could blame the denizens of the two war parties in Congress. The leading Republican and Democrat presidential candidates have a record—and without exception it is a prowar record. McCain froths at the mouth at the prospect of more war. Hillary was there from the beginning and has voted yea on every prowar resolution in the Senate—from authorizing the war to voting for the trillions that have been used to fund the damned thing.

Comparing the votes of Edwards and Obama is especially instructive. When Edwards had a vote in the Senate, his votes declared him prowar. Once without a vote, he said he was against the war—but there was no voting record to show it. He was for it before he was against it. Obama's record is even less defensible. He said he was against the war until he had a Senate vote. Then he voted for each and every prowar appropriation. Hence, Obama was against it before he was for it. In every case, give them a vote and they vote to kill.

But what about the rest of us? We know that the world is bristling with nuclear weapons; and wars and a war mentality threaten us with their use. Nuclear winter threatens all higher life with extinction, and nuclear winter is still all too possible. In fact nuclear winter would make global warming look like a kiddy sandbox.

And beyond the threat to our very survival, empire and the wars that spring from it threaten our civil and political liberties, without which no change, no progress is possible. The Libertarians especially have raised the point that, once empire crowds out a republic, then the days of liberty are gone. The paleoconservatives agree. And the progressives also agree, recognizing as well that valued social programs cannot be funded with enormous wealth plowed into our empire of

757 foreign military bases and 969 domestic bases, none designed for defense but instead for offense to "project power" throughout the empire.

With such strong and varied antiwar sentiment, is it not remarkable that the antiwar movement has come to nothing? Our country is now embroiled in Iraq, in Afghanistan, in countries on Russia's perimeter, in Iran, in many parts of Africa and elsewhere. And the war parties, Democrat and Republican, are itching for a fight with China. Altogether the situation is pretty miserable.

So why the great gap between popular sentiment and effective antiwar action? I submit that the war parties, Democrat and Republican, very effectively use a divide and conquer tactic—and the antiwar forces play into it, usually quite eagerly. So when some on the left have good things to say about Ron Paul, the sterile lefty ideologues quickly change the subject. If that does not work, those who speak favorably of Paul are excoriated for being right wingers in our innermost thoughts, which we ourselves cannot plumb, we are told, although the psychoanalysts of the left can. And if that does not work, the thought nannies tell us that Ron Paul is a Nazi, another Hitler, who is to be opposed at all costs. That kind of stuff emanates especially strongly from the precincts of the *New Republic,* which has been calling for Paul's head ever since he dared say "AIPAC" in public. In so doing the asps at TNR are merely repeating the hate campaign against Pat Buchanan whom they and their allies at the *National Review* labeled an anti-Semite. And so the antiwar left is manipulated into avoiding alliances, which might actually make some headway. Thus we have the spectacle of progressives who eschew alliances that might make—well, progress.

The same is true on the other side. The Paleos and to a lesser degree the Libertarians cannot put aside differences with Greens and other leftists long enough to make headway against war and empire. As soon as common cause begins to be made, then the specter of increased social spending is raised by the Libertarians and of creeping secularism by the Paleos. Because everyone wants only allies that are in complete agreement, no alliances are made. And presto, the ruling war parties have divided and conquered.

Such behavior on the part of the antiwar movement is childish in the extreme. For the sake of ideological purity, we give up on making common cause with others who agree with us only in part. For an impossibly long shot at gaining everything, we sacrifice gaining the most important thing at the moment—an end to war and empire. That is not politics. That is theology—or perhaps more accurately the behavior of spoiled kids. Or perhaps even more accurately behavior unencumbered by the thought process. And it is boring to boot. The crowd one hangs with has all the answers to every question; and no matter how much reality shifts, as with the end of the Cold War, the answers remain the same.

So what is to be done? It is time for the various antiwar groupings and ideologies to get together and to do so in a way that can have an effect on the '08 elections. First we have to begin a conversation to decide on a course of action. And we must do it soon. So far the only places that seem willing to host such a conversation are CounterPunch.com, Antiwar.com and The *American Conservative* (TAC). There are also lots of smaller grass roots groups like AntiwarLeague.com and the Second Vermont Republic, which have made strides at unifying the various antiwar factions. It is clear, however, that UFPJ, ANSWER, "P"DA, *The Nation* and others will never serve this function. They will put loyalty to the Democrat Party over all else. Nor will the DemoGreens or the inside the beltway Libertarians ensconced in their high-priced digs at Cato act to break down barriers. They too put party, whether Democrat or Republican, first.

Perhaps with more debate revolving around the question of how we, the antiwar majority, are effectively marginalized, we can move forward. But to do so we all have to suspend some of our ideological certainties and stereotypes of the other and concede that there are more things in heaven and earth than we have dreamed of—or at least embraced in our theories. And we may find we have more in common than we thought. Why not do this? We have nothing to lose and much to gain. So let us hope that this discussion can begin in earnest. And let's move fast; 2008 is slipping away.

The Silence of the Anti-War Movement is Deafening

Counterpunch, August 26, 2009

By John V. Walsh

Cindy Sheehan will be at Martha's Vineyard beginning August 25 a short way from Obama's vacation paradise of the celebrity elite but very far from the Afghanistan and Pakistan and Iraq where the body bags and cemeteries fill up each day as Obama's wars rage on. She will remain there from August 25 through August 29 and has issued a call for all peace activists to join her there. For those of us close by in the New England states and in New York City, there would seem to be a special obligation to get to Martha's Vineyard as soon as we can.

A funny thing has happened on Cindy Sheehan's long road from Crawford, Texas, to Martha's Vineyard. Many of those who claim to lead the peace movement and who so volubly praised her actions in Crawford, TX, are not to be seen. Nor heard. The silence in fact is deafening, or as Cindy put it in an email to this writer, "crashingly deafening." Where are the email appeals to join Cindy from *The Nation* or from AFSC or Peace Action or "Progressive" Democrats of America (PDA) or even Code Pink? Or United for Peace and Justice. (No wonder UFPJ is essentially closing shop, bereft of most of their contributions and shriveling up following the thinly veiled protest behind the "retirement" of Leslie Cagan.) And what about MoveOn although it was long ago thoroughly discredited as a principled opponent of war or principled in any way shape or form except slavish loyalty to the "other" War Party. And of course sundry "socialist" organizations are also missing in action since their particular dogma will not be front and center. These worthies and many others have vanished into the fog of Obama's wars.

Just to be sure, this writer contacted several of the "leaders" of the "official" peace movement in the Boston area—AFSC, Peace Action, Green Party of MA (aka Green Rainbow Party) and some others. Not so much as the courtesy of a reply resulted from this effort—although the GRP at least posted a notice of the action. (It is entirely possible that some of these organizations might mention Cindy's action late enough and quickly enough so as to cover their derrieres while ensuring that Obama will not be embarrassed by protesting crowds.) We here in the vicinity of Beantown are but a hop, skip and cheap ferry ride from Martha's Vineyard. Same for NYC. So we have a special obligation to respond to Cindy's call.

However, not everyone has failed to publicize the event. The Libertarians at Antiwar.com are on the job, and its editor in chief Justin Raimondo wrote a superb column Monday on the hypocritical treatment of Sheehan by the "liberal" establishment.[1] As Raimondo pointed out, Rush Limbaugh captured the hypocrisy of the liberal left in his commentary, thus:

"Now that she's headed to Martha's Vineyard, the State-Controlled Media, Charlie Gibson, State-Controlled Anchor, ABC: 'Enough already.' Cindy, leave it alone, get out, we're not interested, we're not going to cover you going to Martha's Vineyard because our guy is president now and you're just a hassle. You're just a problem. To these people, they never had any true, genuine emotional interest in her. She was just a pawn. She was just a woman to be used and then thrown overboard once they're through with her and they're through with her. They don't want any part of Cindy Sheehan protesting against any war when Obama happens to be president."

Limbaugh has their number, just as they have his. Sometimes it is quite amazing how well each of the war parties can spot the other's hypocrisy. But Cindy Sheehan is no one's dupe; she is a very smart and very determined woman who no doubt is giving a lot of White House operatives some very sleepless nights out there on the Vineyard. Good for her.

Obama is an enormous gift to the Empire. Just as he has silenced most of the single-payer movement, an effort characterized by its superb scholarship exceeded only by its timidity, Obama has shut down the antiwar movement, completely in thrall as it is to the Democrat Party and Identity Politics. Why exactly the peace movement has caved to Obama is not entirely clear. Like the single-payer movement, it is wracked by spinelessness, brimming with reverence for authority and a near insatiable appetite to be "part of the crowd." Those taken in by Obama's arguments that the increasingly bloody and brutal AfPak war is actually a "war of necessity," should read Steven Walt's easy demolition of that "argument."[2] Basically Obama's logic is the same as Bush's moronic rationale that "We are fighting them over there so we do not have to fight them over here." There is a potential for "safe havens for terrorists," as the Obamalogues and neocons like to call them, all over the world; and no one can possibly believe the US can invade them all. However, the ones which Israel detests or which allow control of oil pipelines or permit encirclement of China and Russia will see US troops sooner or later.

The bottom line is that everyone in New England and NYC who is a genuine antiwarrior should join the imaginative effort of Cindy Sheehan in Obamaland this week and weekend. We owe it to the many who will otherwise perish at the hands of the war parties of Bush and Obama.

[1]See: http://original.antiwar.com/justin/2009/08/23/war-coverage-and-the-obama-cult/ or go to Antiwar.com and make a contribution while you are there. It's almost as good as CounterPunch.com.
[2]See:http://walt.foreignpolicy.com/posts/2009/08/18/the_safe_haven_myth

Fattest Lady Singing

George Wilson

In declaring in his State of the Union address that he won't cut the Pentagon budget, President Obama is like a trainer telling the fattest lady in his class that she need not do her exercises. Why didn't Obama order the fat Defense Department to join the government-wide effort to reduce the deficit by killing off weapons that no longer make sense?

Two-thirds of our casualties in the Iraq War were inflicted by hidden bombs that the bad guys set off by cell phones or other simple devices available at Radio Shack. Neither our new aircraft carriers costing $12 billion apiece nor our new F-22 fighter aircraft costing $350 million a plane can keep our troops from being killed or wounded by cheap improvised explosive devices.

This doesn't mean that deficit cutters should cancel such super weapons willy nilly. More conventional wars than the ones in Iraq and Afghanistan may well be in America's future. But Obama and Congress should at least order Defense Secretary Gates and his deputies to justify every major weapon by expaining what red-hot threat out there justifies spending fresh billions on it.

The GAO drew a good road map for conducting such a review last year in its devastating report on Pentagon cost overruns. Entitled "Defense Acquisitions: Assessments of Selected Weapon Programs," the GAO studied 96 major weapons in 2008 and discovered that the contractors' original price tag had nothing to do with reality.

The cost overruns on the weapons studied totaled $296.4 billion. Just making the contractors, not the taxpayers, eat their own cost overruns would reduce the deficit by almost $300 billion.

Instead of making such a demand, Obama last Wednesday gave defense contractors, their overseers in the Pentagon and Congress a pass: "Starting in 2011 we are prepared to freeze government spending for three years. Spending related to our national security, Medicare, Medicaid and Social Security will not be affected. But all other discretionary government programs will."

Where is Congress in this supposed war against the deficit that Obama just declared? The Founding Fathers in Article I, Section 8 of the U.S. Constitution gave Congress the power to "provide for the common defense," not the president.

When are the lawmakers going to start cutting Pentagon programs like outrageously expensive warships, planes that soar over the price tags contractors originally put on them and missile defenses that have a lot bigger flaws than Toyota's stuck gas pedals?

"Never," is the answer I get from some of the walking wounded who fought in past battles of the Pentagon budget. They say any weapons, whether justified by today's threats or not, get protected by lawmakers as long as they provide jobs back home.

Congress, these vets contend, to reassert its constitutional right to provide for the common defense, should deny money to produce any weapon before it is thoroughly tested; forbid congressional add-ons to the Pentagon budget unless CBO and GAO have determined what the pet project would cost and, if deemed worthy, conduct an open competition to build it; forbid any congressional staffer from vaulting to a job in the Pentagon or defense industry.

Obama did take one step toward making congressional wheeling and dealing on add-ons more transparent by declaring in his address that "I'm calling on Congress to publish all earmark requests on a single Web site before there's a vote so that the American people can see how their money is being spent." That might help some but not much. Voters in the lawmaker's district or state might not object to getting earmarked for goodies.

As one who has studied the military-industrial-political-intelligence complex for almost 50 years now from the front row seat a defense reporter gets, I think the deficit, unemployment, cost overruns on weapons that don't work and/or have nothing to do with winning the war against terrorists—along with voter disgust with Washington's spending binge—will eventually force the president and Congress to rein in their spending on dubious weapons.

The overseers will realize that real national security means fixing the national economy, not letting the Defense secretary and Army, Navy, Air Force, and Marine Corps continue to drive the taxpayers to the poor house in Cadillacs.

As one who spent seven and a half months on an aircraft carrier, let me fuel the eventual battle of the Pentagon budget by asking right here and now whether it makes sense in these economic times to build all three of the new carriers of the class named after the late President Gerald R. Ford.

In its latest Selected Acquisition Report, the Pentagon projects that three of these Ford class carriers will cost a total of $35 billion, or almost $12 billion each. A pilot who really knows carriers from taking off and landing on them thousands of times told me that the bad guys could disable the carrier flight deck with comparatively cheap missiles or do what our own Navy frogmen have already done: Sneak aboard a carrier at night undetected by climbing up its steel sides on magnetic shoes. "They can make it rain longer than we can swim," the pilot said of those bent on dethroning the queen of the Navy fleet.

"Forward Observer," an insider's look at defense and military topics, appears every other Monday in *Congress Daily.*

Special Correspondent George C. Wilson can be reached at gcwilson1@comcast.net.

From Liberty to Empire: The Demise of American Defense

Ben Manski

From liberty to empire: The demise of American defense

> *All you have to do is remember that anti-imperialism is only another name for old-fashioned Americanism, and all will be clear to you. An American who has a settled body of convictions...who with his inherited ideas has an inherited courage, an inherited love of equality and justice...why, he is a natural born anti-imperialist, and it is simply his Americanism that makes him think and act as he does...*
> —New York Evening Post, *May 3, 1902*

Were the British billionaire Rupert Murdoch to read those words today in what is now his *New York Post,* it is possible he might suffer a heart attack. Were we to read them in most any mainstream U.S. daily, we would at least be shocked. That this is the case is a testament to the past century's shift in media ownership, certainly, but more to the point, it speaks to the demise of the American system of national defense.

A century ago, it was natural for the editor of a major newspaper to write that "old-fashioned Americanism" is anti-imperialism. Today, that kind of old-fashioned Americanism is dead, buried, and forgotten. The cost of forgetting is not insignificant: It is acceptance—by foes and advocates of U.S. empire alike—of a military order that would have been forcefully rejected by prior generations.

To see how far we have fallen, it is best to return to the beginning.

In defense of the revolution: The Militia Clause

> *The Congress shall have power...*
> *To provide for calling forth the militia to execute the*

laws of the union, suppress insurrections and repel invasions; To provide for organizing, arming, and disciplining, the Militia, and for governing such Part of them as may be employed in the Service of the United States, reserving to the States respectively, the Appointment of the Officers, and the Authority of training the Militia according to the discipline prescribed by Congress;
—U.S. Const. art. 1, § 8, cl. 15 & 16

The original American defense force was the state local, and independent militia. Its membership included, as recognized by the federal Militia Act of 1792, "every free able-bodied white male citizen of the respective States, resident therein, who is or shall be of age of eighteen years, and under the age of forty-five years...." Its officers were appointed or elected, depending on state law. Its members were trained and armed by authority of Congress. This was the primary defense; for decades, the United States had no real standing army, only a small force numbering in the hundreds.

Defense meant something deeper than the protection of territorial borders; it meant the protection of America as a "land of liberty." By and large, the revolutionary generation was committed to creating a new society in which power was decentralized. They had revolted, after all, against a monarch who in the words of the Declaration of Independence, had, "kept among us, in times of peace, Standing Armies without the Consent of our legislatures.... [and] affected to render the Military independent of and superior to the Civil Power." A force made up of the people themselves was considered the greatest protection against the potential collapse of the American republic into imperial tyranny.

What, Sir, is the use of a militia? It is to prevent the establishment of a standing army, the bane of liberty... Whenever Governments mean to invade the rights and liberties of the people, they always attempt to destroy the militia, in order to raise an army upon their ruins.
—U.S. Rep. Elbridge Gerry, Mass., August 17, 1789

The revolutionary generation provided in the Constitution varied means for common defense. To Congress and the Presidency they gave shared responsibility for diplomacy. To Congress alone they accorded the powers to declare war, maintain a navy, and raise an army (for up to two years at a time). To the President, in times of war, they entrusted the office of Commander in Chief.

Yet among the war powers, the role of the militia was preeminent. Indeed, the Constitution not only guarantees to the American people—we citizen soldiers—the right to keep and bear arms, it specifies clear limits on federal use of the state militias. The Militia Clause of the U.S. Constitution, Article 1, Section 8, Clause 15 & 16, lays out the three purposes for which Congress may call into actual service the militia, these being, "to execute the laws of the union, suppress insurrections and repel invasions." The clause also provides for congressional regulation and maintenance of the militia. In a government of "limited and enumerated powers," the ability of Congress to federalize the state militias was intended to end with the provisions of the Militia Clause, and for more than a century it did.

Note that among the purposes for which Congress is not empowered to call the militia into national service are deployment to, invasion of, or occupation of other countries. The state militia were defensive, not offensive. This was by design. Of U.S. empire, Thomas Jefferson insisted in 1791 that, "If there be one principle more deeply written than any other in the mind of every American, it is that we should have nothing to do with conquest." And a generation later, future president John Quincy Adams laid forth an image of America embodied by Lady Liberty:

> *America's glory is not dominion, but liberty. Her march is the march of the mind. She has a spear and shield, but the motto upon her shield is: Freedom, Independence, Peace. This has been her declaration. This has been, as far as her necessary intercourse with the rest of mankind would permit, her practice.*
> *—U.S. Secretary of State John Quincy Adams, July 4, 1821*

Pretty as those words were, clear as the text of the Constitution was, what gave the words and text weight was the practical reality of militia-based defense. Hundreds of thousands of citizens armed, trained, and organized in state and local militias provided a defense against federal tyranny and a real check on federal imperial ambitions. Citizen soldiers were unlikely to agree to deployment far from home and for dubious purpose. Citizen soldiers were unlikely to enable the enforcement of tyrannical federal laws—such as the Fugitive Slave Act of 1850—in their states and communities. That was the rhetoric of the time, and for the most part, that was the reality.

Here for the sake of clarity is a summary of the original distribution of American defense. First, the American people were armed, trained, and organized in state militia as a defense against foreign invasion, tyranny at home, and empire abroad. Second, the Congress of the United States was entrusted with maintaining peace, regulating the militia, supporting the navy, calling the militia into actual national service for very specific purposes, raising additional armies when war threatened, and alone determining whether the United States was to declare war and engage in military action. Third, the President of the United States held one military role only—that of Commander in Chief in times of war—in order to ensure civil control of the military at the very moment that the military posed the greatest potential threat to civil government.

Imagining what would happen were the militia removed from this three-part arrangement is not difficult; we have seen the results. Congress created a large standing army in place of the state militias. With real standing armies, Congress and the Presidency now were able to act aggressively. And with the militia gone as a popular check on military adventurism, Congress ceded evermore power to the Presidency. The most important war powers question, therefore, is that of what happened to the state militias.

The first 100 years

From 1789 to 1903, the state militias remained the bulwark of American defense. In the War of 1812, following a declaration of war by the United States against Great Britain, Congress called the militia into service. Most state militias responded to the call. Some units, however, initially refused to appear on the ground that Great Britain had not yet invaded the territorial United States; others resisted service throughout the war, declaring that the conflict had been avoidable and was wrongful. And some units refused to participate in U.S. incursions into Canada; as a direct result, those expeditions failed.

A generation later, Congress declared war on the Empire of Mexico. Congress did not, however, call the state militias into service. Even the most diehard war proponents acknowledged that the Militia Clause did not give Congress the authority to use the militia for the invasion of another country (attacks on native peoples within U.S.-claimed territory were another matter). Furthermore, even had Congress attempted to call them into service, it is doubtful that northern militias would have appeared. The invasion of Mexico was deeply unpopular in northern states, as it was seen as furthering the spread of slavery.

The domestic divisions over the invasion of Mexico widened into war a dozen years later in the most significant military event in the history of the United States, the American Civil War. Militias played significant roles in pre-war years. Well known is the role of the state militia of the South in preparing the way for the Confederate States Army. Yet militia by their nature will reflect the character of the people who compose them.

John Brown's militia fought in the conflict over whether Kansas was to become a free or slave state. Later, that militia conducted the raid on Harper's Ferry, ushering in the Civil War.

Hundreds of thousands of anti-slavery men prepared for war in militia units known as the "Wide Awakes," so called because they were 'wide awake' against slave hunters, and sometimes took action to resist implementation of federal fugitive slave laws (see "States Rights for Civil Rights," *Liberty Tree, Vol. 1, Issue 3*).

During the war, Blacks were inducted into the federalized militia for the first time (Blacks had served with some local and independent militia units before then), and a militia made up of Irish republicans struck a blow against the English occupation of Ireland by invading the Dominion of Canada. Following the war, state militia of freed Blacks were organized across the South to enforce the progress of Reconstruction.

A most significant Civil War role of the state militias may be among the least known. As with the War of 1812, at the beginning of the Civil War, the federal government called the state militia into national service. But this time, unlike with the earlier war, the concern for the states was not that the militia had been wrongly called into service, but that they were not being brought into service quickly enough.

Anti-slavery men governed many northern states, particularly in the Great Lakes region. Seeing that the Confederacy had a significant head start in war mobilization, and that the Union army was failing to accept tens of thousands of volunteers for service, these governors worried that the cause of abolition would be harmed by federal incompetence or, worse, lethargy. They convened in Cleveland, Ohio, on May 3, 1861, and elected as spokesperson the governor of a state which only two years earlier had itself considered secession in response to federal slave law, Wisconsin Governor Alexander Randall. In a letter mailed on May 6, 1861, Randall warned President Lincoln that if the federal government failed to channel rising war spirit, the people and the states might take the war into their own hands:

> *[It would be] better for the Government to direct this current than to let it run wild.... The Government must provide an outlet for this feeling, or it will find one for itself.*

Feeling such heat from his party's radical wing, facing an implicit threat of autonomous action by northern militias, and fearful of the war's course himself, Lincoln responded, issuing a call for 300,000 men for the Union war effort.

The militia system was never perfect. While they played positive roles in Reconstruction, Abolition, and the Revolution, the state militias were sometimes directed to purposes contrary to the ends of human progress: Suppressing slave revolts, crushing farmer and labor strikes, and worse, massacring native peoples. The militia system had a key bias against central power, but beyond that bias it was not inherently progressive.

Overall, the militia system meant that for more than a century, the ability of the federal government to project military power abroad was significantly limited. On the cusp of the 20th century, in 1898, 115,000 Americans were enrolled in militia, as against 18,000 in the regular army.

The destruction of the militia

In 1898, the United States warred with Spain and won possession of the former Spanish colonies of Guam, the Philippines, Puerto Rico, and Cuba. The Spanish American war not only sounded the demise of the Spanish Empire, it also brought with it the end of the American system of defense, and the start of modern U.S. imperialism.

For the first time in American history, the federal government called state militia units into national service to send them overseas to fight and occupy foreign lands. Following the war, the federal government turned the Philippines, Guam, and Puerto Rico into U.S. colonies, and established a military "protectorate" over Cuba.

In 1903, the year Congress ratified the Cuban protectorate as well as the U.S. military base at Guantánamo Bay, Congress also adopted the Militia Act of 1903, or Dick Act. The Dick Act was a response to the perceived weaknesses of the militia system in carrying out the new imperial policy. The Act required the various state militia to adhere to U.S. army organization, and began the reidentification of the militia as the "National Guard."

The federalization of the state militia increased pace with the adoption of the National Defense Act of 1916. That wartime Act made mandatory the renaming of the militia as the National Guard, required Guard members to pledge obedience to the President, and in times of war inducted irrevocably the Guard into the U.S. Army Reserve.

Subsequent amendments to the National Defense Act established a National Guard Bureau commanded by federal officers and created our current dual-enlistment system in which Guard members are inducted into the U.S. Armed Forces in times of peace as well as war. (This dual-enlistment system means that upon joining the Guard, an individual enlists in both the National Guard of the several states—e.g., the Nebraska National Guard, Vermont National Guard—and in the National Guard of the United States, being the U.S. Army Reserve or Air National Guard). A final blow to state control of the state militia came with the National Defense Act amendments of 1952 and 1986; these authorized the Department of Defense to call the National Guard into national service in times other than national emergency, and to mobilize Guard units for training and other purposes without the consent of the governor of that unit's state.

The federalization of the militia, the occupation of foreign lands, the use of the militia for purposes other than the repelling of invasion, law enforcement, or suppression of insurrection—all were unconstitutional. Yet despite howls of protest from the anti-imperialists of the day, all were maintained. The new dual enlistment system was eventually held to mean that for Guard units called into national service, in the words of the U.S. Supreme Court in Perpich v. Department of Defense, "the Militia Clause is no longer applicable."

The original American purposes of, in John Quincy Adams' words, "freedom, independence, and peace," now gave way to property, empire, and war. Rep. Elbridge Gerry's fearful warning of those who would, "destroy the militia, in order to raise an army upon their ruins," had come to pass.

Democracy against empire

The United States of America were never intended to become, in the words of Emma Lazarus's The New Colossus, "like the brazen giant of Greek fame, with conquering limbs astride from land to land." Empire was the business of the "ancient world" and its "storied pomp." Yet today the United States is more like the old colossus than the new, and millions of lives, freedom, and economic and ecological destruction have been the price.

How might we end this era of U.S. imperialism and revive American liberty?

To begin, we must insist that the U.S. Armed Forces as they are currently organized are unconstitutional and contrary to the original intent of the revolutionary generation that America be a land of liberty, not empire. The courts that upheld the federalization of the state militia were also the courts that upheld segregation via the judge-made law of separate-but-equal and that struck down worker protections via the judge-made law of the dormant commerce clause. Why, when we reject those holdings today, would we accept similarly repugnant rulings? We should not. We should question the deployment of the Guard for purposes other than those specified in the Militia Clause, we should continue to challenge Congress' delegation of its war-declaring powers to the Presidency, and we should begin to challenge the absurd notion that the wartime office of Commander-in-Chief bestows on the Presidency peacetime military powers that belong to the Congress, the states, and the people alone.

We should, moreover, raise up a renewed vision for American defense defined by defense of liberty, decentralized and democratized, with popular participation understood not as a draft, but a birthright.

We should continue to support members of the U.S. Armed Forces who resist unlawful service. We should build on the anti-war consensus developed in last year's troop withdrawal initiatives and referenda to pass city and county ordinances directing our local government officials to provide safe haven for war resisters and to disallow unconstitutional recruiting activities in our communities. And we should work to win state legislative and gubernatorial action to bring the Guard home.

Finally, we should make these initiatives within the context of building a new American democracy movement. The old militia system did not survive the rise of the corporations, media conglomerates, and federal power. Without the significant democratization of U.S. media, elections, economics, education, law, and culture, there is little reason to hope for the survival of a newly democratized system of defense.

Ben Manski is a Wisconsin attorney and the editor of the *Liberty Tree Journal.*

America Needs an Effective Anti-War Movement

Peace advocacy needs to be broad-based, credible, inclusive and politically independent

By Kevin Zeese

In his State of the Union, Obama did not brag about some record breaking truths of his first year in office. President Obama broke several important records of President George W. Bush. He passed the largest military budget in U.S. history, the largest one-year war supplementals and fired the most drone attacks on the most countries.

He also did not mention that he is on a path to break more records in his second year. He began 2010 asking for another $30 billion war supplemental and with the White House indicating that the next military budget will be $708 billion, breaking his own previous record for war spending.

His State of the Union did make a lot of useful proposals for the nation that if adequately funded could get the county moving again. One he highlighted the day after the speech was rapid rail. The United States has underfunded rail projects for decades resulting in the nation's rail network shrinking to just 94,942 miles, less than half of what it was in 1970, so this investment is a welcome proposal. Obama proposed that 31 states receive funds for rapid rail. How much did he propose? Eight billion dollars. A completed California system alone is projected to cost $45 billion. (There are good reasons to expand conventional rail than rapid rail especially when the budget is so limited.)

Indeed, every domestic program President Obama recommended will be woefully underfunded. The result, if everything the president recommends is put into law it will not be sufficient to get the U.S. economy moving again or create the jobs needed to put America to work.

Why are domestic programs underfunded at this time of economic collapse? One major reason is the record-setting, constantly growing war and weapons budgets. For years, really for decades, the United

States has been feeding the military-industrial complex at the expense of the civilian economy. The cost of war is one reason why our domestic economy has become hollow.

What kind of debate can we expect in Congress about the military budget? With a few exceptions from people like Ron Paul and Dennis Kucinich who are marginalized by their own parties, we can expect the committees that oversee the military to add to the war budget rather than subtract from it. We can expect no one on the Armed Services Committees to urge cuts in military spending. Even though there are $300 billion dollars in cost overruns on weapons contacts—with nearly 70 percent of the Pentagon's 96 largest weapons programs over budget in 2008—will anyone take action to reign in this overspending?

During the presidential campaign some commentators hailed Obama as the peace candidate because he made an anti-Iraq War speech before being elected to the senate. There was no one to point out that he had voted for all the funding for the Iraq War as well as for the DoD budget. No one on the air pointing out that his plan to end the Iraq War would leave tens of thousands of troops and an equal number of private contactor mercenaries in Iraq. When he urged expansion of the Afghanistan War the media did not have people on to explain why that may not be the best course of action.

Why this gap in debate and discussion of war in the Congress and media? There are a lot of reasons beginning with the power of the military-industrial-congressional complex. But in addition, there is no strong, credible, broad-based antiwar advocacy in the United States. This is not because Americans all support war—quite the contrary. Polling actually shows majorities often oppose war and escalation of war. But these views are not represented in government or the media.

In addition, opposition to war is not limited to people on the left it covers the American political spectrum and it always has.

There is a long history of opposition to war among traditional conservatives. Their philosophy goes back to President Washington's Farewell Address where he urged America to avoid "foreign entanglements." It has showed itself throughout American history. The Anti-Imperialist League opposed the colonialism of the Philippines in the 1890s. The largest anti-war movement in history, the America First Committee, opposed World War II and had a

strong middle America conservative foundation in its make-up. The strongest speech of an American president against militarism was President Eisenhower's 1961 final speech from the White House warning America against the growing military-industrial complex.

In recent years the militarist neo-conservative movement has become dominate of conservatism in the United States. Perhaps none decry this more than traditional conservatives who oppose massive military budgets, militarism and the American empire. Anti-war conservatives continue to exist, speak out and organize. Much of their thinking can be seen in the *American Conservative* magazine which has been steadfastly anti-war since its founding in 2002 where their first cover story was entitled "Iraq Folly."

Of course, the left also has a long history of opposition to war from the Civil War to early imperialism in the Philippines, World Wars I and II through Vietnam, Iraq and Afghanistan. It includes socialists, Quakers, social justice Catholics and progressives. Indeed, the opposition to entry into World War I was led by the left including socialists, trade unionists, pacifists including people like union leader and presidential candidate Eugene Debs, Nobel Peace Prize winner Jane Addams and author and political activist Helen Keller. This movement was so strong that Woodrow Wilson ran a campaign to keep the U.S. out of the Great War (but ended up getting the U.S. into the war despite his campaign promises). Opposition to Vietnam brought together peace advocates with the civil rights movement, highlighted by Dr. Martin Luther King, Jr.'s outspoken opposition to the war.

The United States would have a much healthier political discourse if people who oppose war, no matter where they are on the political spectrum, joined together in a unified voice against American militarism. Indeed, this has become an imperative. The cost of U.S. militarism in lives and dollars has become so great that Americans need to consider the cost of war.

What are the ingredients for a successful anti-war, pro-peace movement?

—Broad based. The anti-war movement needs to be a reflection of not just the left but of Middle America and traditional conservatives who oppose war. As noted above their is a long history of opposition to war across the political spectrum. A majority of Americans oppose war and escalation of current wars but that is not reflected in the peace movement.

—Patriotic. A successful anti-war peace movement cannot give up the flag of patriotism. It needs to grab hold of America's patriotic impulses and show the United States can be the nation many imagine us to be—leading by positive example, helping in crisis, being a force for good, rather than propagating military dominance and hegemony. A successful anti-war movement needs to be a place where veterans, from grunts to generals, can openly participate, share their stories and explain the lessons they learned from American militarism. A credible, patriotic anti-war movement, will allow more former military to speak out in a cohesive and effective manner. Patriotism does not mean failure to criticize when the country goes off course, in fact it means criticizing in the best interests of the country.

—Organized ongoing outreach. A well organized anti-war movement will have committees not only reaching out to military and business, but to academics, students, clergy, labor, nurses, doctors, teachers and a host of others. Outreach and organization needs to be an ongoing priority. And, organization must be designed around congressional districts so it can have a political impact. This demonstrates one reason for the need for a right-left coalition; the anti-war movement cannot allow "red" states or districts to go unorganized. We need to keep building the anti-war, pro-peace base in an organized way.

—New tactics. The 1960s tactics of big marches and congressional demonstrations have their role but they are not sufficient. The media and government have adjusted to them. We need to use tools like voter initiatives and referenda to break through and put our issues before the voters. And, we need to learn from around the world what has worked; for example, general strikes, whether of a few hours or a few days, have shown unified opposition to government policy. Also effective in other countries are efforts to shut down their nation's capitol to prevent business as usual when the government is working in the wrong direction. Voters for Peace Project Board member Cindy Sheehan is moving in this direction with Peace of the Action this spring.

—Link war to the economy. Make war relevant to Americans' day-to-day lives by constantly linking the cost of war to their communities, incomes, and bank accounts. People need to learn that Empire is not good for the U.S. economy. The economic impact of war and the military budget will attract the support of business

leaders who recognize that war undermines the American economy. When the United States is spending one million dollars per soldier in Afghanistan it is evident to anyone focused on the bottom line that a teetering U.S. economy cannot afford the cost of war. The U.S. has already spent a trillion dollars in Iraq and Afghanistan when care for the wounded and lost productivity is included the cost is more than doubled. The military expenditures of a decades long "Long War" will cripple the U.S. economy.

—Politically independent. Both parties are dominated by pro-militarist elected officials. The anti-war movement needs to be strong in criticizing candidates who call for a larger military, escalation of war, or other militarist policies. Recently peace activists have been drawn into silence when John "Anybody but Bush" Kerry ran a campaign where he called for escalation of the Iraq War and expansion of the military. And, when candidate Obama promised to escalate the Afghanistan war, attack Pakistan, only partially withdraw from Iraq and expand the U.S. military—many in the peace movement remained silent or criticized his policies but promised to support him anyway. Movements cannot stop and start for elections, nor allow party loyalty to divide them. They must continue to build through the election. Indeed, elections can be prime opportunities to build the movement and push candidates toward the anti-war peace perspective. The peace movement needs to protest candidates from any party who call for more militarism, larger military budgets and more U.S. troops and demand real anti-war positions for their votes. Anti-war advocates need to make all candidates earn the peace vote.

—Long-term commitment. Developing an effective anti-war peace movement is a big task that will take years. U.S. Empire can be traced back to the late 1800s and President Eisenhower warned America of the military industrial complex fifty years ago. The U.S. is currently engaged in a "Long War" supported by neocons, neo-liberals and corporatist politicians. The pro-militarist establishment has deep roots in both major parties and undoing the military machine will take many years of work. Advocacy against war and militarism needs to be persistent; constantly educating the American public that war undermines national security, weakens the rule of law and contributes to the collapsing economy. We need to show how investment in militarism rather than civil society undermines livability of American communities, weakens the economy and puts basic necessities like education and health care financially out of reach.

The peace movement cannot continue to keep doing the same thing over and over again and expect different results. We need to look at the effectiveness of our work, question it, and improve on it. The facts are on the side of the anti-war peace advocates, now we must build organizations that represent the patriotic, anti-militarist impulses of the American people.

The "Long War" Quagmire

Tom Hayden

The doctrine, which posits an 80-year or so war against insurgents in the Middle East to South Asia, needs more scrutiny.

Without public debate and without congressional hearings, a segment of the Pentagon and fellow travelers have embraced a doctrine known as the Long War, which projects an "arc of instability" caused by insurgent groups from Europe to South Asia that will last between 50 and 80 years. According to one of its architects, Iraq, Afghanistan and Pakistan are just "small wars in the midst of a big one."

Consider the audacity of such an idea. An 80-year undeclared war would entangle 20 future presidential terms stretching far into the future of voters not yet born. The American death toll in Iraq and Afghanistan now approaches 5,000, with the number of wounded a multiple many times greater. Including the American dead from 9/11, that's 8,000 dead so far in the first decade of the Long War. And if the American armed forces are stretched thin today, try to conceive of seven more decades of combat.

The costs are unimaginable too. According to economists Joseph E. Stiglitz and Linda Bilmes, Iraq alone will be a $3-trillion war. Those costs, and the other deficit spending of recent years, yield "virtually no room for new domestic initiatives for Mr. Obama or his successors," according to a *New York Times* budget analysis in February. Continued deficit financing for the Long War will rob today's younger generation of resources for their future.

The term "Long War" was first applied to America's post-9/11 conflicts in 2004 by Gen. John P. Abizaid, then head of U.S. Central Command, and by the retiring chairman of the Joint Chiefs of State, Gen. Richard B. Myers, in 2005.

According to David Kilcullen, a top counterinsurgency advisor to Army Gen. David H. Petraeus and a proponent of the Long War doctrine, the concept was polished in "a series of windowless offices deep inside the Pentagon" by a small team that successfully lobbied to incorporate the term into the 2006 Quadrennial Defense Review, the nation's long-term military blueprint. President George W. Bush declared in his 2006 State of the Union message that "our own generation is in a long war against a determined enemy."

The concept has quietly gained credence. *Washington Post* reporter-turned-author Thomas E. Ricks used "The Long War" as the title for the epilogue of his 2009 book on Iraq, in which he predicted that the U.S. was only halfway through the combat phase there.

It has crept into legal language. Federal Appeals Court Judge Janice Rogers Brown, a darling of the American right, recently ruled in favor of holding detainees permanently because otherwise, "each successful campaign of a long war would trigger an obligation to release Taliban fighters captured in earlier clashes."

Among defense analysts, Andrew J. Bacevich, a Vietnam veteran who teaches at Boston University, is the leading critic of the Long War doctrine, criticizing its origins among a "small, self-perpetuating, self-anointed group of specialists" who view public opinion "as something to manipulate" if they take it into consideration at all.

The Long War has momentum, though the term is absent from the 2010 Quadrennial Defense Review unveiled by Defense Secretary Robert M. Gates in February. One commentator has noted the review's apparent preference for finishing "our current wars before thinking about the next."

Still we fight wars that bleed into each other without clear end points. Political divisions in Iraq threaten to derail the complete withdrawal of U.S. troops scheduled for 2012.

As troop levels decline in Iraq, they grow to 100,000 in Afghanistan, where envoy Richard C. Holbrooke famously says we'll know success "when we see it." The Afghan war has driven Al Qaeda into Pakistan, where U.S. intelligence officers covertly collaborate with the Pakastani military. Lately our special forces have stepped up covert operations in Yemen.

It never ends. British security expert Peter Neumann at King's College has said that Europe is a "nerve center" of global jihad because of underground terrorists in havens protected by civil liberties laws. Could that mean NATO will have to occupy Europe?

It's time the Long War strategy was put under a microscope and made the focus of congressional hearings and media scrutiny. The American people deserve a voice in the strategizing that will affect their future and that of their grandchildren. There are at least three important questions to address in public forums:

—What is the role of the Long War idea in United States' policy now? Can the Pentagon or president impose such war-making decisions without debate and congressional ratification?

—Who exactly is the enemy in a Long War? Is Al Qaeda (or "Islamic fundamentalism") considered to be a unitary enemy like the "international communist conspiracy" was supposed to be? Can a Long War be waged with only a blanket authorization against every decentralized group lodged in countries from Europe to South Asia?

—Above all, what will a Long War cost in terms of American tax dollars, American lives and American respect in the world? Is it sustainable? If not, what are the alternatives?

President Obama has implied his own disagreement with the Long War doctrine without openly repudiating the term. He has pledged to remove all U.S. troops from Iraq by 2012, differing with those like Ricks who predict continuing combat, resulting in a Korean-style occupation. Obama also pledges to "begin" American troop withdrawals from Afghanistan by summer 2011, in contrast to those who demand we remain until an undefined victory. Obama told West Point cadets that "our troop commitment in Afghanistan cannot be open-ended, because the nation that I'm most interested in building is our own."

Those are naive expectations to neoconservatives and to some in the Pentagon for whom the Long War fills a vacuum left by the end of the Cold War. They will try to trap Obama in a Long War by demanding permanent bases in Iraq, slowing American withdrawals from Afghanistan to a trickle and defending secret operations in Pakistan. Where violence flares, he will be blamed for disengaging prematurely. Where situations stabilize, he will be counseled it's because we keep boots on the ground. We will keep spending dollars we don't have on wars without end.

The underlying issues should be debated now, before the future itself has been drafted for war.

Tom Hayden, a former California state senator, teaches a course on the Long War at Scripps College. He is the author of "The Long Sixties: From 1960 to Barack Obama."

30,000 Wrongs Won't Make It Right

Cindy Sheehan

I have had to reluctantly watch many presidential speeches since my son was killed in Iraq in 2004. I was even dragged out of a Bush State of the Union speech in 2006, that I didn't want to go to anyway, for just wearing a shirt with an anti-war message.

Now, I knew that Obama was going to announce that he would be condemning 30-35,000 more troops to Afghanistan(Pakistan): that wasn't exactly a state secret. I also knew that his speech would be filled with jingoistic propaganda—that's a given with presidential speeches—and the Pope of Hope is no different. However, I was not prepared for the physical sickness that overcame me while he was speaking. His delivery was wooden and not convincing, but the words tore my heart apart like I was a newby to presidential calumny.

I did not support Obama when he ran for president because he said he was going to send more troops to Afghanistan. He is a rare bird: a president that fulfills a campaign promise. I am not surprised, or disappointed, but I am filled with anger.

I am angry that thousands of more mothers will, without reason or rhyme, be served the unending pain of burying a child.

I was watching O'Bomber's speech tonight at a bar in Las Vegas after our protest at the Federal Building there and I was punched in the gut with Obama telling the Cadets at West Point that he has:

"As President, I have signed a letter of condolence to the family of each American who gives their life in these wars. I have read the letters from the parents and spouses of those who deployed. I have visited our courageous wounded warriors at Walter Reed. I have travelled to Dover to meet the flag-draped caskets of 18 Americans returning home to their final resting place. I see firsthand the terrible wages of war."

Just like goddamned George Bush and his evil vice-president, Obama has no freaking idea what the "terrible wages of war," are. Signing letters, or saluting caskets, or meeting with the wounded are NOT the same thing as receiving one of those letters, lying in one of those caskets or being maimed for the rest of your life. He has only "witnessed" the "terrible wages of war," from a remote viewing location that is filtered through the gauze of a deep disconnect from the violent pain that he is imposing.

Another thing—no one in our armed forces are "giving" their lives. No one has "given" his or her life for decades now, if ever, in our history. The people who have been killed in the Racket of War have had their lives STOLEN from them and their futures denied by chicken hawks who sign condolence letters in comfortable offices surrounded by millions of dollars of protection and by Congress members who also have no idea of the never-ending ache that is not dulled by time. Don't even start with the bullshit that our troops are "volunteers." If they are "volunteers" then I would suggest every one of them, or any one of them try to "volunteer" not to be deployed to Afghanistan.

December 7, 1941 was a day that has lived in "infamy" but it was not used to justify the waging of unending wars, even though our permanent bases still remain in Germany and Japan after 65 years. However, Obama again uses the attacks on 9-11 to justify this absolutely bat-shit crazy occupation of Afghanistan—no matter what he says, it IS an occupation. Tonight, in the speech he gave in front of his Cadet "props," Obama said that the attack on 9-11 was "vicious."

I agree that 9-11 was awful and it's a day that we surely will never forget, but if that was "vicious" then what does Obama call what America has been doing in Iraq-Af-Pak now for twice as many years as WWII lasted? What's worse than "vicious?" Genocide, that's what.

Genocide is the systematic killing of a racial or cultural group and please don't waste your time telling me that Obama has a "good heart" or "great intellect" because if he had either one of those things, the troops would be coming home by now.

Obama is just another coward that has risen to the highest office in the world and I am tired of having to be shoved by crazy people, chased and shot at by police, tear-gassed, arrested, called names that make even me blush, scrimping for every penny to stay afloat in this peace business, traveling and protesting to the point of exhaustion, etc. Not only did Obama condemn 30,000 troops to horror, with just one speech, he also condemned the real anti-war movement that was opposed to his policies from the beginning, to many more years of our sacrifices.

Well, I am not going to stop protesting and doing all of the above things, but I am not doing them for the rest of my life. If you believe in the mythical "drawdown" that Obama has just lied through his teeth about, then I ask you where did the "one combat battalion per month" out of Iraq go? Remember that promise? There has been no significant "drawdown" of troops from Iraq at all.

No matter what Obama says, these wars aren't "just" and we aren't "right" and we only have the "might" of the War Machine to open those "new markets" he talked about in his speech.

No matter what Obama says, these ARE open-ended wars, but I am NOT an open-ended anti-war activist.

We have to end them as soon as possible. We have to escalate our peace as the War Machine escalates its violence.

I Dreamed I Saw Casey Sheehan Last Night—to the Tune of Joe Hill (by Earl Robinson)

Submitted by Cindy Sheehan

I dreamed I saw Casey Sheehan last night
alive as you and me
Says I, "But Casey, you're two years dead,"
"I never died," says he, "I never died," says he.

"The oil bosses killed you my boy,
for greed and power they sent you to die"
"Takes more then greed to kill a man,"
Says Casey, "I didn't die," says Casey, "I didn't die."

And standing there as big as life
And smiling with his eyes
Casey, "What they forgot to kill
My mom went on to organize, she went on to organize."

"Casey Sheehan ain't dead," he said to me,
Casey Sheehan is now alive in all the people that I see..

From San Diego up to Maine
In every part of this land
Where people work for peace and our troops
It is there where I make my stand.......

Where people work for peace and our troops
It is there where I make my stand.

BUILDING AN ACROSS THE POLITICAL SPECTRUM MOVEMENT OPPOSED TO WAR AND EMPIRE

Delusions of Empire

(In the Spirit of William Appleman Williams)

Paul Buhle and Dave Wagner

The Situation Now

Our moment may be defined as a crisis of empire, of unsustainable expansion in the direct and residual costs of war.

Our delusion leads us to ignore impending bankruptcy, the fragility of a currency exposed to the mercy of competitor nations and the danger of the idea that wars may be pursued indefinitely without consequence: We imagine that continual war and occupation abroad and social improvements at home can be borne by a national government that remains solvent and limited.

Our political life is a stalemate. Our parties are held in low esteem because of the absence of either a true conservative party or true liberal party that can function independently of narrow interests. Each party promises movement, either backward into an imaginary past or forward into an equally imaginary future. Meanwhile, each successive administration continues the policies of its predecessor in a reckless plunge into unconstitutional government. One party discredits any change in social relations as a form of moral decline, the other promises changes it is unwilling or incapable of making. Each is dominated by corporations that have no loyalty to locale, region or nation. No social improvement (as in public health) is permissible unless it is defined as a technical adjustment in relations between predatory corporations and obese federal bureaucracies.

Because of the political myopia that is the cost of empire, no class is capable of working in the national interest. Our intellectual class relies on corporate foundations and declining government budgets, our financial class on government policies that guarantee not merely private incomes but unimaginably precarious risk. Our middle class holds itself hostage to a captive electoral system, and our working and impoverished classes are unable to assert their interests against those of empire, regardless of circumstance.

Erected on this trembling social fretwork is a foreign policy that is both naïve and brutal, based on the establishment of naval bases at every oceanic chokepoint to monitor the resource trade and on military bases established in virtually every country with a strategic topography and most aggressively in the Middle East and South Asia, with Iran the single prize beyond our grasp. Conservatives idealize this power while liberals ethicize it. Each side of the Moebius strip reveals its identity with the obverse and conceals the fact that it provides no end point and no escape.

The situation requires decisive change that grows out of a commitment to sustained action over the long term. We define the necessary change in the following eight points.

Toward the Demobilization of Empire: Eight Points

1. Demobilize and withdraw all U.S. troop from the Middle East, Asia, Africa and Europe.

2. Redeploy U.S. naval forces to the waters of the United States, territories and possessions.

3. Abolish covert intelligence operations as an instrument of executive authority.

4. Abolish all military treaties.

5. Withdraw from the WTO, NAFTA, CAFTA and related organizations and renegotiate hemispheric treaties based on fair trade at fair prices and reciprocal wages.

6. Dismantle resource corporations that require U.S. military assistance for the recovery, transportation or processing of any goods. Break up vertical integration in any industry as a matter of policy.

7. Dismantle the largest U.S. banks and retract the bank charter of all former investment banks to close their access the federal discount window. Defund Treasury guarantees of all proprietary investments, including derivatives. Create publicly owned clearing houses for and require the public registration on the Internet of all instruments of collateralized and sercuritized debt.

8. Convert idled military resources where feasible to pure scientific research and applied technology dedicated to a rapid, climate-appropriate reindustrialization of the U.S. economy, supported by trade, tariff, tax and credit policies.

Organizing against Empire—Where Left and Right Meet...Amicably

Paul Buhle

Over a conference table at a Washington hotel on February 20, a couple dozen antiwar activists and intellectuals, yours truly included, met to hash out the beginnings of a most unusual movement. We wanted to end American war and American Empire, against the evident bipartisan determination to keep both of them going.

There never was such a boundary-crossing event before, at least not in my 50 year political lifetime or any historical incident that I can recall.

Not quite true. The Populists, arguably the one literal grassroots movement that most nearly overturned the two party system in a handful of states, brought together a kind of cultural conservatism, bathed in scorn of city life, and political radicalism. The antiwar movement of the 1910s made Republican German-and Scandinavian-Americans of the northern Midwest and Great Plains states turn to the Farmer-Labor movement, under a variety of names, and again, in the middle 1930s, to join campus antiwar activists in resisting the militarization of American culture. Even as Pearl Harbor drew close, Norman Thomas stood on platforms with outspoken conservatives urging some other solution than US entry with the inevitable counterparts of conscription, loss of civil liberties, etc. They were wrong about the war but, at least after Truman came to power, right after all about the doleful consequences of mobilization for war. The big state, with its military-industrial part not at all benign, was here to stay.

Even these past sagas, now relegated to a kind of pre-history, seem very different from the little gathering of magazine editors, journalists, youth activists against war. We live in a time so strange that several nineteen year olds joined us, devotees of maverick Texas congressman Ron Paul, who had been at the conservative CPAC convention the day before, on their feet cheering Paul's call for an end to US occupations overseas while neocon elders sat in their chairs, glowering. A time so strange that these kids sat a few seats away from Jon Berger, the SDSer on hand, reminding me of my own SDS days and the historic moment when isolationists joined us against the Vietnam War. The shared sentiment never became a real movement forty years ago, but this time it might.

The editors of *The Nation, American Conservative, Reason,* The Progressive Review (on line), Black Agenda Report (on radio) and the *Veterans for Peace Newsletter* were all very much were on the scene, although perhaps not so prominent as notables Ralph Nader or William Greider. The event-coordinator, Kevin Zeese, is director of Voters for Peace but perhaps better remembered as a longtime, prominent figure urging an end to the drug war.

The premise was simple, if difficult to grasp entirely at first: the crisis of empire has generated a wave of distrust, making a sense of outrage simultaneous among erstwhile Leftwing enthusiasts of Obama (this writer included) and Rightwingers who get labeled "Isolationist" but cannot be pinned down precisely on issues beyond their opposition to US interventions, occupations and military bases abroad. Well, it does sound simple. Perhaps the real problem has been a lack of trust among varied opponents of war, a combination of the usual Lesser Evil voting and a growing, parallel if not mutual sense of political despair.

There proved ample room for agreement as well as disagreement, summed up for me in one exchange. I proposed a return to the late 19th century title, "American Anti-Imperialist League," set up by Boston Brahmins to oppose the bloody war on the Philippines. A conservative sitting improbably to my left complained that the phrase "anti-imperialist" brought visions to his reader of Jane Fonda, whereas "opposition to empire" would give them a proper perspective. (I was loath to mention what recovered past visions of Jane Fonda might do to, or for, me.) In other words, the invasions of Iraq and Afghanistan made us both rage and weep, while the remembrance of the 1960s made him rage and me weep…with nostalgia.

We had, however, the same goal: bring the troops home now. And we had better learn to work on that together, somehow or other, if we didn't want rightwingers gulled by Sarah Palin and leftwingers waiting, waiting and waiting hopelessly for Obama to do the right thing globally.

It's easy for either side to project nuttiness in the other. Speaking only for myself, I have a useful yardstick for these particular conservatives' favorite politician: I ask myself whether Ron Paul is crazier than my evangelical relatives. The answer is personally satisfying, even when Paul goes off on a tangent about abolishing the Fed (well, not a bad idea) or something about immigration that I do not like at all.

Veteran peace mobilizers, like Sam Smith, Mike McPherson of Veterans for Peace, and young peace mobilizers, like the SDS activist Jon Berger from the University of Maryland, offered some of the most useful, i.e., practical reflections and questions of the day. How would a multiracial coalition of antiwar conservatives and radicals operate? And how would they overcome what remains a crucial distinction between distaste and disillusion toward a president whose election seemed so promising (alternatively: threatening, at least frustrating) but whose global military strategy was and is dead certain to remain both catastrophically expensive and just plain awful?

There aren't any easy answers, but the route toward them must lie in a better understanding, and that, at least, seems to have been achieved.

At the end of this day, the presence of the vanden Heuvel-style mover-shakers on various points of the spectrum might well have been the most impressive fact in evidence. It wasn't, because their affable expressions mirrored something deeper, the ground changing beneath all our feet.

Somehow, the delayed crash of Cold War Liberalism may finally have happened, as it could not happen under either Clinton (the male one) or Bush. It is awfully hard to see what lays on the other side, but as aging Pan African giant CLR James wrote after reading *The Gulag Archipelago:* "at least we know." The bipartisan military-industrial empire has hit the skids and may be in ruins the day after tomorrow, so to speak. At any rate, their Demo-Republican credibility is gone. Now the rest of us had better speak up and begin organizing alternatives.

Paul Buhle, founder-editor of the SDS journal *Radical America* in the 1960s, is a historian of the American Left and in recent years, an editor of nonfiction comic books, including *The Beats: a Graphic History.*

The Heroic Left-Right Peace Conference

Matt Cockerill at 8:11 AM, February 25, 2010

Dan McCarthy of the *American Conservative* invited YAL's Nick Leavens, Shaun Bowen, and me to attend a bipartisan peace conference last week. Attendees came to the meeting hoping to form a broad antiwar coalition. Disagreements arose, but we were unified in opposition to Obama's wars and the bipartisan foreign policy of empire.

The meeting, organized by Voters for Peace chair Kevin Zeese, and former Pat Buchanan campaign official George O'Neill, included in its guestlist:

An economist from a naval war college who previously served as the chief energy economist in President Reagan's Council of Economic Advisers.

Two officials of Veterans for Peace, including the organization's chief executive.

Katrina vanden Heuvel, publisher of *The Nation,* aka "The flagship of the left."

A regular contributor to *Rolling Stone,* and a contributing editor at *The Nation.*

A Senior Fellow at the Cato Institute.

An editor from *Reason* magazine.

Independent Journalist Sam Smith of *Progressive Review.*

Peace activist Murray Polner, who coauthored a book with Tom Woods.

A student leader of the famous Students for a Democratic Society (SDS).

Ralph Nader. Yes, that Ralph Nader.

Author Bill Kauffmann, who seeks to revive Old Right-style antiwar conservativism

American Conservative senior Editor Dan McCarthy, along with us YAL kids.

Sound bipolar? You have no idea. Yet our interactions were cordial and productive. Good ideas that attendees came up with included:

A bipartisan press release of sorts, against the wars and the empire.

Establishing a website with a cohesive, unifying mission statement.

A cross-country campus tour, whereby liberal and conservatives activists would together speak against the wars.

Pro-peace student groups on the left and the right working together.

Outreach to key groups such as veterans, academics, and business leaders.

I bet a formidable coalition will come out of this. These weren't political hacks, but true believers in peace. Keep your eyes pealed for future updates about this at yaliberty.org. We'll be looking for authentic and articulate anti-war folks of all ideologies.

Peace coalition aside, meeting Ralph Nader by itself was worth attending the conference. He was smart, authentic, and a real gentleman.

Carl Oglesby Was Right

Daniel McCarthy, March 05 2010, *American Conservative*

The tail end of last week was a busy time for TAC staff. Thursday, which was also the first day of CPAC, was our print date. I made it to the conclave just long enough to emcee Thomas DiLorenzo's talk, "Lincoln on Liberty: Friend or Foe?", before hotfooting it back to the office for a last round of proofreading.

As big as CPAC was this year, particularly with Ron Paul's stunning straw-poll win, for me the biggest event of the weekend was a 40-person conference I attended on Saturday, a gathering of progressives, libertarians, conservatives, and radicals opposed to militarism. Some of the other attendees have already blogged about their impressions (vide Jesse Walker, Michael McPhearson, Sam Smith, David Henderson, and co-organizer Kevin Zeese). For my part, I've been sanguine about the prospects for Left-Right cooperation against the warfare state since the run-up to the Iraq War in 2002. Subsequently it's only become more obvious that the old political-cultural divisions established during the 1960s are now moot. Neither the Cold War nor the culture war tells us much about what needs to be done in a world wracked by terror, hot wars, and teetering financial systems. These crises are not novel in the abstract, but their manifestations today—under conditions of U.S. hegemony and the rise of nonstate actors—are profoundly different from what Americans experienced in the mid-to-late 20th century.

Moreover, the strategic and economic crises confronting the U.S. are not entirely separate beasts. One theme that emerged at the conference from both Left and Right was the recognition that we cannot afford the foreign policy we have. Libertarians, conservatives, and progressives would all like to have that "peace dividend" we were promised after the fall of the Berlin Wall, even if we might put it to different uses. Almost any use would be better than perpetuating our self-destabilizing attempts to manage the globe, from Mesopotamia to the Caucasus to Latin America.

Surprisingly, the shift from the previous Left-Right spectrum to a new continuum has already had practical consequences. Ron Paul and Barack Obama both attest to this, albeit in radically different ways: Paul was sidelined in the old Left-Right fights, as a strict constitutionalist whose interests in monetary policy and noninterventionism seemed out of place in the era of identity politics. Yet suddenly he's become a timely figure, a hero not only to libertarians and Old Right conservatives, but to a fair number of progressives. Obama also received support from some unexpected quarters, including conservative dissidents like Jeffrey Hart and Christopher Buckley and others not accustomed to voting Democratic (or at all), though Obama swiftly betrayed whatever hopes his new supporters had for him. The Democrats' meteoric descent illustrates just how poorly Obama and the congressional majority understood the forces that had elected them.

Ralph Nader, by contrast, who spoke at Saturday's gathering, has a pretty firm grasp on what's going on. His talk impressed me on a number of scores. At times, in emphasizing the primacy of Congress in the constitutional system and the importance of localism, he sounded almost like Willmoore Kendall. Even his anti-corporate philosophy is not something conservatives or libertarians ought to dismiss too readily. His objections to corporate personhood are very much in line with Felix Morley's objections. Morley didn't want to attack corporations, but he understood that the abuse of the 14th Amendment was giving the federal government and corporations together power to steamroll over the states and individuals. (See Morley's *Freedom and Federalism* for more on this.)

Nader's views on campaign-finance restrictions, on the other hand, I find quite unpalatable. David Henderson has some notes on that here. I don't think it's too much of a barrier to cooperation on other issues. (What's more, there is some very quiet pro-campaign-finance-reform sentiment on the Right, though I'm in the anti camp myself.)

I'm skeptical of what under-funded advocacy groups can achieve in politics, but there are at least a few steps a Left-Right coalition can take toward cracking the ideological ice of contemporary politics. There are significant differences of principle among the journalists, intellectuals, and activists who attended the meeting, but that doesn't mean cooperation has to be unprincipled. As my headline suggests, I think Carl Oglesby was on to something when he suggested that the Old Right and New Left have (some) common ground. Oglesby's 1967 thoughts on the topic (from *Containment and Change*) were included in the conference's reading packet, and they're worth quoting at length:

It would be a piece of great good fortune for America and the world if the libertarian right could be reminded that besides the debased Republicanism of the Knowlands and the Judds there is another tradition available to them—their own: the tradition of Congressman Howard Buffett, Senator Taft's midwestern campaign manager in 1952, who attacked the Truman Doctrine with the words: "Our Christian ideals cannot be exported to other lands by dollars and guns... We cannot practice might and force abroad and retain freedom at home. We cannot talk world cooperation and practice power politics." There is the right of Frank Chodorov, whose response to the domestic Red Menace was abruptly to the point: "The way to get rid of communists in government jobs is to abolish the jobs." And of Dean Russell, who wrote in 1955: "Those who advocate the 'temporary loss' of our freedom in order to preserve it permanently are advocating only one thing: the abolition of liberty... We are rapidly becoming a caricature of the thing we profess to hate." Most engaging, there is the right of the tough-minded Garet Garrett, who produced in 1952 a short analysis of the totalitarian impulse of imperialism which the events of the intervening years have reverified over and again. Beginning with the words, "We have crossed the boundary that lies between Republic and Empire," Garrett's pamphlet unerringly names the features of the imperial pathology: dominance of the national executive over Congress, court, and Constitution; subordination of domestic policy to foreign policy; ascendency of the military influence; the creation of political and military satellites; a complex of arrogance and fearfulness toward the "barbarian"; and, most insidiously, casting off the national identity—the republic is free; the empire is history's hostage.

This style of political thought, rootedly American, is carried forward today by the Negro freedom movement and the student movement against Great Society-Free World imperialism. That these movements are called leftist means nothing. They are of the grain of American humanist individualism and voluntaristic associational action; and it is only through them that the libertarian tradition is activated and kept alive. In a strong sense, the Old Right and the New Left are morally and politically coordinate.

Yet their intersection can be missed. Their potentially redemptive union can go unattempted and unmade. On both sides, vision can be cut off by habituated responses to passé labels. The New Left can lose itself in the imported left-wing debates of the thirties, wondering what it ought to say about technocracy and Stalin. The libertarian right can remain hypnotically charmed by the authoritarian imperialists whose only ultimate love is the subhuman brownshirted power of the jingo state militant, the state rampant, the iron state possessed of its own clanking glory.

"Just War" Is Just Words

By Ralph Nader

Friday, December 11. 2009
In the Public Interest

President Obama, the Afghan war escalator, received the Nobel Peace Prize in Oslo, Norway, and proceeded to deliver his acceptance speech outlining the three criteria for a "just war" which he himself is violating.

The criteria are in his words: "If it is waged as a last resort or in self-defense; if the force used is proportional; and if, whenever possible, civilians are spared from violence."

After 9/11, warmonger George W. Bush could have used the international law doctrine of hot pursuit with a multilateral force of commandoes, linguists and bribers to pursue the backers of the attackers. Instead, he blew the country of Afghanistan apart and started occupying it, joined forces with a rump regime and launched a divide-and-rule tribal strategy that set the stage for a low-tiered civil war.

Eight years later, Obama is expanding the war within a graft-ridden government in Kabul, fraudulent elections, an Afghan army of northern tribesmen loathed by the southern and south-eastern tribes of 40 million Pashtuns, an impoverished economy whose largest crop by far is a narcotic, and a devastated population embittered by foreign occupiers and non-existent government services.

President Obama's national security adviser, former Marine General James Jones, said two months ago: "The al-Qaeda presence is very diminished. The maximum estimate is less than 100 operating in the country, no bases, no ability to launch attacks on either us or our allies."

Since Mr. Obama repeats George W. Bush's reason for going into Afghanistan—to destroy al-Qaeda—why is he sending 30,000 more soldiers plus an even greater number of corporate contractors there in the near future at a cost stated by the White House of one million dollars per solider per year? Is this "proportional force"?

Always small in number, al-Qaeda has moved over the border into Pakistan and anywhere its supporters can in the world—east Africa, north Africa, Indonesia. The gang is a migrant traveler.

Is Obama pouring soldiers into Afghanistan so that they and our inaccurate, civilian-destroying drones can expand the fighting across the border in Pakistan, as indicated by the *New York Times*? Beyond the violations of international law and absence of constitutional authorization involved, this could so roil Pakistanis as to make the U.S. experience next door look like a modest struggle.

Obama has emphasized weakening the Taliban as the other objective of our military buildup with its horrible consequence in casualties and other costs. Who are the Taliban? They include people with different causes, such as protecting their valleys, drug trafficking to live on, fighters against foreign occupiers or, being mostly Pashtuns, protecting their tribal turf against the northern Tajiks and Uzbeks.

How many Taliban fighters are there? The Pentagon estimates around 25,000. Their methods make them unpopular with the villagers. They have no air force, navy, artillery, tanks, missiles, no bases, no central command. They have rifles, grenade launchers, bombs and suiciders. Unlike al-Qaeda, they have only domestic ambitions counteracted by their adversarial tribesmen who make up most of the Afghan army.

Robert Baer, former CIA officer with experience in that part of Asia, asserted: "The people that want their country liberated from the West have nothing to do with al-Qaeda. They simply want us gone because we're foreigners, and they're rallying behind the Taliban because the Taliban are experienced, effective fighters."

To say as Obama inferred in his Oslo speech that the greater plunge into Afghanistan is self-defense, with proportional force and sparing civilians from violence is a scale of self-delusion or political cowardliness that is dejecting his liberal base.

For as President Eisenhower stated so eloquently in his 1953 "cross of iron" speech, every dollar spent on munitions and saber-rattling takes away from building schools, clinics, roads and other necessities of the American people.

The Afghan War and the Iraq war-occupation—already directly costing a trillion dollars—are costing the American people every time Washington says there is not enough money for neonatal care, occupational disease prevention, cleaner drinking water systems, safer hospitals, prosecution of corporate criminals, cleaner air or upgrading and repairing key public facilities.

Even the hardiest and earliest supporters of his presidential campaign in 2008 are speaking out. Senior members of the Congressional Black Caucus, such as John Conyers (D-MI) and Maxine Waters (D-CA) have recently criticized the President for not doing enough to help African-Americans weather the hard times.

In a stinging ironic rebuke to the first African-American President, Rep. Waters declared "We can no longer afford for our public policy to be defined by the worldview of Wall Street."

According to Congressman Conyers, an upset Barack Obama called to ask why the Michigan lawmaker was "demeaning" him. Conyers has been increasingly turned off by the President's policies—among them health care reform, the war in Afghanistan, slippage on Guantanamo and the extension of the Patriot Act's invasive provisions.

The 80-year old Congressman spent most weekends in 2007 and 2008 tirelessly on the campaign trail trying to get Obama elected.

White House aides are not troubled by the rumblings from the moderate Left. They said they have all of 2010 to bring them back into the fold by the November Congressional elections. Besides, where else are they going to go?

Well, they could stay home. Remember 1994 and the Gingrich takeover.

Left and Right Against War

Murray Polner

"Ours is a world of nuclear giants and ethical infants. We know more about war than we know about peace, more about killing than we know about living."
—General Omar Bradley

"Canada must be ours [say the war hawks]. We have nothing to do but to march into Canada and display the standard of the U.S., and the Canadians will immediately flock to it."
—Rep. Samuel Taggart, 1812

The United States of America has historically been addicted to war, an addiction that persists today more than ever with a vast "national security" apparatus, over 700 military bases, and a nation torn between those who believe in military intervention for humanitarian causes and those who extol war as a way of maintaining the country's worldwide hegemony. Now we are faced with endless wars in the Middle East as the drums are beating for war against Iran in Washington, Jerusalem and western European capitals.

Several years ago Thomas Woods, Jr. asked me to collaborate with him in a book we titled *We Who Dared to Say No to War: American Antiwar Writing from 1812 to Now* (Basic Books, 2008). We intended to portray a broad American antiwar tradition often absent from classrooms, films, television and the new media. Tom is a libertarian and conservative and I a left-liberal and believer in nonviolent activism. We differ on some things but not on our opposition to our nation's reliance on war and conquest (as well as our mutual support for civil liberties).

We have no illusions that our book can deter contemporary warmakers or outwit the fabrications and manipulations of governments and propagandists past and present. We were (and are) instead motivated by the hope that arguments for war might be critically examined, as the men and women of different political persuasions we include in the book did in their time. To quote from our introduction, we intend the book to be "a surprising and welcome change from the misleading liberal-peace/conservative-war dichotomy that the media and our educational establishment and popular culture have done so much to foster."

During our efforts to find appropriate and effective essays, speeches and documents, I turned to Americans who had shaped my own thoughts about war: Randolph Bourne, the physically handicapped prophet who died far too young (at 32) but memorably wrote that "war is the health of the state"; Robert A. Taft, bitterly assailed as an isolationist—in truth, he was very suspicious about military interventions—who rightly condemned the undeclared entry into the Korean War, where some 38,000 GIs died, many more were wounded in body and mind and several million Korean civilians killed, saying "the President has no right to involve the United States in a foreign war"; Russell Kirk, the founder of postwar American conservatism, urging "a policy of patience and prudence" against "preventive war" and decrying how "a handful of individuals...made it their business to extirpate the populations of Nagasaki and Hiroshima"; and a man I proudly voted for in 1972, George McGovern, who publicly excoriated his pro-war senatorial colleagues by describing each of them as "partly responsible for sending 50,000 young Americans to an early grave." "This chamber," said this onetime World War II bomber pilot unforgettably, "reeks of blood," adding Edmund Burke's cautionary words: "A conscientious man would be cautious how he dealt in blood."

Unsurprisingly, we found that the arguments used for war today are the same ones that have been employed in all our wars. We begin with Daniel Webster's speech in December 1814 after the War Hawks (a term coined during America's aggressive war to capture Canada) urged a draft: "Where is it written in the Constitution," he asked, "in what article or section is it contained, that you may take children from their parents, and parents from their children, and compel them to fight the battles of any war in which the folly of the wickedness of Government may engage it?"

For the U.S. government's war of aggression against Mexico in 1846–48 we include (among numerous others) the abolitionist William Goodell, who called President Polk's invasion a "war for slavery." In another selection then-Representative Abraham Lincoln denounced the Mexican War, calling Polk's war message "the half-mumbling of a fever dream" and Polk a "bewildered, confounded, and miserably perplexed man."

Before the U.S. entered World War I, Eugene Debs, the Socialist labor leader, spoke truth to power: It is "the working class who freely shed their bloods and furnish the corpses." Debs received a ten-year prison sentence for that speech. Senator George Norris, the progressive Republican from Nebraska (the Midwestern states once had many such Republican politicians) who condemned U.S. entry into WWI and their advocates, likewise condemned war profiteering: "Their object in having war and in preparing for war is to make money."

That, incidentally, isn't a problem that has gone away. Think of contemporary war profiteers who have made so much money in Iraq and Afghanistan, while a threatened war with Iran promises untold riches as well. Add to this the hysteria generated during the Cold War, a frenzy which consistently and deliberately exaggerated Soviet military capabilities while frightening many Americans. (See, for example, the declassified documents released in September 2009 by George Washington University's private National Security Archive.)

These are tough words, echoed by so many men and women (Helen Keller, Jane Addams, Jeannette Rankin, Rep. Barbara Lee, Gold Star mothers, etc.) whose words we sought to rescue from obscurity. Had we more room we would also have written about the military decimation of our Native American tribes and the habitual interference in the affairs of Caribbean and Central American states.

What we learned in writing this book was that lies, deliberate manipulation of patriotic feelings, scare tactics, a compliant, often indifferent media, and bribery of legislators kept and keeps the war machine oiled and too many decision makers in clover. Virtually everything heard in the past is still heard today. We quoted William Jay's observation after the invasion of Mexico: "We have been taught to ring our bells, and illuminate our windows and let off fireworks as manifestations of our joy, when we have heard of great ruin and devastation, and misery, and death, inflicted by our troops upon a people who never injured us, who never fired a shot on our soil and who were utterly incapable of acting on the offensive against us."

And we concluded, "Everything we've seen recently, we've seen before. Time and again."

In the end, I have personal favorites: William Graham Sumner, an irascible Yale academic who opposed the Spanish-American and Philippine-American wars and the nation's growing appetite for imperial conquest and world power; Marine Commandant David Shoup, who said of our Vietnam adventure, "Let's Mind Our Business"; and W. D. Ehrhart, a combat Marine veteran of Vietnam, who enlisted at age 18 and years later told students at a Pennsylvania school, "I am no longer convinced that what I owe to my country is military service whenever and wherever my government demands it… if I owe something to my country, my country also owes something to me…it owes us the obligation not to ask for our lives unless it is absolutely necessary." Then there is Howard Zinn, WWII bombardier turned pacifist, who argues, "We need to refute the idea that our nation is different from, morally superior to, other imperial powers of world history" and instead "assert our allegiance to the human race, and not to any one nation." Libertarian Lew Rockwell writes, "Do we reject war and all its works? We do reject them." Especially moving is the contribution of Andrew Bacevich, a Vietnam War veteran, Boston University professor, and father of a son killed in Iraq, whose distressing "I Lost My Son to a War I Oppose; We Were Both Doing Our Duty" is unforgettable.

Our book will not change the course of history. Still, it reflects our mission, our passion: to encourage debate and discussion, in our nation's classrooms as well as among our compatriots, now drowning in a mass culture that celebrates trivia—"amusing themselves to death" in the late Neil Postman's incisive words. Tom Woods and I would like to encourage an alternative patriotism that goes not abroad every few years to seek and destroy real and imagined "enemies" while sacrificing a new generation of our young.

October 1, 2009

Eight Hours in the Basement for Peace

Sam Smith

Progressive Review

Last Saturday I spent eight hours with three dozen other people in a basement conference room of a Washington hotel engaged in an extraordinary exercise of mind and hope.

The topic was, by itself, depressingly familiar: building an anti-war coalition. What made it so strikingly different was the nature of those at the table. They included progressives, conservatives, traditional liberals and libertarians. Some reached back to the Reagan years or to 1960s activism, some—including an SDS leader from the University of Maryland and several Young Americans for Liberty—were still in college.

In a time when politics is supposed to be hopelessly polarized along the lines proposed by Glenn Beck and Keith Olbermann, the most heated debate occurred not between left and right but over tactics between Ralph Nader and Bill Greider.

There was an economics professor from a naval war college and the executive director of Veterans for Peace; there was Katrina vanden Heuvel, editor of the *Nation,* me from the *Progressive Review,* and editors from the *American Conservative* and *Reason* magazine.

The session had been conceived by long time activist and current head of Voters for Peace, Kevin Zeese, along with artist George D. O'Neill, Jr. who had been chair of the Rockford Institute, a leading traditional conservative intellectual think tank in the 1980s, and who had worked on Pat Buchanan's 1992 presidential campaign.

What we shared was an antipathy towards war. It was not so much that we were anti-war as we were seeking a post-war world. Our approaches might differ but our goals were, at worst, next door.

As Zeese put it in an introduction to the session, it was about "views from the right, left and radical center, views that reflect those of many Americans which are not represented in the political dialogue in Congress or the White House, or the mainstream media. Throughout American history there have been times when movements developed that were outside the limited political dialogue of the two major parties…

"Polling actually shows majorities often oppose war and escalation of war. But these views are not represented in government or the media. In addition, opposition to war is not limited to people on the left; it covers the American political spectrum and it always has. There is a long history of opposition to war among traditional conservatives. Their philosophy goes back to President Washington's Farewell Address where he urged America to avoid 'foreign entanglements.' It has showed itself throughout American history. The Anti-Imperialist League opposed the colonialism of the Philippines in the 1890s. The largest anti-war movement in history, the America First Committee, opposed World War II and had a strong middle America conservative foundation in its make-up. The strongest speech of an American president against militarism was President Eisenhower's 1961 final speech from the White House warning America against the growing military-industrial complex. In recent years the militarist neo-conservative movement has become dominate of conservatism in the United States. Perhaps none decry this more than traditional conservatives who oppose massive military budgets, militarism and the American empire.

"Of course, the left also has a long history of opposition to war from the Civil War to early imperialism in the Philippines, World Wars I and II through Vietnam, Iraq and Afghanistan. It includes socialists, Quakers, social justice Catholics and progressives. Indeed, the opposition to entry into World War I was led by the left including socialists, trade unionists, pacifists including people like union leader and presidential candidate Eugene Debs, Nobel Peace Prize winner Jane Addams and author and political activist Helen Keller…

"Opposition to Vietnam brought together peace advocates with the civil rights movement, highlighted by Dr. Martin Luther King, Jr.'s outspoken opposition to the war…

"What are the ingredients for a successful anti-war, pro-peace movement?

—The anti-war movement needs to be a reflection of not just the left but of Middle America and traditional conservatives who oppose war.

—A successful anti-war peace movement cannot give up the flag of patriotism. It needs to grab hold of America's patriotic impulses and show the United States can be the nation many imagine us to be—leading by positive example, helping in crisis, being a force for good, rather than propagating military dominance and hegemony.

—A successful anti-war movement needs to be a place where veterans, from grunts to generals, can openly participate, share their stories and explain the lessons they learned from American militarism.

—A well organized anti-war movement will have committees not only reaching out to military and business, but to academics, students, clergy, labor, nurses, doctors, teachers and a host of others.

—The 1960s tactics of big marches and congressional demonstrations have their role but they are not sufficient. The media and government have adjusted to them. We need to use tools like voter initiatives and referenda to break through and put our issues before the voters. And, we need to learn from around the world what has worked; for example, general strikes, whether of a few hours or few days, have shown unified opposition to government policy

—Make war relevant to Americans' day-to-day lives by constantly linking the cost of war to their communities, incomes, and bank accounts. People need to learn that Empire is not good for the U.S. economy.

—Both parties are dominated by pro-militarist elected officials. The anti-war movement needs to be strong in criticizing candidates who call for a larger military, escalation of war, or other militarist policies."

Clips from the bios of those at the session suggest the unusual cross-ideological and cross-cultural presence:

—A Senior Fellow at the Cato Institute. He also is the Robert A. Taft Fellow at the American Conservative Defense Alliance and served as a Special Assistant to President Ronald Reagan.

—His leading work includes a biography of historian William A. Williams, the *Encyclopedia of the American Left,* five volumes on the lives and work of the Hollywood Blacklistees,…and eight volumes of nonfiction comic art (adaptations of Howard Zinn and Studs Terkel, graphic biographies of Isadora Duncan and Emma Goldman, *The Beats, The Art of Harvey Kurtzman,* etc).

—He has been a regular contributor to *Rolling Stone,* and currently covers national security for its National Affairs section. He is a contributing editor at *The Nation,* a contributing writer at *Mother Jones,* and a senior correspondent for *The American Prospect.*

—An associate professor of economics at the Naval Postgraduate School in Monterey, California and a Research Fellow with the Hoover Institution at Stanford University. From 1982 to 1984, he was the senior economist for health policy, and from 1983 to 1984 he was the senior economist for energy policy, with President Reagan's Council of Economic Advisers.

—Founding member of the Washington chapter of the National Association of Black Journalists; executive board member of the National Alliance of Third World Journalists…

—Founding Managing Editor and current Executive Editor of *The American Conservative.* Research director of Pat Buchanan's 2000 campaign.

—Executive Director of Veterans For Peace. His volunteer social and economic justice activist work include membership in Military Families Speak Out, coordinating committee member for the Bring Them Home Now campaign against the U.S. occupation of Iraq and Co-Chair of United for Peace and Justice.

—Legislative aide for the armed services for Senator Robert Taft, Jr., of Ohio from 1973 through 1976 and held a similar position with Senator Gary Hart of Colorado from 1977 through 1986. An opponent of the Iraq War, has written for the *Marine Corps Gazette,* and *Defense and the National Interest…*

—For over four decades has exposed problems and organized millions of citizens into more than 100 public interest groups to advocate for solutions…

—Active within the Democratic, Republican, and Green parties at various times. As a boy, he supported George McGovern for president in 1972 partly because of the Democrat's anti-war stance. In the mid 1970s, he became a conservative who backed Ronald…

—Managing editor of *Reason* magazine, is the author of *Rebels on the Air: An Alternative History of Radio in America.*

Notably absent from the session were members of the extremist center, liberal professors seeking to prove their manhood by backing yet another war, legislators afraid to challenge the Pentagon, belligerent bullies and the cowardly complacent. And everyone in the room was trying something different.

Which, when you come to think of it, is just what happens when you make peace. People who have been shooting at each other sit down and find a way to share some space. One might expect that anti-war activists would understand this, but too often we all regard our political beliefs not as the product of imperfect and struggling minds but as our sacred identity, our justification and our privileged demographic. We reduce politics to the theology of the self-righteous rather than as an imperfect search for better times.

As I sat around that table, I tried to recall those few occasions when I had experienced something close to this—few, that is, since the days when I sat around the family table as the third child of six and learned about living with those different from oneself and more than willing to say so.

Some of the later times worked; some didn't. One that worked was the anti-freeway coalition of the 1960s and 70s that kept Washington from becoming another Los Angeles. It was started by among the least likely activists—black and white middle class homeowners whose neighborhood was about to be ruined. It expanded to include those of us in the civil rights group SNCC as well as the all white Georgetown Citizens Association. I once wrote of the leader, "By all rights, Sammie Abbott should have been disqualified as a DC leader on at least three grounds: he was too white, he was too old, and he lived in the suburbs. Instead, this short man with a nail-file voice became the nemesis of public officials for years. Abbott, the grandson of Arab Christians who fled Turkish persecution in Syria, had been a labor organizer, a bricklayer and a World War II veteran with a Bronze Star."

There was only one qualification to join the anti-freeway movement: opposition to freeways. And the success of our effort—rare among such highway protests—left a mark on a city colony devoid of rights and helps to explain how—just two years after the riots—we were able to form a biracial third party that would hold seats on the city council and/or school board for 25 years.

I would come to think of it as existential politics—in which one defined one's existence by one's actions rather than by one's ethnicity, class, party registration or magazine subscriptions. And it was a sort of politics that would become increasingly rare.

But it didn't always work. In the mid sixties, I was editing a neighborhood newspaper in Washington's biracial Capitol East. Things were already well beyond the capacity of any one community to solve. America's cities were starting to burn and you could feel the heat even in Capitol East. In September 1967, anti-poverty activist Lola Singletary convinced the white businessmen of H Street to form a organization dedicated to involvement in community problems.

In late 1967 I came up with the idea of pulling together the various leaders of Capitol East into an informal leadership council with the possibility of forming a major neighborhood coalition. Fourteen people attended a meeting on January 31: 7 white and 7 black. Among our purposes:

—To share our group differences so we can increase our knowledge of one another's group positions, plans and needs.

—To increase opportunities to share our group concerns so that we can better support one another's group efforts.

—To unite in common action where we have agreement.

It was too late. A little more than two months later, the riots broke out and Capitol East had two of the four major riot strips, including H Street. Hope had burned up as well.

Then in 1995, as part of the Green Politics Network, I joined a number of other Greens in hosting a conference of third party activists. Over a hundred showed up, ranging from one of the founders of the American Labor Party to Greens, Libertarians, Perot backers, Democratic Socialists of America, and followers of Lenora Fulani. It was a recklessly dangerous idea for a Washington weekend, but John Rensenbrink, Linda Martin, and Tony Affigne seemed to know what they were doing and I was happy to go along. We established two basic rules:

—We would only discuss issues on which we might find some agreement.

—We would reach that agreement by consensus.

I was one of the kickoff speakers and said:

"As a simple empirical matter you can say that one of the great characteristics of Americans is not merely opposition to a system of the moment but antipathy towards unnatural systems in general—opposition to all systems that revoke, replace or restrain the natural rights of humans and the natural blessings of their habitats.

"This, I think, is why we are here today. If nothing else binds us it is an understanding of the damage that heartless, leaderless, mindless systems have done to the specifics of our existence…

"Further, in our distaste with the systems suffocating our lives, we are very much in the mainstream. These systems have done half our work for us, they have lost the people's faith…

"We must stake out a position with real programs for real people, with our enthusiasm on our sleeve and our ideology in our pocket, with small words and big hearts, and—most of all—with a clear vision of what a better future might look like. We must tackle what Chesterton called the "huge modern heresy of altering the human soul to fit its conditions, instead of altering human conditions to fit the human soul."…

"This then is our task. Let's embrace it not as sectarians or as prigs but as a happy fellow members of a new mainstream. Not as radicals permanently in exile but as moderates of an age that has not quite arrived. Let's laugh and make new friends and be gentle with one another. Let's remember Camus' dictum that the only sin we are not permitted is despair…"

Despite the wide range of views present, despite the near total absence of Robert's Rules of Order, the final document, with full consensus, called for nothing less than a major transformation. The group unanimously agreed to support proportional representation, campaign finance reform "to provide a level playing field in elections;" initiative, referendum and recall; better ballot access; the end of corporate welfare; strong environmental policies; sexual and reproductive freedom; an end to the war on drugs and treatment of addiction as a health matter rather than as a crime; a dramatic cut in military expenditures; workplace democracy and the maximum empowerment of people in their communities "consistent with fairness, social responsibilities and human rights."

Not bad for a meeting at which nobody yelled at anyone.

Interesting stories but how rare.

Now Kevin Zeese and George O'Neill have to try to build on the spirit in that basement last Saturday and turn it into something that all can see. Perhaps it will be a catalyst as was, say, the Seneca Falls conference was for women's rights. Perhaps it will be nothing but another nice try that didn't work out.

We may never know. After all, only two women who attended Seneca Falls conference lived long enough to vote.

We do know, however, that good futures are built on the efforts of those unafraid of failure. At a time when a majority of Americans consider their system broken, we can either consign ourselves to being victims or we can, as we did last Saturday, come together in new ways, with new ideas and new allies and start replacing a failed system with communities that work.

COME HOME AMERICA: PROSPECTS FOR A COALITION AGAINST EMPIRE

by Jeff Taylor, March 12 2010

Front Porch Republic, Jacksonville, AL

I was privileged to be at the February 20 anti-empire, anti-war conference in DC. The meetings included two other Front Porchers—Bill Kauffman and Allan Carlson—and at least a couple FPR fellow travelers (Dan McCarthy and Jesse Walker). The session itself has been well described by participants from various perspectives: conservative (Dan), libertarian (Jesse, Matt Cockerill, David Henderson), and liberal (Kevin Zeese, Sam Smith, Paul Buhle). So, I'll just briefly summarize my impressions of the meeting. I'll deal at length with the theoretical and historical context of the coalition-building effort.

As usual, Bill gave an eloquent presentation of his thoughts, which have been collected for posterity in *America First!; Look Homeward, America;* and *Ain't My America.* (Do you notice a recurring theme?) The second book is subtitled *In Search of Reactionary Radicals and Front-Porch Anarchists,* which provided our website's name, although the black flag of anarchy has been lowered a bit. Bill's content was wonderful in both style and substance. Prose that sounded like poetry. Allan focused on the baneful effects of militarism and empire on families and communities. His perspective is counterintuitive to most modern Americans although, on some level, many must recognize the obvious truth of what he says. Allan has a nice touch when speaking and it's always good to hear a fellow Iowan.

It was fun talking music, philosophy, and real-world politics with Jesse and Dan. George O'Neill Jr. was a gracious host and he brought along his delightful children. George is a veteran of the Buchanan '92 campaign. Co-organizer Kevin Zeese was a manager of Nader's 2004 campaign. He and Linda Schade are the driving forces behind Voters for Peace. Linda reminded me of some of my old friends in the Green Party—a certain Green vibe that Sam also possessed.

Ralph Nader gave a fiery speech during lunch, sprinkled with humor and just the right amount of sarcasm. He was with us for the rest of the afternoon. During the group meetings, I sat between Michael McPhearson and Mike Ferner of Veterans for Peace. I couldn't have asked for better neighbors. Bill Lind, friend and co-worker of the late Paul Weyrich, contributed some useful thoughts on language and gave an interesting summary of the Fourth Generation War theory. On a personal level, it was exciting to get to know some of my political journalism heroes, including Sam Smith and Bill Greider.

I recognized Paul Buhle's name as editor of the *Encyclopedia of the American Left,* but I did not immediately realize that Murray Polner co-edited, with Tom Woods, the great reader *We Who Dared to Say No to War*. Socializing on Friday night, Paul regaled us with tales of ex-Communists writing episodes of Lassie. An example of reactionary radicals? Over breakfast, Murray and I compared notes as ethical vegetarians. John Walsh from Boston is affiliated with the Antiwar League, a group founded by the visionary Doug Fuda. John's sense of humor and logic added to the proceedings. The input from the college-age students—mostly Ron Paul-influenced Young Americans for Liberty, with one Student for a Democratic Society—was informative. It's important to learn from history, but we are living in 2010 and the next generation has something to say.

With all the permutations of Left and Right present among the 40 participants, I thought there was only one conferee who was dogmatically ideological in a knee-jerk way. Even that person presented one good idea. Sure, there were a few comments about social and economic issues that ruffled a few feathers, but for the most part the group stayed focused on foreign policy and reached consensus more often than not. Certainly the common enemy was recognized: the bipartisan Center of wealth and power, of empire and war.

The gathering was not meant to be an exclusive get-together of the best and the brightest. It was a start. Obviously, the goal is to bring more people in. A meeting of forty is not going to change U.S. foreign policy. A movement of forty million might. The potential is there. The American people have a deep "isolationist" streak, a common-sense nationalism that is wary of policing the world or meddling in other people's business in distant countries with strange names. A Pew Research Center opinion survey released in December 2009 shows that a plurality of Americans think that the U.S. should "mind its own business internationally and let other countries get along the best they can on their own" (49 percent—an all-time high). Of course, elite opinion stands in contrast to popular sentiment: 69 percent of Council on Foreign Relations members "support the United States playing an assertive role in global affairs."

The extent of American isolationism—which really means reluctance toward entangling political and military alliances—varies from year to year, but there is an America First instinct that remains constant. Public opinion partly accounts for why the U.S. did not enter World War I in 1915 or World War II in 1939. Wilson and Roosevelt certainly wanted to push the nation into those conflicts earlier than was possible. Of course, we ended up fighting anyway. Americans' disinterest in having themselves and their loved ones put in harm's way overseas also hindered plans to send a large amount of ground troops to the Balkans in the 1990s. A decade later, it meant that McCain's contention that "We are all Georgians" was met with more laughter than seriousness.

Muscular American imperialism is not a winning issue for any political party. Politicians usually cloak their imperial designs while campaigning because the idea of expending American blood and money in obscure places halfway around the world does not appeal to average Americans. They care far more about practical domestic issues. The U.S. government acting as policeman of the world has never been a popular idea among Americans. It is costly and implies that our own society has reached such a state of perfection that we can easily afford to look elsewhere for problems to solve. Meddling in other people's affairs creates enemies and can actually make our own people less safe. There is a difference between being a helpful big brother and being an arrogant empire. Even if we concede the existence of good intentions on the part of our government, perception becomes reality for people in the rest of the world.

The Iraq War was never really popular. A vast majority of Americans rallied around the president when the invasion began in 2003, but there was widespread resistance throughout 2002 when the idea was first publicly raised because many Americans did not see Saddam Hussein as a genuine threat to the country. After the much-touted WMDs failed to materialize and the American death count continued to rise after Bush's declaration of Mission Accomplished, opposition to the war grew. During the fall 2004 campaign, half of Americans believed the war was a mistake. (Despite claims to the contrary by both Bush and Kerry.) A year later, a majority felt that way. According to a 2005 Harris poll, 53 percent said taking military action against Iraq was the "wrong thing to do," and only 34 percent thought it was right. The shift in opinion, depending on circumstances, indicates that support for the war had always been soft and conditional.

Americans are not pacifists. The vast majority are not even close to the quasi-pacifism of a William Jennings Bryan. We live in a country that glorifies the military. Still, it must be said that most Americans are also not as callous and martial as those who rule in Washington; after all, it is their loved ones who are personally experiencing the brutality and bloodletting. Presidents may fret about wars while photographers snap pictures and reporters note their burdened souls, but they do not send their children into combat. Like the Bush Jr. administration, most Americans are unilateralists. In fact, they are unilateralists of an isolationist, not internationalist, sort, so it is a unilateralism that exceeds that of Republican leaders. Unlike many Democrats, they do not think we need the permission of Kofi Annan, Jacques Chirac, or any other foreigner to wage war in defense of ourselves.

The question is, Was this truly the case with Iraq or were there other motives behind the attack and occupation? Many patriotic citizens either opposed the war from the start or soured on it when they realized that the Iraqi government had been no threat to us. Americans who support more of an interventionist foreign policy tend to view our government as a Good Samaritan on the global stage. In most cases, they wrongly attribute their own well-meaning attitudes and Judeo-Christian values to their leaders. They assume that these leaders are acting on the basis of moral idealism. This is a largely mistaken impression.

Regardless of the rhetoric used as policy justification, our leaders are usually guided by the principles of political realism and their less than altruistic policies have led to the widespread international perception of the U.S. not so much as a Good Samaritan as a Schoolyard Bully. Most people are not grateful for U.S. intervention because it is often accompanied by military violence and political domination. Scores of sincere Americans cannot understand this natural reaction of others. "Why do they hate us?" "We're damned if we do and damned if we don't." et cetera.

Unfortunately, many patriotic Americans are easily fooled by U.S. government propaganda. This is especially true for evangelicals, who tend to be politically unsophisticated, particularly when the nation is ruled by a Republican president (who, by definition, must be "a good Christian"). Sarah Palin is a case study in this naïve phenomenon. From her correct and populist intuition that loyalty and patriotism are good, she moves dogmatically to an embrace of propaganda and jingoism. She does not realize that most wars are imperial and aggressive in nature, hence the opposite of the national defense she cherishes. Neoconservatives and gunboat liberals exploit this confusion, in Palin and millions of other well-meaning Americans.

Opposition to an ongoing war is a complicated thing, emotionally and intellectually. Americans find it difficult to believe that friends and family members are wounding and being wounded, killing and being killed for ignoble reasons. Even if it might be true, the cognitive dissonance is far too great for most to embrace such a thought. Cindy Sheehan, mother of Army Specialist Casey Sheehan, and Andrew Bacevich, father of Army Lieutenant Andrew Bacevich Jr., are exceptions. Their sons were killed in Iraq for no good reason and they have been able to embrace this truth despite its horror. This is rare.

For the rest of us, we too can oppose the bad foreign policies for which the troops are serving as pawns without despising the good personal qualities that often motivate and are often exhibited by the individuals in uniform. In other words, we can recognize the fictional and exploitative nature of the "fighting for our freedom" cliché while honoring the patriotism, bravery, and sacrifice of combat veterans. I can disagree with the Vietnam War while respecting Colonel George "Bud" Day USAF and Major Ed "Eagle Man" McGaa USMC. This is what Professor Bacevich has done with his own son, but obviously on a much deeper level. If you have not read what he wrote three years ago, you should. His poignant essay is a rare example of truth on the op-ed pages of *The Washington Post.*

Having several editors of *The American Conservative,* the managing editor of *Reason,* and the editor-publisher of *The Nation* present at the DC conference made me think of the golden age of political mass-circulation magazines from the 1910s through the 1940s: *The Commoner* of William Jennings Bryan, La Follette's *Weekly* (later: *The Progressive*) of Robert La Follette, *The Nation* of Oswald Garrison

Villard, *The Christian Century* of Charles Clayton Morrison, *The Freeman* of Albert Jay Nock, *Saturday Evening Post* of Garret Garrett, and *The American Mercury* of Lawrence Spivak. *Politics* of Dwight Macdonald had a smaller circulation but it was a classic periodical. One component of a successful anti-war coalition is the ability to get the message out to a wide range of citizens.

In some ways, things were simpler one hundred years ago. The demos were less divided. Yes, there were partisan, sectional, and ethnic divisions, but in many cases the common people were able to rise above those differences to see what they had in common. For example, the bloody shirt was sometimes transcended. The People's (Populist) Party had strength among both ex-Federals and ex-Confederates. In the South, Populists had some success in establishing a biracial coalition to oppose aristocratic Democrats ("Bourbons"), which is one reason Jim Crow laws targeted both blacks and poor whites.

In the early 1900s, elitists who represented corporate wealth were conservatives. In the parlance of the Progressive Era, they were reactionaries, standpatters, or plutocrats. Just about everyone else went by various names indicating support for a democratic republic, a non-entangling foreign policy, individual rights, the common good, and fidelity to the Constitution: populists, progressives, insurgents, or liberals. The latter camp was spread throughout the Democratic and Republican parties, and, to a lesser extent, various third parties. They were the heirs of Thomas Jefferson, John Taylor, and Samuel Adams.

Although there were some differences in emphasis and some electoral rivalry, liberal Democrats like W. J. Bryan and liberal Republicans like R. M. La Follette cooperated on most of the major issues of the day, both domestic and foreign. Often times, they endorsed a candidate for congressional reelection of the opposing party when their own party fielded a reactionary. Commitment to common principles trumped party loyalty. In 1896, Bryan had the support of Democrats, Populists, and Silver Republicans. In 1924, La Follette united liberal Republicans with Socialists under the Progressive banner. At the turn of the century, principled conservatives like Grover Cleveland, Charles Francis Adams Jr., and Andrew Carnegie were even willing to work with liberals in the American Anti-Imperialist League.

By the early 1920s, greater factionalization had taken place among the citizenry. More and more, Americans were defining themselves by occupation. Commonweal was giving way to special interest groups ("pluralistic democracy"). In the political realm, American populism had split by the early 1940s in response to co-optation and changing of the word liberalism by Franklin Roosevelt in the Democratic Party and Wendell Willkie in the Republican. Roughly speaking, populists who valued justice more than liberty remained "liberals," while populists who valued liberty more than justice became "conservatives." The libertarian Old Right of the New Deal years was an offshoot of Bryan-La Follette liberalism. It had nothing in common with the Hamiltonian conservatism of the past, which had rather suddenly morphed into "liberalism"—exchanging an unpopular label for a designation more popular and trendy.

Both occupational identity politics and semantically-confusing ideology meant that Jeffersonian cousins who ought to have been natural allies instead grew further estranged from one another throughout the coming decades. The emergence of anti-Communism in the late 1940s and Counterculturalism in the late 1960s further strained relations among anti-Establishment citizens. The Power Elite used these divisions as a form of conflict displacement, as political scientist E. E. Schattschneider referred to earlier examples of popular in-fighting. The old divide-and-conquer strategy.

There was a brief moment, in 1940-41, during which a bipartisan popular coalition thwarted a bipartisan elite coalition. The America First Committee was mostly led by new-style conservative populists like Robert Wood of Sears, Roebuck; Robert McCormick of the *Chicago Tribune;* Robert Douglas Stuart of Quaker Oats; book publisher William Regnery; and aviator Charles Lindbergh Jr., but it also included many old-style liberal populists like Amos Pinchot, John T. Flynn, Alice Roosevelt Longworth, and Oswald Garrison Villard. Villard, former owner-editor of *The Nation,* was a veteran of the Anti-Imperialist League. He opposed the Spanish-American War, World War I, and World War II. Consistency incarnate. Grandson of abolitionist William Lloyd Garrison, co-founder with W.E.B. DuBois of the NAACP. A truly great, if now-forgotten, man.

Memory of OGV was one reason I was pleased to see Katrina vanden Heuvel at the table in DC. *The Nation* has a distinguished legacy and plays an important role in the liberal movement, despite occasional lapses into Democratic lesser-evilism. Other liberal populists, including historian Charles Beard and Norman Thomas of the Socialist Party, assisted the anti-intervention cause from outside the AFC. Conservative thinker Russell Kirk would cast his presidential ballot for Thomas in 1944 to reward him for his anti-war stance.

Military veterans in prominent AFC roles included Brigadier General Wood (former acting quartermaster general of the Army), Colonel McCormick, Colonel Lindbergh, and Major General Hanford MacNider (former assistant secretary of war and national commander of the American Legion). This was certainly not an anti-war movement that could be easily dismissed by epithets of tie-dyed hippie peaceniks or effete Hollywood glitterati. This was a movement that could appeal to Middle America, with its patriotism, common sense, and traditional values. While mostly sympathizing with England, in 1940, about 80 percent of the American people were opposed to war and Franklin D. Roosevelt—like his role model Woodrow Wilson twenty-four years earlier—was reelected on a pledge to keep our boys out of the European bloodletting.

Ultimately, the America First Committee was unsuccessful. In hindsight, many would say that was for the best. Whether it was or not, we can still learn some lessons from AFC. It was a coalition that united influential, well-placed, and genuine representatives of a common people that were divided along established party and nascent ideological-label lines. It became tainted by accusations of ethnic prejudice because elite interventionists—men who tended, ironically, to be respectably anti-Semitic themselves—exploited real or imagined failings of Lindbergh and others. In the end, the movement could not prevent the presidential nomination of pro-war candidates by both the Democrats and Republicans; could not overcome the power and propaganda of FDR, the British Empire, Wall Street, and the corporate press; and could not stop Pearl Harbor and the natural rush to war that resulted.

There were ad hoc efforts by both Left and Right to stop the Cold War, the Vietnam War, the Persian Gulf War, and the Iraq War, but none of these efforts were very successful. They were less broad-based than the anti-WWII effort and there were no national umbrella organizations that approached the stature of AFC.

Although their presidential campaigns approached the subject from different perspectives, conservative Robert Taft ("Mr.

Republican") and liberal Henry Wallace (VP under FDR) were the two most prominent opponents of Cold War foreign policy in 1948 within their respective parties. For example, both would oppose the founding of NATO the following year. In a July 1950 letter, Senator Taft wrote that he had the feeling that the U.S. was "in real danger of becoming an imperialistic nation," noting, "The line between imperialism and idealism becomes very confused in the minds of those who operate the system" (Ronald Radosh, *Prophets on the Right: Profiles of Conservative Critics of American Globalism,* 174). In a speech given in 1951, Taft said, "I certainly do not think we should be obligated to send American troops to defend Indo-China [Vietnam] or Burma or Thailand where they would become involved in a much more serious war than we have been forced into in Korea" (Ibid., 192-93).

Taft had impeccable all-American credentials—grandson of a secretary of war, son of a president and chief justice, friend of Herbert Hoover, champion of small business and free enterprise—and yet this did not prevent W. Averell Harriman from calling him "the Kremlin's candidate" for president in 1952. Taft was genuinely anti-communist, which is one reason he opposed allying our government with Stalin in World War II, but he was not willing to use a reputed global crusade against communism to mask U.S. imperialism. That was his unpardonable sin in the eyes of Harriman, former Soviet ambassador and commerce secretary, future New York governor, and, most important of all, international investment banker (Brown Brothers, Harriman & Co.—the firm of GW's grandfather Prescott Bush). Of course, Harriman and his fellow "Wise Men" were hypocrites, since they had linked themselves to the Kremlin and been senior partners in a Popular Front with U.S. communists from 1940 to 1945. Their "anti-communism" was highly selective and thoroughly opportunistic.

Unlike his father, Bob Taft was not a product of the Rockefeller machine of Ohio and had not befriended the east coast establishment. He was a Main Street Republican, not a Wall Street Republican. This fact had foreign policy implications that doomed Taft's ability to gain his party's presidential nomination in 1940, 1948, or 1952. It forever tainted him in the eyes of those whom Phyllis Schlafly would later call "the kingmakers." (Through her nationalist-populist-moralist-libertarian choices for president, Schlafly symbolizes the true line of conservative descent within the party, despite variations of emphasis and purity, from Taft to Goldwater to Ashbrook to Reagan to Buchanan.) Taft had been the unofficial leader of his party in the Senate for years and he served as majority leader for six months before dying of cancer in July 1953. Taft was no anomaly among conservatives of his generation. Colonel McCormick also criticized the "imperialism" of the U.S. government and Senate Minority Leader Kenneth Wherry (R-NE) also opposed NATO.

Robert Welch was an active Taft '52 man within the Massachusetts GOP. Welch and the John Birch Society were excommunicated from the mainstream conservative movement by William F. Buckley Jr. and *National Review* in the mid 1960s not so much because of their supposed racial prejudice and political extremism, but more so because of their petit-bourgeois lack of respectability and their principled opposition to the Vietnam War. In 1964, Welch was opposing war in southeast Asia...several years before johnnies-come-lately like Eugene McCarthy, Robert Kennedy, and George McGovern. It is hard to imagine anyone more anti-communist than Robert Welch, but his skepticism toward foreign intervention was consistent with his Old Right heritage. The anti-war sentiment of the JBS has popped up with Vietnam, the Gulf War, and the Iraq War. *The New American* even opposed the Panama invasion.

In the Senate, the only two votes against the pro-war Gulf of Tonkin Resolution in 1964 were from liberals Wayne Morse (D-OR) and Ernest Gruening (D-AK). Morse, Gruening, and even Welch (by way of Taft) were all more-or-less descended from the La Follette tradition of liberal Republicanism. This tradition, from which Taft, McCormick, Frank Gannett, and others would emerge in the late 1930s to create a new-style conservatism indebted to Jefferson rather than Hamilton, had always been linked to national sovereignty, international neutrality, defense but not war, and domestic emphasis. In September 1924, the perspective of La Follette's party was spelled out in the pages of the CFR journal *Foreign Affairs:* "It is historically characteristic of governments devoted to conservative measures and the maintenance of the status quo in domestic affairs to develop an aggressive policy in foreign affairs, and similarly for governments whose chief outlook is toward the progressive improvement of existing conditions to seek to disembarrass themselves from the complications of foreign policy."

The New Left-inspired grassroots movement against the Vietnam War did put pressure on the power structure and it did have some importance within the Democratic Party, but the White House did not begin to change its war approach until 1967, when Wall Street and their Wise Men mouthpieces began raising economic objections to the status quo. After three decades, military conscription (the draft) was ended more by libertarians like Martin Anderson and Milton Friedman than by left-wing peace demonstrators in the streets.

Opposition to the Persian Gulf War, in 1990-91, included the populist Left (Brown), Right (Buchanan), and Middle (Perot). We've seen a similar anti-war configuration during the past twenty years with Ralph Nader and Howard Phillips, Dennis Kucinich and Ron Paul. And yet, in all of the pivotal war election years, the nominees of both major parties have been pro-war (WWI-1916, WWII-1940, Cold War-1948, Vietnam-1964, Balkans-1996, Iraq-2004, Afghanistan-2008). Divisions over secondary-but-emotional cultural/social/moral issues have prevented sustained efforts by the Left and Right to work against empire. We've seen an occasional joint press conference by activist leaders to denounce a specific war, but nothing lasting and nothing that includes millions of average Americans.

In the estimation of Bill Kauffman, excepting the Murray Rothbard-Leonard Liggio Left and Right attempt to bring about cooperation between the libertarian Old Right and the New Left in the 1960s, the meeting in DC represented the first real attempt at a Left-Right antiwar coalition since the America First Committee seventy years ago. The conference brought together a relatively small number of journalists, activists, intellectuals, and students. One thing lacking was politicians. Or, perhaps I should say statesmen if we're talking about the "good guys." There were no elected leaders. That's okay for the time being, but if we hope to be successful in the long run in creating an effective coalition to stop war and dismantle empire, we will have to bring politicians on board. We need to have someone in Washington listening to us when we speak from the hinterland. Folks with a forum who can amplify our message. People with power who can translate our concerns into legislation.

It is not wise to put all of our eggs in one basket by concentrating on presidential races. A run for the White House can raise a standard under which citizens from across the land can assemble. This is useful. But it is unrealistic to think that either major party is going to be captured in the short run via a national nominating convention, or that a third party will capture the presidency itself. Congress is less glamorous and obviously the branch has abdicated much of its power to the de facto emperor, but individual legislators can still play an important defensive role in the struggle against empire. Cicero and his allies did it in ancient Rome. Senate Foreign Relations Committee Chairman Charles Sumner (R-MA) was instrumental in killing U. S. Grant's plan to annex Santo Domingo in 1870. In the run-up to World War I entry, House Majority Leader Claude Kitchin (D-NC) and Senate FRC Chairman William Stone (D-MO) worked with ex-Secretary of State Bryan to prevent war.

There were many self-styled liberals and conservatives, on both sides of the aisle, who worked to stop World War II entry, including Senators William Borah (ID) (ranking Republican on the FRC), Hiram Johnson (CA) (running mate of TR in 1912 and Borah's successor as senior Republican on the FRC), Robert La Follette Jr. (WI) (son of Fighting Bob), Charles McNary (OR) (1940 vice presidential nominee), Arthur Capper (KS), Henrik Shipstead (MN), Ernest Lundeen (MN), Gerald Nye (ND), Lynn Frazier (ND), and William Langer (ND). That was just the liberal GOP contingent in the upper chamber!

We could also think of conservative Republicans such as Senator Robert Taft (OH) and Representatives Howard Buffett (NE) (father of Warren), Hamilton Fish (NY), B. Carroll Reece (TN), H.R. Gross (IA), George Bender (OH), and Henry Dworshak (ID). Liberal Democrats who were anti-war included Senators Key Pittman (NV) (chairman of the FRC), Burton Wheeler (MT) (running mate of LF in 1924), David Walsh (MA), Bennett Champ Clark (MO), Edwin Johnson (CO), Morris Sheppard (TX), and Homer Bone (WA).

Where are the Borahs and Johnsons, Wheelers and Clarks, and all the rest, in the U.S. Senate today? There's Russ Feingold (D-WI), Jim Webb (D-VA), Jon Tester (D-MT), and Bernie Sanders (I-VT). That's about it. They are good but they are backbenchers. None chair relevant committees. The most sincerely conservative Republicans—Tom Coburn (OK), Jim DeMint (SC), David Vitter (LA), and Jim Bunning (KY)—are hawks. Chuck Grassley (IA) was one of two Republicans, along with Mark Hatfield (OR), to vote against the Persian Gulf War, but unfortunately Grassley backs the current wars.

There's a handful of anti-war Republicans in the House, led by the incomparable Ron Paul (TX) and including Walter Jones (NC) and Jimmy Duncan (TN). There are more anti-war Democrats, from Dennis Kucinich (OH) to Barbara Lee (CA), but many pull their punches when a Democrat is the commander in chief. Kucinich's March 10, 2010 resolution directing the president to remove U.S. armed forces from Afghanistan was defeated 65-356. A paltry five Republicans voted Yea. Although 60 Democrats supported it, three times more were opposed. We need a Senator Rand Paul (R-KY?), a Senator John Hostettler (R-IN?) , and dozens more like them in Congress. Liberals, conservatives, Democrats, Republicans. Maybe even a Green, Libertarian, or Constitution party member.

For a successful coalition, we need people + power, grassroots + government, pressure from below + action from above. As for We the People, at some point we have to get off our front porches, or stop being transfixed by our screens, in order to recover our republic. This is never easy. The decline of social interaction and civic engagement by Americans during the past sixty years makes it even more difficult. But it is possible. The coalition needs a narrow focus. Divisive issues briefly raised their heads at the conference in DC. Things like campaign finance reform, same-sex marriage, abortion, and tea partiers. That way lies destruction.

The message of the coalition should be broad in the sense that it deals with the bipartisan foundation of U.S. foreign policy. Opposition to empire is better than opposition to war because the problem is not a specific war started by a specific president of a specific party. It is a systemic tendency toward war for the sake of empire maintenance. You could compare it to an alcoholic: the specific bout of drinking-to-excess is less important than the alcoholism itself. We must get to the root of the problem, and do it in a way that does not come off as unpatriotic, kooky, or partisan. That's as broad as we should get. Beyond that, all other issues should be set aside. Coalition members are free to think and do as they please on their own time, but they should not produce divisions within the movement over non-relevant issues.

For me, the CPAC victory of Ron Paul was an unexpected ray of sunshine in Washington. The Across-the-Spectrum conference was a second ray. We still have to move beyond discussion to action. We need to have lots more people join us under the "Come Home,

America" tent as we work toward building a mass movement with friends in Washington. It's easy to be cynical, considering past failures. It would be easy to be discouraged by the daunting odds. But, as Kevin Zeese puts it, "This is a long-term, not short-term, effort that should be measured in years, not in months."

Left, Right and Miscellaneous

Published in *Reason* magazine

By Jesse Walker

Last Saturday I sat down for an eight-hour conversation with a couple dozen writers and activists from different parts of the political spectrum. We were a diverse bunch, united only by our belief that the U.S. needs—to borrow a phrase—a more humble foreign policy. Another attendee, Sam Smith of *The Progressive Review,* has posted a wrapup of the event on his site. I encourage you to read the whole thing, but for now a few excerpts will do:

"The topic was, by itself, depressingly familiar: building an anti-war coalition. What made it so strikingly different was the nature of those at the table. They included progressives, conservatives, traditional liberals and libertarians. Some reached back to the Reagan years or to 1960s activism, some—including an SDS leader from the University of Maryland and several Young Americans for Liberty—were still in college.

"In a time when politics is supposed to be hopelessly polarized along the lines proposed by Glenn Beck and Keith Olbermann, the most heated debate occurred not between left and right but over tactics between Ralph Nader and Bill Greider...

"As I sat around that table, I tried to recall those few occasions when I had experienced something close to this...One that worked was the anti-freeway coalition of the 1960s and 70s that kept Washington from becoming another Los Angeles. It was started by among the least likely activists—black and white middle class homeowners whose neighborhood was about to be ruined. It expanded to include those of us in the civil rights group SNCC as well as the all white Georgetown Citizens Association...There was only one qualification to join the anti-freeway movement: opposition to freeways."

Smith calls this "existential politics—in which one defined one's existence by one's actions rather than by one's ethnicity, class, party registration or magazine subscriptions."

I was likewise impressed with the discussion. It was the sort of event that was going to be interesting even if it ended in a great big food fight, and was all the more interesting because it wound up being generally amicable instead. It helped that the folks around the table were, for the most part, more interested in listening than in talking, a rare thing among people professionally engaged in politics. Maybe it was the fact that we all knew going into the room that it would be filled with deep-set philosophical disagreements. When there's little chance of converting someone to your point of view, you just might spend some time focusing on the things you can do, like figuring out ways to work together in the areas where you're already aligned.

Next Steps

By John V. Walsh

I do not minimize the importance of a name. I think PostWar Coalition is too vague—and it has the unfortunate initials, PC. The name should have punch, put our ideas out there and make people grapple with them. The Ant-Empire League or Anti-Empire Coalition or Coalition to End Empire (CEE), something that makes people confront Empire right off the bat. Unlike you I was not surprised that the Right liked the word Empire but not Imperialism. The latter has been since Lenin's pamphlet associated with the Left and at times unfortunately used to loosely. Empire not only describes the modern era but the Empires of the past, England and Rome, which no one likes. And the Conservatives, like their heroes the Founders, are driven by examples from the ancient world and the idea that Empire and Republic cannot co-exist for long. And of course the Left easily accepts Empire, seeing it as another word for Imperialism. It is a great term and many, probably most, Americans would agree that we operate an Empire. Our slogan as opposed to our name should be "America, Come Home." (I also like the term Isolationism but I think that it would be an uphill battle to get that word back to a point of respectability.)

I think we need to map out a propaganda campaign with multiple steps. I think of PNHP which began with its 1987 statement of goals for Single-Payer, appearing in *JAMA* or *NEJM* and signed by the founders and others. I think the idea of a Manifesto is a great one so long as we keep it focused and clear and catholic. Where woud it appear? I do not like the idea of an advert as a first step. I would like us to publish it in a place like the *Atlantic,* or perhaps there is a better place along those lines. (Fallows might even be approached—perhaps by Ralph.) After that there might be an ad or series of ads. And of course our gathering of writers should be banging out articles for every Left and Right outlet imaginable. But the Manifesto needs thought and it should contain some stirring and inspirational words. It should hold out the vision of America as peaceful island, interacting vigorously with the world but never, except in clear defense, in a military fashion. It should be presented as something new and exciting and anti-establishment. I do NOT think an anti-corporatist theme should be part of it nor a class theme.

Then we need something like a standard presentation, much like the PNHP slide show for campus and other presentations. This could be built upon Empire of Bases and other work like that. It should be as factual and historical as possible.

Finally, we might need to move forward with a grass roots effort, perhaps even piggy backing onto Ralph's non-partisan Congress Watch.

And if we were lucky some author would come along to write a novel that would inspire an anti-Empire effort.

But in summary I think the first effort must be to fund you and some assistants, come up with a Manifesto and wage a battle of ideas. (The Left has, except for the successful revolutionaries, underestimated the importance of ideas IMHO.)

E-mail to Kevin Zeese following the February 20, 2010 conference.

Naomi Wolf Thinks the Tea Parties Help Fight Fascism—Is She onto Something or in Fantasy Land?

Justine Sharrock

In her bestselling *End of America,* Naomi Wolf outlines the 10 warning signs that America is headed toward a fascist takeover. Using historical precedents, she explains how our government is mimicking those of Mussolini, Hitler and Stalin through practices like the surveillance of ordinary citizens, restriction of the the press, development of paramilitary forces and arbitrary detention.

The book was lauded by liberals under George W. Bush: the Independent Publishers gave it the Freedom Fighter Award; John Nichols at the *Nation* named it the most valuable political book of 2007. Now, under President Obama, Wolf's book is providing ammunition for the Tea Partiers, Patriots, Ron Paul supporters and Oath Keepers, who also warn of impending tyrannical government. Even when the book first came out pre-Obama, Alex Jones, Michael Savage and Fox News invited her on their shows, and agreed with her.

It's not just her message. She speaks their language, referring to the Founding Fathers and American Revolution as models, admitting to a profound sense of fear, warning of tyranny, fascism, Nazism and martial law. When Glenn Beck warns of these things we laugh. When Wolf draws those same connections, we listen. How can both sides be speaking the same language, yet see things so differently? Or are we just not listening to each other? I telephoned Wolf to ask her what it means when your book ends up bolstering policies you oppose.

Justine Sharrock: First off, is your book still relevant under Obama?

Naomi Wolf: Unfortunately it is more relevant. Bush legalized torture, but Obama is legalizing impunity. He promised to roll stuff back, but he is institutionalizing these things forever. It is terrifying and the left doesn't seem to recognize it.

JS: Did you realize that your book is being lauded within the Tea Party and patriot movements?

NW: Since I wrote *Give Me Liberty,* I have had a new audience that looks different than the average Smith girl. There is a giant libertarian component. I have had a lot of dialogue with the Ron Paul community. There are [Tea Partiers] writing to me on my Facebook page, but I figured they were self-selective libertarians and not arch conservatives. I am utterly stunned that I have a following in the patriot movement and I wasn't aware that specific Tea Partiers were reading it. They haven't invited me to speak. They invited Sarah Palin.

JS: If they did invite you, would you speak at a Tea Party?

NW: I would go in a heartbeat. I'll go anywhere to talk about the Constitution. I believe in trans-partisan organizing around these issues. When I went on Fox News people asked me why I was going on those shows. Are you kidding? You have to go, especially to people you don't agree with. We need to get back into grappling with people we disagree with if we want to restore the Republic.

I was invited by the Ron Paul supporters to their rally in Washington last summer and I loved it. I met a lot of people I respected, a lot of "ordinary" people, as in not privileged. They were stepping up to the plate, when my own liberal privileged fellow demographic habituates were lying around whining. It was a wake-up call to the libertarians that there's a progressive who cares so much about the same issues. Their views of liberals are just as distorted as ours are of conservatives.

JS: Why do you think the sides don't understand each other?

NW: Frankly, liberals are out of the habit of communicating with anyone outside their own in cohort. We have a cultural problem with self-righteousness and elitism. Liberals roll their eyes about going on "Oprah" to reach a mass audience by using language that anyone can understand even if you majored in semiotics at Yale. We look down on people we don't agree with. It doesn't serve us well.

There is also a deliberate building up of two camps that benefits from whipping up home team spirit and demonizing the opposition. With the Internet there is even more fractioning since we are in echo chambers. With so much propaganda it is hard to calm down enough to listen.

JS: What do you think is the biggest misconception about the Tea Parties?

NW: The Tea Party is not monolithic. There is a battle between people who care about liberty and the Constitution and the Republican Establishment who is trying to take ownership of it and redirect it for its own purposes.

JS: In your essay, "Tea Time in America" you said that some of the Tea Party's proposals are "ahead of their time." What are some examples?

NW: I used to think "End the Fed people" were crackpots. The media paints them as deranged. But it turned out we had good reason to have more oversight. Or take their platform about states' rights. Demographically, I'm a hippie from San Francisco and I'm not culturally inclined to be sympathetic to states' rights. My cultural heritage is FDR and Medicare and federal government solutions. But if you think through the analysis, strengthening state rights is a good corrective of the aggregation of an over-reaching federal power. Take California's challenge of the Patriot Act or states like Vermont leading the way with addressing the corruption of the voting system. It's a good example of the Tea Party thinking out of the box on how to address a problem.

JS: That's interesting because strengthening states' rights is key to their entire platform, including protesting health care reform. Would you call yourself pro-Tea Party?

NW: Even though I'm appalled when racism surfaces, and I personally don't agree with certain policy solutions and a lot of what they believe in, as someone who is very concerned about reinvigorating democracy the Tea Parties are an answer to what I asked for.

I was basically saying don't sit around waiting for the two corrupted established parties to restore the Constitution or the Republic. The founding generation was birthed by the rabble of all walks of life that got fed up and did risky things because they were captivated by the breath of liberty. There is a looming oligarchy and it is up to the people to organize a grassroots movement and push back. You guys have to do it yourself. Their response is the most visible and the initiative they show is the most recognizable. People of all kinds are waking up. Even people passionate for Obama realize that knight on a white horse isn't enough to roll back the oligarchy.

I'm seeing a lot of action on the left as well that is never reported. But the Tea Party response is the most visible and the initiative they show is the most recognizable.

JS: How do you feel about your books bolstering a fight for policies you don't agree with?

NW: If people are taking my book seriously and organizing, getting into office, caring about the constitution, and not waiting for someone else to lead them, I think, God bless them. All of us should be doing that. The left should be doing that. There is always the risk in advocating for democracy that the first people to wake up might not be your team, but that is a risk worth taking. I would rather have citizens I don't agree with organized and active than an oligarchy of people that I agree with.

JS: These days the kinds of comparisons you make in your book between America and Nazis and fascists are mostly coming out of the mouths of people like Glenn Beck and Alex Jones. What do you make of the commonality of the rhetoric?

NW: There is no question that the right-wing idea machine saw how that message was resonating in the run-up to the last election. A YouTube video of a speech I gave went viral and got 850,000 hits. I'm not saying that is the only thing that caused this, but there is no question that the Republican and the right wing are quick to co-opt the strategic language that's resonating on the other side and turn it against itself.

JS: How is your comparison of Obama to Hitler any different from someone at a Tea Party holding up a placard of Obama with a Hitler mustache?

NW: Those signs are offensive. If only the Holocaust was just about imposing health care on my people. Obama has done things like Hitler did. Let me be very careful here. The National Socialists rounded people up and held them without trial, signed legislation that gave torture impunity, and spied on their citizens, just as Obama has. It isn't a question of what has been done that Hitler did. It's what does every dictator do, on the left or the right, that is being done here and now. The real fight isn't left or right but between forces of democracy across the spectrum and the forces of tyranny.

JS: People criticize Beck's use of that kind of language as incendiary and hyperbolic. Why is your use any different?

NW: Every time I use those analogies, I am doing it with a concrete footnoted historical context. When people like Glenn Beck throw around the word Nazi without taking that kind of care, they are engaging in demagoguery. There's an important difference.

JS: What about your warnings about concentration camps and martial law? How do they compare to conspiratorial fears about FEMA concentration camps?

NW: With the FEMA rumor, I have heard some suggestive first-person accounts that some good reporters should follow up on. But until I see two well-documented sources of it, I can't speak to it at all.

JS: Well, more generally, you talk about the possibility of concentration camps and martial law.

NW: I think we have gone very far down that road. I met Muslim immigrants in Brooklyn who were swept up in 9-11 raids, held in abusive conditions, beaten, denied rights. That's how things started in Germany. Guantanamo was modeled after what Stalin developed for the Gulag. Why are we engaged in psychological denial that it's not a concentration camp? In terms of martial law, my god. Since the book came out they deployed a brigade in the U.S. and suspended the Posse Comitatus Act. There is no question that it's something to take seriously. People have a histrionic view of what martial law will look like.

I'm not worried that tomorrow there will be a battalion outside your Greenwich Village apartment. I'm worried about things like the McCain Liberman bill that would define enemy belligerents so loosely it would include Americans, which is just like Stalin and Hitler and Mussolini. If Obama tries people with military tribunals, setting that precedent, that is what a military state does. That is what martial law looks like. From a constitutional point of view Bush passing through the Patriot Act is no worse than Obama renewing it.

Peace Activists Extend an Olive Branch to the Tea Party to Talk About War

Medea Benjamin

On Tax Day, Tea Party members from around the country will descend on the nation's capitol to "protest big government and support lower taxes, less government and more freedom. CODEPINK, a women-led peace movement advocating an end to war and militarism, will be sending some representatives. While we come from the opposite end of the political spectrum and don't support the goals and tactics of the Tea Party, there is an area where we are seeking common ground: endless wars and militarism.

As Tea Partiers express their anger at out-of-control government spending and soaring deficits, we will ask them to take a hard look at what is, by far, the biggest sinkhole of our tax dollars: Pentagon spending. With the Obama administration proposing the largest military budget ever, topping $700 billion not including war supplementals, we are now spending almost as much on the military as the rest of the world combined.

Perhaps the Tea Party and peace folks—unlikely allies—can agree that one way to shrink big government is to rein in military spending. Here are some questions to get the conversation going:

—At the Southern Republican Leadership Conference on April 10, Congressman Ron Paul—who has a great following within the Tea Party—chided both conservatives and liberals for their profligate spending on foreign military bases, occupations and maintaining an empire. "We're running out of money," he warned. "All empires end for financials reasons, and that is what the markets are telling us today…We can do better with peace than with war." Do you agree with Congressman Paul on this?

—Every taxpayer has already spent, on average, a staggering $7,367 for the wars in Iraq and Afghanistan. Now Obama plans to send another 30,000 troops to Afghanistan, with a price tag of one million dollars per soldier per year. Opposition to these wars ranges from liberal Congressperson Dennis Kucinich to conservative Tea Party leader Sheriff Richard Mack. During a Congressional vote to end the war in Afghanistan that was defeated but got bipartisan support, Rep. Dennis Kucinich said, "Nearly 1000 U.S. soldiers have died. And for what? Hundreds of billions spent. And for what? To make Afghanistan safe for crooks, drug dealers and crony capitalism?" Do you think Congress should turn off the war spigot and bring our troops home?

—The Cold War has been over for 20 years, yet we maintain 800-plus bases around the world, have troops stationed in 148 countries and 11 territories. Conservative commentator Pat Buchanan asks, "How we can justify borrowing hundreds of billions yearly from Europe, Japan and the Gulf states—to defend Europe, Japan and the Arab Gulf states? Is it not absurd to borrow hundreds of billions annually from China—to defend Asia from China?" Should we begin to dismantle this global web of bases?

—Far and away the largest recipient of US foreign aid is Israel, a wealthy country (the 11th wealthiest in the world) that gets $3 billion a year from Uncle Sam with no strings attached and no accountability. We also give the repressive Egyptian government over a billion dollars a year to buy their support for a Middle East peace plan that is going nowhere. Are you in favor of continuing this taxpayer largesse to Israel and Egypt?

—An area where Pentagon spending has mushroomed is the payment of private security contractors. While many soldiers who risk their lives for their country struggle to support their families, private security company employees can pocket as much as $1,000 a day. High pay for contract workers in war zones burdens taxpayers and saps military morale. Moreover, military officers in the field have said contractors often operate like "cowboys," using unnecessary and excessive force that has undermined our reputation overseas. Rep. Jan Schakowsky introduced the Stop Outsourcing Security Act that would phase out private security contractors in war zones. Do you support that?

—Experts on the left and the right say we could cut our military budget by 25%, including closing foreign bases, winding down the wars, and ending obsolete weapons systems, without jeopardizing our security. Do you agree? If we could make significant cuts to the military budget, how should those funds be reallocated? To pay down the debt? Increase security at home? Rebuild our infrastructure? Stimulate the economy through tax breaks?

We are not naïve to think that it would be easy for the Tea Party and the peace movement to work together. Our core values are different. We have had our battles in the past. We would certainly part ways in terms of how to redirect Pentagon funds, with progressives wanting more government investment in healthcare, jobs, clean energy and education—which is exactly what the Tea Party opposes.

But building peace means reaching out to the other side and trying to find common ground even with those people whose beliefs contradict so many of our own. If the Tea Party is really against runaway government spending, then certainly we can work together to cut a slice out of the military pork that is bankrupting our nation. In extending the olive branch to talk about war, the conversation can hopefully be enlightening on other issues as well, such as banks run amok and undue corporate control of our government.

Who knows what kind of potent brew could emerge when folks on the left and the right—both alienated by a two-party system that doesn't meet our needs—sit down for tea?

Beyond Left and Right: the New Anti War Populism

by Justin Raimondo

The War Party is running scared—and with good reason. Writing in the *Washington Post,*[1] neocons Danielle Pletka and Thomas Donnelly are in a panic that the rising "tea party" movement, which upended the Republican establishment at the polls, is about to abandon "the defense of freedom" in faraway Afghanistan in favor of rescuing what's left of our freedom closer to home:

> *"Since World War II, a touchstone of American conservatism has been the defense of freedom. The freedoms of others were regarded as essential to secure and enjoy our own. In 2010, however, the conservative movement—and the party that seeks to represent it—is at a crossroads. One path continues in this direction; the other leads backward, seeking to defend freedom only at home. The choice conservatives make will go a long way toward defining America and the world, still more toward defining the future of the right."*

As the nation sinks into an economic depression that looks to rival and even exceed that of the 1930s, the cost of maintaining an overseas empire is taking a big bite out of the federal budget—economist Joseph Stiglitz estimates the cost of the Iraq war at three trillion dollars and counting[2]—and conservatives are beginning to wake up to the fact that being the world's policeman can only end in national bankruptcy.

The Pletka-Donnelly tag team, however, will have none of this: Pletka is a longtime top official of the American Enterprise Institute, and was, you'll recall, one of Ahmed Chalabi's loudest promoters, going so far as to attack the Bush administration when her hero

[1] Danielle Pletka and Thomas Donnelly, "Is Freedom's Price Too High for the Right?", *Washington Post,* September 24, 2010.

[2] Linda J. Bilmes and Joseph E. Stiglitz, "The Iraq War Will Cost Us $3 Trillion, and Much More," Washington Post, March 9, 2008; see also, Bilmes and Stiglitz, *The Three Trillion Dollar War: The True Cost of the Iraq Conflict,* W. W. Norton, 2008.

was charged with espionage—on behalf of the Iranians—and his headquarters in Iraq raided by US troops.[3] Donnelly has long been the neocons' go-to man for coming up with reasons why we always need more "defense" spending—because spending more on the military than all other nations on earth combined isn't enough. It's never enough, as far as the neoconservatives are concerned, and the rising dissent from this view on the right is abhorred by this duo as rank heresy:

> *"The road backward beckons in an almost Calvinistic call to fiscal discipline; austerity is its virtue even before national security in a time of war. Libertarians and Tea Party darlings such as Ron and Rand Paul and conservative stalwarts such as Tom Coburn have long inhabited this political territory. Members of the GOP vanguard such as Indiana Gov. Mitch Daniels and, possibly, insurgent Tea Party candidates are joining them.*
>
> *"Thin threads bind these cloth-coat Republicans. Some simply wish to spend less; if that means under-resourcing the war in Afghanistan, so be it. To them, the Defense Department is another case of wasteful government and bureaucratic collusion that has, in Coburn's words, 'allowed the military-industrial complex to make things unaffordable.' For others, doctrinaire fiscal conservatism blends easily with a renewed isolationism. As one GOP up-and-comer told us recently, 'America has borne the burden of making the world secure for 60 years; it's someone else's turn.'"*

Oddly, Pletka and Donnelly come off sounding like liberal Democrats—is trying to rein in spending at a time of severe economic crisis really "Calvinistic," or just plain common sense? Yet it isn't so odd when one considers the history of the neoconservatives, a political sect of which they are exemplars: the neocons started out as Henry "Scoop" Jackson Democrats, cold

[3] Elisabeth Bumiller, "Conservative Allies Take Chalabi Case to the White House," *New York Times,* May 29, 2004.

war Social Democrats who combined fervent anti-communism and interventionism with support for Lyndon Baines Johnson's big spending "war on poverty." The growing influence of antiwar forces in "their" party led them out of the Democracy and into the GOP, where they hitched a ride on the Reagan revolution and ensconced themselves in the conservative movement, which they soon began to dominate with their ideological ferocity and access to big money.[4]

They never bought into the free market, anti-government radicalism of the traditional right, or the tea partiers of today: the decision to go into the GOP was motivated solely by their horror at the takeover of the Democratic party by anti-interventionist supporters of George McGovern in 1972. Indeed, the neocons' house organ, *The Weekly Standard,* raised high the banner of "big government conservatism," as *Standard* senior editor Fred Barnes proudly (and accurately) deemed it, which didn't abjure spending like a drunken sailor—as long as big corporations and military contractors got the lions' share of the goodies, and poor people got the crumbs, if that.[5] This label gave way, during the post-cold war years, to "national greatness conservatism,"[6] which combined the monument-building of the pharaohs with the megalomania that motivated *Weekly Standard* editor Bill Kristol to proclaim in his foreign policy manifesto that the US should seek to establish a "benevolent global hegemony."[7] Where Alexander failed, the neocons would succeed.

Except it didn't turn out that way. Energized by the 9/11

[4] For a good account of the Trotskiyist origins of neoconservative thought, see Alan M. Wald, *The New York Intellectuals: The Rise and Decline of the Anti-Stalinist Left,* University of North Carolina Press, 1987. and also *Peter Drucker, Max Shachtman and His Left: A Socialist's Odyssey Through the 'American Century,'* Humanities Press, 1994. For a review of more contemporary history, see Jacob Heilbrun, *They Knew They Were Right: The Rise of the Neocons,* Doubleday, 2008. For the story of how they came to dominate the American conservative movement, see Paul Gottfried and Thomas Fleming, *The Conservative Movement,* Twayne, 1988, and also Justin Raimondo, *Reclaiming the American Right: The Lost Legacy of the Conservative Movement,* Center for Libertarian Studies, 1993.

[5] Fred Barnes, "Big Government Conservatism," *The Weekly Standard,* August 18, 2003.

[6] David Brooks, "A Return to National Greatness: A Manifesto for a Lost Creed," *The Weekly Standard,* March 3, 1997.

[7] William Kristol and Robert Kagan, "Toward a Neo-Reaganite Foreign Policy," *Foreign Affairs,* July/August 1996.

terrorist attacks, and in place at key points in the administration of George W. Bush, they did indeed succeed in getting us bogged down in seemingly endless wars of occupation in Iraq and Afghanistan—and discrediting themselves in the process. When the country discovered they had been hoodwinked by the mirage of Iraq's "weapons of mass destruction," and the "cakewalk" promised by neocon armchair generals failed to materialize, the desire for change—any kind of change—swept the GOP from power. The conservative movement woke up, on November 5, 2008, to find a world in which eight years of neoconservative rule had led to bigger government on the home front and a foreign policy that made us less safe, more hated, and nearly bankrupt.

Aside from a generalized desire for "change," the Obama-crats took the Democratic presidential nomination—and the presidency—largely on the strength of their candidate's alleged antiwar credentials. Barack Obama's opposition to the Iraq war was the line of demarcation that set his campaign apart from that of his main rival, Hillary Clinton. What his antiwar supporters didn't know—or want to know—was that this opposition was based on his often-stated contention that we were fighting a war *on the wrong front:* Afghanistan, he averred, is the main battlefield in our generations-long "war on terrorism." Iraq was merely a "diversion"—and, he suggested, we ought to go into Pakistan, if necessary, an idea that horrified even John McCain, who denounced it as "irresponsible."[8]

People believe what they want to believe, however, and the left fell into line behind Obama, who by this time had become a kind of cult figure around which liberals and self-identified "progressives" could rally after eight years in the political wilderness. What they didn't notice was that shortly after his election, which was greeted by the right with despair, the "progressive" Center for a New American Security—the source of many high level appointments by the Obama administration—held a joint conference with Kristol's newly-created "Foreign Policy Initiative, which hailed Obama's decision to escalate the Afghan war.[9] The participants busied themselves with the intricacies of CNAS's new counterinsurgency doctrine—essentially

[8] Andy Merten, "McCain Paints Obama as Too Hawkish?", MSNBC News, February 20, 2008, http://firstread.msnbc.msn.com/_news/2008/02/20/4438617-mccain-paints-obama-as-too-hawkish.

[9] Michael Brendan Dougherty, "Neoconned Again," *The American Conservative,* April 20, 2009.

a "nation-building" scheme to set up a semi-permanent colony in the wilds of Afghanistan, and extend the war further into the heart of Central Asia.

If the 9/11 terrorist attacks gave the neocons' agenda of perpetual war a terrible momentum, the crash of 11/11 stopped them dead in their tracks. As the great financial houses came crashing down, along with the stock market and the hopes and dreams of ordinary Americans—who were to lose their jobs, their homes, and their capacity for hope in the subsequent fallout—so did the untrammeled hubris that had empowered the War Party for a decade.

In retreat, and discredited on the right as well as in the eyes of the country at large, these dead-ender neocons are lashing out at the alleged "Calvinists" of the tea party, who are threatening to take away their expensive toys. When Sen. Cobun (R-Oklahoma) attacks the military-industrial complex, he's attacking their meal ticket: Pletka's American Enterprise Institute, otherwise known as Neocon Central, owes its very existence to the willingness of major military contractors like Boeing and Lockheed to shell out big bucks. In the case of the neocons' fervent defense of a bloated "defense" establishment, the key explanation is "follow the money."

Donnelly, for one example, was the author of a position paper put out by the Foreign Policy Initiative's predecessor, the Project for a New American Century, "Rebuilding America's Defenses," which called for more than doubling military spending.[10] From PNAC to Lockheed-Martin, the nation's biggest military contractor, was a natural transition for a policy wonk who promoted permanent war.[11] From there he went to AEI, where he and Pletka spend a lot of their time worrying about the rebellion against rampant militarism in the conservative ranks.

Forced to pay lip service to the idea of fiscal sanity and the restoration of limited government, the neocon duo aver that "the road forward embraces small government and a renewal of private enterprise but sees an equally exceptional American enterprise abroad." This awkward formulation, they assure us, "has been the mainstream position of conservatives and Republicans since 1945, expressed in Sen. Arthur

[10] Thomas Donnelly, "Rebuilding America's Defenses: Strategy, Forces, and Resources for a New Century," Project for a New American Century, September 2000.

[11] Rightweb, "Thomas Donnnelly," http://www.rightweb.irc-online.org/profile/Donnelly_Thomas.

Vandenberg's rejection of 'isolationism' and embrace of 'internationalism.'"

This stunning revision of conservative history is the complete opposite of the truth: Vandenberg was one of the first RINOs[12], who—together with the Eastern establishment wing of the GOP, exemplified by Henry Cabot Lodge—allied with the Truman Democrats to keep wartime economic controls after WWII, maintain the level of taxation required to fund the growing welfare state as well as an enormous and growing "national security bureaucracy, and usher in conscription as a permanent policy. Like most Republicans in Congress, Vandenberg had been ostensibly opposed to interventionism, but did a turnabout when President Truman unveiled his "Truman Doctrine" which entailed aid to Greece, Turkey, and Iran in order to resist an alleged Soviet threat. On this question, the real leader of the conservatives in the GOP, Sen. Robert A Taft, was skeptical, but Vandenberg, head of the Senate Foreign Relations Committee, took up Truman's cause. As Ralph Raico points out:

> *"After the landslide Republican victory in the congressional elections of 1946, Truman had to deal with a potentially recalcitrant opposition. The Republicans had promised to return the country to some degree of normalcy after the statist binge of the war years. Sharp cuts in taxes, abolition of wartime controls, and a balanced budget were high priorities.*
>
> *"But Truman could count on allies in the internationalist wing of the Republican Party, most prominently Arthur Vandenberg, a former "isolationist" turned rabid globalist, now chairman of the Senate Foreign Relations Committee. When Truman revealed his new 'doctrine' to Vandenberg, the Republican leader advised him that, in order to get such a program through, the president would have to 'scare hell out of the American people.' That Truman proceeded to do."*[13]

"If we desert the President of the United States at [this] moment,"

[12] Right-wing slang meaning "Republican In Name Only."

[13] Ralph Raico, "Truman: Advancing the Revolution," in *Reassessing the Presidency: The Rise of the Executive State and the Decline of Freedom,* Ludwig von Mises Institute, 2001.

thundered Vandenberg, "we cease to have any influence in the world forever." Not to be outdone in the hyperbole department, Henry Cabot Lodge declared that rejecting Truman and his overblown "doctrine" would be a crime akin to treading the American flag underfoot. Some things never change.

Vandenberg, described by James B. Reston as "a big, loud, vain, and self-important man, who could strut sitting down," and whose "written statements were masterpieces of confusion," is an unlikely candidate for valorization.[14] His much-touted "conversion" to interventionism was not the ringing declaration of principle Pletka and Donnelly make it out to be, nor did it have much to do with the conservative principle of limited government. While conservative Republicans rose in opposition to Truman's proposed loan of $3.75 billion to bankrupt socialist Britain, in 1946, Vandenberg and a passel of northeastern Republicans supported the measure. The "foreign aid" gravy train was beginning to flow, and the "internationalists" supported it under the very thin veneer of "national security" and anti-communism.

However, the real political and economic motivation behind this support was not hard to fathom: as the historian Justus Doenecke put it: "Representatives of the coastal states, with ties to commerce and international finance, undoubtedly backed the loan...in the hopes of gaining a thriving export trade." Pressure from northeastern labor unions were a factor in garnering support from regional Republican congressmen, and "former isolationists in Michigan were undoubtedly influenced by those market-conscious automobile companies that dominated the state's economy. Vandenberg himself commented as he endorsed the loan, 'One out of five workers in my own State of Michigan normally depends upon export orders for his job.'"[15]

Those dollars—extracted from the pockets of American taxpayers by the tax-happy Truman Democrats—would be poured back into the pockets of his constituents. Or so the theory went: in practice, however, it was quite another matter. The British couldn't pay back the loan on even the most generous terms—two percent interest—nor could London afford to carry out the major trade concessions that were supposed to have been part of the deal. Vandenberg's corporate

[14] http://www.senate.gov/artandhistory/history/common/generic/Speeches_Vandenberg.htm.

[15] Justus Doenecke, *Not to the Swift: The Old Isolationists in the Cold War Era,* Associated University Press, 1979, pp. 65-66.von Mises Institute, 2001.

backers among the automakers were disappointed, but there were other ways to make the new conservative "internationalism" turn a profit.

The neocons' affection for Sen. Vandenberg is understandable, given their own penchant for "defense"-profiteering, but the rest of the conservative movement, and especially the tea partiers, are likely to find his "internationalism"—including Vandenberg's enthusiasm for the United Nations, which he and Alger Hiss helped found—a rather tepid source of inspiration.

No doubt aware of this, Pletka and Donnelly team wheel out the time-honored icon of American conservative to buttress the case for an "internationalism" of the right:

"Washington's chattering classes have tried to imagine a battle between the heirs of Eisenhower and Reagan. In this myth, Ike was a war-hardened vet who had the 'political will and willingness... to make hard choices,' as Defense Secretary Robert Gates intoned recently. Reagan, in this telling, was a profligate 'supply-side' quack who gave his defense secretary America's credit card."

We are then treated to some pretty dubious statistics, which treat military spending as a percentage of GDP—a ruse that big spenders always use to justify whatever boondoggle they want to put over. This expenditure, they argue—whatever it might be—amounts to "only" a small percentage of GDP—this is how "foreign aid" is routinely justified, for one example—but the reality is that this measure includes all government spending without subtracting the debt governments incur to finance the spending. In short, the productive sector—i.e. the private sector, the true source of all wealth-producing economic activity—is much smaller than the bloated "official" government GDP totals. This is statistical sleight-of-hand any real conservative will surely see through. Which means the percentages they cite—military spending at 10 percent under Eisenhower, and 5.8 percent under Reagan—are actually much higher. Today, under the "stimulus"-happy Obama administration, as we pass from recession to full-fledged depression and the productive sector shrinks, the percentage is astronomical—and rising.

Another problem with pulling Reagan out of a hat is that it's no longer "morning in America"—not with the economy in free fall. If one is a fiscal conservative, it's more like twilight—but then, again, the neocons aren't conservatives in any meaningful sense of the term.

They are radical Jacobins, as professor Claes Ryn rightly calls them, whose hubris is the polar opposite of the conservative temperament.[16] Yet Pletka and Donnelly have the gall to declare that "nothing less than a fight for the soul of conservatism is underway." Well, yes, it is indeed, but the heirs of Arthur Vandenberg—and Scoop Jackson—have no valid claim to the conservative mantle, which is why they are losing.

The neocon mandarins of AEI are fighting a rearguard action against those "many young-gun conservatives" who are "from another school." Yes, they are indeed from another school—they are Old School conservatives, who think the concept of "big government conservatism" is an oxymoron, and who aren't fooled by the Pletka-Donnelly funny numbers which tell us "defense is not the source of the deficit." Government spending is the source of the deficit, and the onerous taxes we pay—and military spending, including veterans' benefits and the "defense" portion of the interest on the debt, accounts for 54 percent of all federal spending.[17]

We can't have an empire, and a balanced budget at the same time: it is one or the other. A return to fiscal sanity means we need real change in our foreign policy. That's what the battle for the conservative soul is all about. The neocons are counting on their evaluation of the tea partiers as "Don't Tread on Me nationalists" rather than "budget balancers," but this calculation comes up short when one takes into consideration the central meme of the tea party movement: that it's the federal government which is treading on us all and sucking the life blood out of the economy—while the Pletkas and Donnellys grow fat on corporate contributions and government contracts.

What's important to note here is that there is a widening split on the American right, between the ultra-nationalist "big government conservatives" who have dominated the movement since the days of Arthur Vandenberg, and the "Old Right" which is so old that it's new, and is making a comeback in a major way, much to the chagrin—and panic—of the neocons.

On the left, too, a split is developing, between those who support Obama's wars—the so-called "national security Democrats" over at CNAS, who are buddying around with Bill Kristol, and the

[16] Claes G. Ryn, *America the Virtuous: The Crisis of Democracy and the Quest for Empire,* Transaction, 2003.

[17] http://www.warresisters.org/pages/piechart.htm

traditional left which opposes interventionism and wants to keep our tax dollars in this country. Sen. Joe Lieberman, a Democrat who supported the neocons' wars, was driven out of his party by anti-interventionists, and it's no accident that he, too, constantly invokes Vandenberg's shade as a rationale for his pro-war, big-spending stance: the neocons, no matter which party they formally adhere to, are nothing if not consistent. As I put it in a column published at the tail end of 2005:

> *"The Democrats, according to Lieberman's logic, must be 21st-century Vandenbergs: Politics, as the turncoat Vandenberg put it, must 'stop at the water's edge.'*
>
> *"What this really means, and always has meant, is that all debate must end: it's okay, as Lieberman says, to discuss "tactics," but the fundamental premise that we must be in the business of "regime change" throughout the Middle East and the world must never be challenged. This is Lieberman's niche in the neocon division of labor: he exists to quash any and all signs of dissent that might crop up in the Democratic Party when it comes to foreign policy. He is, in effect, charged with policing the party for any signs of dreaded 'isolationism.'"*[18]

With Lieberman policing the Democrats, and Pletka and Donnelly policing the Republicans, the idea is to stamp out any and all debate over the fundamentals of US foreign policy. Yet that debate is coming, whether they like it or not, and it looks like neither Lieberman and the tiny clique of "national security Democrats," nor the neocons and their fast-shrinking constituency, have the political weight to stop it.

Lieberman wound up a pariah in his own party. The neocons, too, are fast approaching pariah status. Oh, they try to mount an argument in favor of the political utility of warmongering, albeit without much success. Pletka and Donnelly cite a rather biased-sounding Gallup poll, which asked respondents whether "national defense is stronger

[18] Justin Raimondo, "Lieberman's 'War Cabinet'", http://original.antiwar.com/justin/2005/12/14/liebermans-war-cabinet/.

than it needs to be." Isn't it just like a "big government conservative" to equate throwing money at a government program with "strength"? A more accurate reading of the public mood was taken by the Pew polling organization, which noted, in 2009, that "for the first time in more than 40 years of polling, a plurality (49%) says the United States should 'mind its own business internationally' and let other countries get along the best they can on their own."[19]

This is the majority opinion in America, and it is high time both conservatives and progressives noted it—and took action. Against the Vandenbergian faux-"conservatives," and the Vandenbergian fake-"progressives," there is an opening for anti-interventionists of both the left and the right to challenge the Washington establishment and bring America home.

I would also note that the Pew poll cited above revealed that the elites, embodied by the membership of the Council on Foreign Relations, disagree emphatically with the majority of ordinary Americans: they are all *for* minding everybody else's business but our own. Indeed, not a single CFR "expert" thought minding our own business was even an option.

This radical split between the people and the elites is reflected across the board, politically, on virtually every issue: it is fueling the populist rebellion brewing in the country, which is threatening to throw out incumbents en masse and raise up a whole new generation of political leaders. Disgust with politicians, with crony capitalism, and with the two political parties which constitute the "left" and "right" wings of the War Party, is the zeitgeist of the new era.

An antiwar movement that unites these elements can and will forge a mighty instrument on behalf of peace, and lead us out of the dead end of imperialism which has brought us to the edge of financial—and moral—bankruptcy. This is what the neocons fear the most. They know their time is up. But before a popular mass movement can take off, one that can reclaim and renew the foreign policy of a free nation, the arbitrary divisions and sectarian fixations of both conservative and liberal anti-interventionists must be dispensed with, which is why a single-issue focus is so important.

The War Party would like nothing better than to divide us, to separate out the "tea partiers" who question the expense of empire from the progressives who oppose Obama's wars, and set them one

[19] http://people-press.org/report/569/americas-place-in-the-world

against the other. This is how they've managed to maintain their dominance in spite of the views of the American majority. "Divide and rule" is an old game indeed, and they know how to play it. However, even that gambit is wearing a bit thin, as the crisis looms ever larger—and we are faced with the spectacle of a mighty "empire" with a standard of living that is falling, precipitously, to the level of the Third World.

Contra Vandenberg and the neocons, politics cannot and must not stop at the water's edge: American foreign policy ought to be the concern of every citizen, and the debate is just beginning. If we are to win that debate, anti-interventionists must defy the old paradigm of "left" versus "right," mount a challenge to the elites who think they have an unlimited mandate, and forge a new American consensus around the idea that minding one's own business is the only way to survive and prosper in a dangerous world. The unintended—and intended—consequences of a foreign policy that is motivated to right every wrong and fight every battle will continue to be visited upon us in ways we can only begin to imagine. It's time to bring our elites up short, restrain their world-saving—and self-interested—delusions, and bring America back to the foreign policy of the Founders.

In their panicked screed against "isolationism," Pletka and Donnelly denounce conservative opponents of global intervention as "a combination of George McGovern and Ebeneezer Scrooge," to which one can only reply: better McGovern and Scrooge than Vandenberg and Darth Vader.

The United States Needs a Broad-Based Anti-War Movement

By Kevin Zeese, Voters for Peace
February 24, 2010

Can the Right and Left Work Together to Oppose War and Empire?

There has to be a better way to stop wars and reduce military spending. Polls show U.S. voters at worst divided on current wars and more often show majority opposition to them. Yet, when Congress "debates" war the widespread view of Americans is muffled, not usually heard.

For the last decade, with President Bush in office the peace movement has been politically left and Democratic leaning. The right wing has been kept off the stage as a result the anti-war movement does not reflect the breadth of American opposition to war. For too long the peace movement has been like a bird with only a left wing. It can barely fly and when it does it seems to go in circles. Perhaps a bird with two wings will fly better?

This past weekend Voters for Peace sponsored a meeting of 40 people from across the political spectrum who oppose war and Empire. The people attending see the U.S. military as too big and too expensive and recognize spending $1 million to keep a soldier in Afghanistan for one year is a symptom of mistaken militarism that weakens U.S. economic and national security.

The purpose of the meeting was to see if we could work together. Could we put aside our differences on other issues and focus on reducing American militarism and in the long run ending reliance on war?

The conversation began with discussions of the history of anti-war advocacy in the United States and what we can learn from it. One point repeatedly made by people on the left and right was that historically there have been conservatives who opposed war and empire. Today those voices are heard in a whisper, if at all. Before the Spanish American War, World War I and World War II, strong opposition to foreign intervention not only came from progressives but also from traditional conservatives rooted in the recommendation of George Washington's farewell address—"avoid foreign entanglements." How can we re-awaken that common sense conservatism and forge a broad based anti-war movement?

What would a broad based anti-war movement look like? Some of the conservatives in the room warned against this 21st Century movement looking like the anti-Vietnam war protests of the 60s. Many on the left and right acknowledged that the mass weekend protests against Iraq were large in size but ineffective in result. While there is a role for such protests, they are not sufficient for the task at hand. Some conservatives warned against describing the United States as imperialist—that would get up the hackles of many Americans. But, they were comfortable describing the United States as an Empire.

Personally, I found that of interest. Americans never hear discussed in the media whether or not our country is an Empire. And, if we were to have such a discussion the critical questions would be is Empire good for us, for our national security, for our economy, for our democracy? Having those questions debated would be a breakthrough in political dialogue.

It is hard to deny the American Empire. The U.S. has more than 2,500,000 DoD personnel deployed across the planet and 761 military bases on foreign soil not counting more than 100 in Iraq and more than 400 American and NATO bases in Afghanistan. U.S. troops are now stationed in 148 countries and 11 territories according to DoD's "Active Duty Military Personnel Strengths by Regional Area and Country." America has spawned a military network larger than the Roman Empire, which at its height had 37 major military bases, and the British Empire which had 36. More bases are planned; billions spent building bases in far off lands while large swaths of American cities degrade into impoverished zones and the infrastructure of the nation crumbles.

When the Cold War ended, rather than reducing troops in Germany, Japan, Korea, Italy, the Philippines, and so many other nations; ending the NATO alliance which was designed to combat the now non-existent Soviet Union; and shrinking the weapons and war budget, the U.S. decided to seek to become the sole superpower on Earth. U.S. military spending is now as much as the whole world combined. The U.S. Navy exceeds in firepower the next 13 navies combined. When all the budgets are accounted for—the Pentagon, the wars, the 16 intelligence agencies, the super-sized embassies—total Empire spending is more than $1 trillion annually.

And, the Empire has deep roots. General Smedley Butler, the most decorated Marine in history joined the Marines in 1898 and served 34 years in China, Nicaragua, Haiti, Cuba, Mexico and other nations as part of the early American Empire. When Butler retired and thought about his career he described himself as a "racketeer" for U.S. business interests around the world and said "war is a racket."

But, this massive Empire is not discussed. It is the elephant in the living room of American foreign policy. And, the entrenched military-industrial complex that President Eisenhower warned us about in 1961 is now so powerful that cutting the military budget is off the table in Washington, DC—despite cost over-runs of hundreds of billions in weapons contracts, the GAO consistently describing the Pentagon as un-auditable and budgets filled with waste, fraud and abuse. The war budget grows and grows despite a fragile if not collapsing economy at home.

After a long day of discussion it became evident that people from across the political spectrum, despite differences on other issues, could in fact work together to challenge American militarism. Some in the room who had been working on these issues for forty years thought such a coalition was decades past due. Some of the students in attendance had their eyes opened to the history of traditional conservative anti-war efforts as in their lifetimes it had not been heard from.

In discussing this publicly, so far I have only heard from one person on "the left" who opposes it. He was a co-founder of Progressives for Obama and he lumps everyone on the conservative side into what he calls "racist populism." Such broad stroke descriptions of people are prima facie evidence of prejudice and certainly not consistent with people I have met from across the spectrum. But, his opposition shows the challenge on "the left"—too many are unwilling to stop their support for the Democrats and Obama.

The challenge on the right is also difficult. The Neocons have taken over almost all significant conservative organizations. How can we attract traditional conservatives to anti-war advocacy? The day after the conference, the surprise land slide victory of the anti-war conservative, Ron Paul, at the CPAC convention gave hope that there were more right wing peaceniks than we may have imagined.

While our task is urgent—something which the 1000th death of a U.S. soldier in Afghanistan and the weekend's killing of two dozen more civilians in an aerial attack brings home—our job is immense. Undoing a century old Empire that is larger than any that ever existed is no easy task, but for citizen patriots it is an essential one for the survival of the nation and the benefit of the world.

Attendees of the February 20th Across the Political Spectrum Conference Against War and Militarism

Doug Bandow

Jon Berger

Shaun Bowen

Paul Buhle
Paul_Buhle@brown.edu

Allan Carlson

Matthew G. Cockerill

Robert Dreyfuss

Mike Ferner

Glen Ford

William Greider

David R. Henderson

Kara Hopkins

Bill Kauffman
P. O. Box 266
Elba NY 14058-0266
bkbatavia@yahoo.com

David Kunes

Nicholas Leavens

William Lind

Daniel McCarthy

Lewis McCrary

Michael McPherson

Ralph Nader

George D. O'Neill, Jr.
P.O. Box 1108
Lake Wales FL 33859-1108
goneilljr@gmail.com

Murray Polner

Andy Richards

Linda Schade

Joseph Schroeder

Sam Smith

Jeff Taylor

Katrina Vanden Heuvel

John V. Walsh

Jesse Walker

George Wilson

Alex Zeese

Kevin Zeese
2842 N. Calvert Street
Baltimore MD 21218
kbzeese@gmail.com

For further information please visit our web site: ComeHomeAmerica.us

Author Index

* indicates post-conference contribution

Made in the USA
Lexington, KY
21 December 2010